PROBLEMS OF LITERARY EVALUATION

YEARBOOK OF
COMPARATIVE CRITICISM

VOLUME II

Problems

of Literary

Evaluation

Edited by

Joseph Strelka

THE PENNSYLVANIA STATE
UNIVERSITY PRESS
University Park & London   1969

Copyright © 1969 by The Pennsylvania State University
All rights reserved

Library of Congress Catalog Card Number 68–56136
Standard Book Number 271–00085–6
Printed in the United States of America
by Heritage Printers, Inc.

Designed by Marilyn Shobaken

CONTENTS

TENTATIVE CONCLUSIONS

FOREWORD

"WHAT IS POETRY?—POETRY! THAT PROTEUS-LIKE IDEA, WITH AS MANY appellations as the nine-titled Corcyra!"[1] This statement may be applied not only to poetry but to literature in general. This convoluted, multifaceted complexity makes literary evaluation a highly problematic and difficult task even for those whose profession it is. Some time ago a student newspaper in Hamburg perpetrated a hoax by sending to a dozen publishing houses a chapter of a novel written by one of the best-known European writers of the present century. Only the names of the characters were changed; nevertheless, all but one of the publishers rejected the work as lacking in talent and totally useless. The "untalented" author in question was Robert Musil, who himself had sprinkled ironic remarks about the problems of literary evaluation throughout his novel *The Man Without Qualities*. In one instance, for example, he remarked that a novelist would have to find a really considerable number of people in Germany who had ideas in common with himself in order to count as an uncommon writer. In another instance he has one of his characters, General Stumm von Bordwehr, toy with the idea of holding a democratic poll in the Austrian army in order to find out what book the soldiers rate as the best. He drops the idea because of his not entirely unjustified suspicion that the majority, after having dutifully voted the Bible into first place, would pick that little booklet which mail carriers in the Austro-Hungarian Empire used to give their customers at New Year's in return for their seasonal gratuity and which, besides containing a list of all current postal charges, also incorporated an extensive collection of rather primitive jokes.

The hoax perpetrated by the Hamburg students has, of course, its serious side as well, and it requires no great powers of imagination to see that a large part of the literature put out by the publishers who were deceived in this manner is strictly ephemeral. We must, however, consider the fact that these publishers have to be guided in their day-to-day behavior by commercial considerations, and by

judgments as to the nature of current popular taste, however much
we may deplore it. Unfortunately, we will be almost as disillusioned
if we hope to find more solid judgment and critical knowledge among
most scholars and professional critics. Indeed, if we look at the matter more closely, we can see that even among the scholars and critics
there is a marked tendency to arrive at critical judgments on comparatively superficial grounds. It is thus perhaps no coincidence that
the most reliable and lasting judgments are to be found in the personal criticisms of an all too small number of scholars and critics who
manage to combine an innate feeling for art with profound historical knowledge, wide experience, and the ability to make critical
distinctions.

In these times of uncertainty about values, when we can hardly
expect to find any solid critical ground to stand on, we must seek at
least a plank to clutch in the swamp of doubt. If David Daiches is
correct in his assertion that literary evaluation is an art rather than
a science, then we must conclude that this "art," like the others, has
its periods of ebb and flow. The increasing concern with the problem
of literary evaluation at the present time might indicate that this "art"
is approaching one of its transitional stages. The intensity with which
any matter is questioned is an indication of its topicality, for we are
little inclined to discuss matters about which we have reached some
degree of certainty. On the other hand, lack of discussion does not
necessarily imply certainty: it may simply be an inability to recognize
the existence of the problem. There is no point, however, in hiding
one's head in the sand and hoping that the problem will go away. On
the contrary, only a constant and intensive concern with the problem
will lead us to at least some tentative conclusions.

To be sure, some people will complain about the uncertainty of
values at all times. This is hardly surprising, since everything is constantly in a state of flux. Indeed, each generation is faced anew with
the task of making its own decisions about art and culture, and in a
certain sense the whole world is re-created in each person's life.
These simple facts are intimately connected with, among other things,
the problem of changing values, with the problem of literary works
which, whether justifiably or not, have been forgotten and—again
whether justifiably or not—are now being rediscovered. However
many people at all times have complained about the uncertainty of
values, there can be no doubt that this uncertainty looms particularly
large today. Even in the free world there is occasionally a tendency to
flee from this chaotic uncertainty to the safety of a dogmatic attitude;

and even in the free world we have seen instances of attempts to form movements ranging from small cliques to great totalitarian ideologies with the purpose of subordinating free and independent judgment to their collective egoisms. We may hope, therefore, that our consideration of the problem of evaluation at this time is not merely excusable but even desirable, since it provides an opportunity to contrast as wide as possible a spectrum of attitudes and opinions.

This collection of essays has been divided into three principal sections, with the contributors arranged alphabetically within each section. The essays in the first section are primarily concerned with the basic problems, difficulties, and general principles of literary evaluation. The second section deals with various attitudes towards the methods of literary evaluation. The third section is concerned with summaries of tentative solutions to the problem. Some of these solutions may, of course, be found in the essays in the first and second sections, the differentiation being frequently merely a matter of emphasis.

At this point I should like to describe more fully the essays in the second section, since those in the first and third sections are self-explanatory. Stephen C. Pepper's attempt at aesthetic integration and Roman Ingarden's phenomenologically directed essay approach the problem of literary evaluation from the philosophical viewpoint. Two of the essays are psychologically oriented, the Jungian Mario Jacobi's exclusively, the Freudian Leonard Manheim's partially. Walter Hinderer's contribution might, in a certain sense, be designated as anthropological.

Wladimir Weidlé uses as his starting point that "second language,"[2] akin to Humboldt's ἐνέργεια, as a result of which the literary work is differentiated from pure communication. This "second language" is at one and the same time immanent in literary works and the means whereby they are created. Luc Benoist represents that esoteric tradition stemming from the work of René Guénon, which derives timeless human values from the study of comparative religion, whereas David Daiches's essay in the third section deals with the necessity of using certain historical perspectives in the study of literary evaluation.

René Wellek has rightly stated that "the literary student is confronted with a special problem of value; his object, the work of art, is not only value-impregnated, but is itself a structure of values. Many attempts have been made to escape the inevitable consequences of this insight, to avoid the necessity not only of selection but of judgment, but all have failed and must, I think, fail unless we want to reduce literary study to a mere listing of books, to annals or a chronicle."[3] Although not only most scholars but all people actively interested in literature will agree with this statement, the practical solution to the problem is nonetheless far more difficult than the simple recognition of its existence. The work of the critic in his attempt to understand and evaluate the constantly burgeoning and developing body of world literature resembles the building of the Tower of Babylon. It is thus no coincidence that the present collection begins with a remark of George Boas which emphasizes the difficulties of the problem by referring to the possibility of a more than "eightfold confusion," and ends with Emil Staiger's demonstration of an important limit to the possibilities of literary evaluation when he speaks of a paradox that characterizes the nature of absolute beauty: "Consequently, when we look at something which is perfectly beautiful, we observe the paradox that it is simultaneously inimitable and exemplary."

While it is certain that there is no timelessly valid table of absolute critical norms, literary evaluation is nonetheless one of the most essential aspects of literary studies, and is indeed indirectly practiced even by those critics and scholars who look upon it as unscientific if not absolutely impossible. As a matter of fact, in each age certain critics produce interpretations which, despite their entirely subjective origins, turn out to be far more than merely subjective; they become valid for the whole age and sometimes even for those to come. The lack of an absolute norm thus does not necessarily indicate the opposite extreme of a purely subjective dead-end and chaotic anarchy. A quotation from Edgar Allen Poe might simplify the problem to some extent at this point: "Among a tribe of philosophers who pride themselves excessively upon matter-of-fact, it is far too fashionable to sneer at all speculation under the comprehensive *sobriquet* 'guesswork.' The point to be considered is, *who* guesses."[4] Is that not the way it is in literature itself? Even the greatest writer with the most powerful imagination may sometimes miss the point, but the insignificant writer will probably never be able to find it. The problem can, of course, be looked at from the opposite point of view as well: a writer is great because he writes great works. However that may be, who can decide what is great? Here, too, it comes down to the fact of *who* is doing the evaluating. In this connection it would appear to be significant that several of the most distinguished contributors to this volume, from Benoist to Staiger, consciously reject the confinement of literary evaluation to external formalistic aspects and emphasize the relationship of literary values to universal human values in aesthetic sublimation.

Two invited contributors—Professor Walter Mueller-Seidel of the University of Munich and Professor Stanley R. Townsend of The Pennsylvania State University—were unfortunately unable to participate. It is regrettable that we do not have these contributions.

I wish to express my thanks for the understanding and financial aid the Yearbook series continues to receive from the Institute for the Arts and Humanistic Studies at The Pennsylvania State University under the direction of Professors John M. Anderson and Henry Johnstone.

JOSEPH P. STRELKA

January, 1969

Notes

1. E. A. Poe, "Letter to B—," in *The Works of Edgar Allen Poe,* Vol. 10, (New York and London, n.d.), p. 149.
2. See W. Weidlé, "Die zwei 'Sprachen' der Sprachkunst," in *Jahrbuch für Aesthetik und allgemeine Kunstwissenschaft,* Vol. XII, No. 2, pp. 154–91.
3. R. Wellek, *Concepts of Criticism* (New Haven, 1965), p. 15.
4. Poe, "Eureka," in *Works,* Vol. IV, p. 224. This is much more than the witty *bon mot* of an author who aims at a rhetorical effect rather than the communication of a truth. Recent literary theory has provided the scientific basis for this position, particularly the work of Roman Ingarden. He has shown in his book *Vom Erkennen des literarischen Kunstwerks* (Tübingen, 1968) that we must distinguish in every work of literary art between artistic and aesthetic values. The latter depends to a great extent on the potential concretion of a given work on the part of the reader or critic whose respective ability and competence participate in the realization of this concretion. This does not by any means signify a hopeless relativizing and surrender of the problem of evaluation to an unbridled and arbitrary subjectivism, for Ingarden has likewise demonstrated that scientific objectivity is definitely possible in the comprehension of literary-aesthetic objects (p. 313 and pp. 314–42).

BASIC PROBLEMS
AND THE CONTEXTS
OF LITERARY EVALUATION

George Boas

THE PROBLEM OF
LITERARY EVALUATION

IN TURGENEV's *Fathers and Children* BAZAROV SAYS TO MME ODINTSOV, in Constance Garnett's version: "All people are like one another, in soul as in body; each of us has brain, spleen, heart, and lungs made alike; and the so-called moral qualities are the same in all; the slight variations are of no importance. A single human specimen is sufficient to judge of all by. People are like trees in a forest; no botanist would think of studying each individual birch-tree." What Bazarov said was typical of what many writers were thinking in the nineteenth century. And, indeed, for the purposes of natural science he may well have been right. But of course there are other purposes. And the slight variations, whether in the internal organs of a human being or the psychological traits, cause most of our moral problems. As a matter of fact, medicine—as distinguished from physiology—is confronted by the same slight variations, for what distinguishes the stomach, lungs, spleen, and heart of one man from another fills our hospitals. Nor can the doctor find the answer to such problems in any general textbook on human anatomy. On the one extreme we find an interest in what all members of a class have in common, and on the other an equally legitimate interest in what individuates these members. The latter is the source of what I can only call practical problems, therapy being one example.

Intellectual tradition has set up the general classes which scientists study. But scientists have always been more or less ready to modify the classifications. To see this, one has only to think of how radically chemical substances were reclassified in the sixteenth century, how zoological classes were modified at about the same time. A good

insect is now one which fits into the classification that modern ento-
mologists have accepted. The same is true of good fishes, good mam-
mals, good primates. But when it is a question of aesthetic classes,
the situation is quite different. For here the classifications that began
with Aristotle are still accepted as guides to our thinking and, especially in the case of tragedy, his definition not only serves to tell
us whether a play is or is not a tragedy, but whether it is a good one.
Moreover, aesthetic categories are ambiguous, being not only general
terms for lumping things together, but terms that are also eulogistic.
You do not praise an insect for having six legs; you simply note it.
But you do praise a tragedy for being serious, having five acts, observing certain unities, and purging or not, according to your translation of *catharsis*, the spectator of pity and fear.

In *A Primer for Critics* I tried to point out that the sentence, "This
is a good book," meant in practice eight different things, depending
upon whether one was taking the point of view of its author or that
of the reader, whether one was thinking of its inherent (terminal)
value or of its instrumental value, whether one was thinking of the
book as the end product of the process of writing or of the process
of writing (the literary technique) itself. My distinctions fell flat,
and to the best of my knowledge no one paid the least attention to
them when it was a question of actual evaluation. Yet the eightfold
confusion was in fact too much of a simplification, for writers, the
process of writing, and the instrumental value of books are much
more various than I indicated. Many a critic has striven to discover
what the author had in mind when he wrote his book before trying
to find out whether he had written a good book or not; the critic thus
acted as if the type of ending was of no importance. Literature as an
end, they held, was a self-enclosed universe. On the other hand, for
centuries critics had maintained that the end of all literature was
moral edification and the book that was ethically neutral or which
could be said to be morally harmful was therefore a bad book. Similarly some critics have said that since all art is self-expression, so long
as a writer really expresses himself, sincerely and honestly, to that
extent his book is a success. To set down all the other differences in
values would be not only tiresome but would end in fourteenth-
century logomachy—the last thing in which I want to indulge.

The prestige of generalization has been so great that critics have
attempted to classify types of literature as though they were taxonomists. The result has been that endless disputes have arisen over
whether such a play was "really" a tragedy or a tragicomedy. But

Polonius ended, at least for some of us, that sport. The *genres tranchés* made for easy evaluation, for if a given work did not fit into the criterion of class membership, there was no difficulty in outlawing it as bad literature. Similarly some critics of painting have said that collages were bad paintings, were not really paintings, were illegitimate paintings, for they were not made of pigments but of bits of colored materials stuck on a board. That being admittedly true, one need not be bothered with them. They were visual objects to be sure and some people enjoyed looking at them and some of them were very beautiful. But since they did not meet the requirements of the class, they could be ignored. A man of my age can recall faculty meetings at which analogous remarks were made about courses which were said to be not really history but sociology, not really philosophy but theology, not really English literature but philology. The value of an individual was to be determined by its adequacy as a member of a class.

Now it is true that in science a two-headed cat is a monster and need not be considered by students of the feline genus. Mermaids, satyrs, chimeras, griffons, centaurs are no longer included in texts on zoology. But the classes in natural science are set up for two reasons: a general scheme of organization based on generally accepted theories, such as evolution, and empirical observation. If two-headed cats occurred more frequently, an attempt would be made to establish a species of two-headed cat. The taxonomist has in mind a general scheme which is supposed, let us say, but only supposed, to be the phylogenetic arrangement of certain forms of life. The reason he has set up a class of vertebrates is because there is believed to be a genetic relation among all the phylae which are listed under vertebrates and furthermore because he can find animals which actually are vertebrates. He may, if he wishes, praise an animal for being a perfect specimen of vertebration, but he usually does not, at least in print. His definition of the order is not based on what some ancient writer has said, but on what investigations, genuine unprejudiced investigations, have shown to be the case. He does not accept the classification of all animals that was based upon their habitat, thus ending up with terrestrial, aqueous, and aerial animals, beasts, fishes, and birds—some taxonomists even included igneous animals, the salamander—in spite of the historical fact that the Great Tradition did so.

In literature the classes that have been established were established by human beings and did not exist *in rerum natura*. No one, moreover, has yet been able to find perfect exemplifications of any of them. An eminent Harvard professor, who shall be nameless, was asked by one of his students whether there was anything in Occidental literature that he fully admired. The reply was, "Yes, most of *Antigone* and the third act of Racine's *Phèdre.*" There are two comments to be made about this: (1) his standard of excellence was so inapplicable that most European literature was below par; (2) like a good Romantic, horrible to relate, he was setting up his personal taste as a standard for the rest of the human race. The first comment need not be taken seriously unless one is in search of standards that will be generally accepted. One usually assumes, and it is only an assumption, that there is a body of literature, including such works as *De Rerum Natura, The Divine Comedy, Hamlet,* probably *Faust,* perhaps *Madame Bovary,* maybe *The Brothers Karamazov*—the yardstick wobbles as one goes on—which is great without qualification. If then one has a standard which excludes some of these works, one is said to be too narrow. The older generation remembers how outraged readers were when T. S. Eliot said that *Coriolanus* was a greater artistic success than *Hamlet.* Everybody knew that *Hamlet* was the greater and that was the end of it. But when one looks at the usual list of the great books, one sees that there are lumped together so great a variety of works that they seem to have next to nothing in common. To read *De Rerum Natura* and *The Divine Comedy* objectively, leaving personal enjoyment out of the question, all one can conclude is that both are poems, long poems, on cosmological themes, but in every other respect they differ. How then can one apply a single adjective to them both and expect others to accept the application?

The second comment raises the question of whether individual taste can ever be omitted in making critical appraisals. The answer is in the affirmative if one is willing to agree on certain impersonal characters, formal or ethical or what not, which are not determined by a reader's pleasure or pain. That is, if one agrees that moral edification is a criterion of excellence, then it can be said that Johnson's *London* is a great poem whether one enjoys reading it or is bored to death by it. I have heard people talk about *Faust* as a great ethical treatise showing that the love of a pure woman can redeem the foulest sinner. The love of Gretchen does redeem Faust and that cannot be disputed. If that is the lesson that Goethe was trying to teach his readers, then I fail to see how one could say the play was a failure. Again, if formal perfection is the standard, then *Vanity*

Fair with its balance of good and evil, the equilibrium of opposites, would be a very great book, whether anyone enjoyed reading it or not. The same would be true of most of Horatio Alger's stories.

It seems paradoxical to say that a book may be great and boring at the same time. The gambit at this point is to evaluate the critic, not the book. Human beings now become members of classes, and the well-read man, the intellectual, one of the Happy Few, or, on the other hand, the fresh, naïve, innocent man of the people, the red blooded, two fisted he-man, becomes the arbiter of taste. Popular art may be thought of as inherently low or inherently good, if history is any testimony. Lycophron's *Alexandra* is usually said to be too remote from ordinary experience to be good; *Barrack Room Ballads* not remote enough. With some reservations this was the attitude of Matthew Arnold. It was certainly the attitude of Irving Babbitt. In short, the man who has had a university education and has read a great many books is supposed to be a better judge of good literature than is a man of the people. So men say that one who has studied the history of art is a better judge of a painting than one who comes to a gallery with an innocent eye. But just what are the two men judging?

It is easy enough to find several critics who will agree that the *Odyssey* is a great poem, but when you ask why, you will get as many answers as there are critics. Often the answers, when you can get them, will vary with that vague thing known as the times in which the critic is living. That is particularly true of the fortunes of Vergil, as everyone knows, and no one would maintain that a book which is used to predict a course of action, as in the *sortes Vergilianae*, is great in the same respect as one which is the glorification of a dynasty. This is an extreme case to be sure, but sometimes extreme cases are test cases. Now since it is difficult to define a time in such a way as to show its influence on criticism, that is, on evaluation, we may as well omit any attempt to explain why critics select those aspects of the book which seem to them of outstanding interest. Let us simply note that they do. I am not speaking of disagreement about the ultimate value of a work of literature. I am speaking of cases where critics agree in their general praise of a book, but disagree about the reason for their praise. Criticism of Hamlet, Shylock, and of Othello, the characters, not the plays as wholes, illustrates my point. If one is going to see in Shylock the symbol of a persecuted race, one is not seeing what Shakespeare saw in him nor what any Elizabethan would have seen in him. The critic who saw Shylock as a superb rendition of a rapacious, revengeful Jew did not admire him because he bore the insults of the Christians with assumed resignation. Anyone familiar with Shakespearean criticism will recognize what I am writing about and those who do not need only glance at the appendices to the *Variorum* Shakespeare for enlightenment.

The case of critics who disagree about values is too familiar to require detailed discussion. When one reads Matthew Arnold on Chaucer, one sees that something is either lacking in Arnold or in oneself. Arnold was right in saying that there is no high seriousness in Chaucer. The question is really that of using high seriousness as a test of literary greatness. Of course a sense of humor sometimes covers greater seriousness than does a long face. For there is plenty of criticism of life in Chaucer, more for that matter than in either the *Iliad* or the *Odyssey*. But critics would disagree about the manner of expressing such criticism of life. This cannot be adjudicated here and I have no intention of trying to do so. Rather, my point is that, whether one likes it or not, the personal character of the critic is going to participate in his judgments. I suppose that what I mean by personal character is what used to be called taste. If I avoid the term, it is because of a belief that taste suggests something immediate and unreflective, like smell or touch. There is indeed something unreflective in a person's reactions to any work of art, whether it be a poem, a picture, a building, a dance, or what not, but that something is far from being the whole story. For everyone who is serious about artistic criticism has certain principles of judgment which make him say, for instance, that *Richard III* is a greater play than *Titus Andronicus*. These principles, however, do not leap out of the plays, like light from a candle, but have been absorbed from one's reading, one's conversation, one's education as a whole. Psychologically they become integrated into and influence one's immediate reactions. They are part of that total discipline which is the process of maturity. When those things that the principles disapprove of are discovered, one not only disapproves of the work of art but dislikes it too, in all probability. The conflict in taste is surely nothing extraordinary. It is analogous to the conflict in behavior: seeing and approving the better and doing the worse.

So much is banal. But the trouble is that one hesitates to see the implications for literary judgments inherent in the situation. These implications are in part that the total culture must influence one's taste, an apparently innocent enough conclusion. What is not so innocent is the fact that, if this is true, then the value of the work of art is not embedded in the work of art itself but is partly contributed to it by the culture in which critics live. I do not mean by this simply that people vary in their judgments, but that there is no value in the absence of human beings who do the valuing, that the words on the page have no value whatsoever until they are interpreted by a reader. It will be granted that they carry meanings and are not just shapes and sounds. The interpretation made by the reader is not a function of a man divorced from the society in which he has grown up. Hence whatever goodness or badness he finds in the work is projected into the work as a function of the psychophysical organism known as a critic, plus all the principles of good and bad that he has absorbed through his education.

My conclusion will be named subjectivism and relativism, bad words both. What of it? Neither implies that one book is as good as another unless the words good and bad are meaningless. To argue that way, as some of my critics have done, is to say that because a stone has one weight at a certain altitude and another at a different altitude, therefore you can assign to it any weight you please. Relativistic statements are simply more accurate than absolutistic ones. Values are values for human beings, not for angels or mathematical entities. And a human being living in the Athens of the fifth century B.C. is not identical with one living in the United States in the twentieth century A.D. As biological specimens the two are of course highly similar, indistinguishable if one wishes. But as readers, and that is what counts, they are very different. A man today cannot turn into an Athenian, for he is likely not to believe in the existence of Zeus, of the Titans, of the Daughters of Danaüs, and of their interrelations. For that matter it is hard enough to read Lucretius and accept all that he says about Venus, atoms and the void, primitive man, the delight of standing safe on the shore watching a fellowman struggling for his life in the waves. Even his key word, *religio*, has to be explained in a footnote. But for that matter one has to adjust to the ghosts in Shakespeare, to the social organization of the society in which Henry James sets his novels, to the Anglicanism of T. S. Eliot, before reading their works with that full sympathy which understanding requires. That we make this adjustment with a certain ease is not because it is trivial but because we are educated men and women. Why not admit this as an integral element in appreciation? One does not have to resort to the Man from Mars or even to the Man from Iceland to prove the cultural limitations of such authors. The man from South Boston or Harlem will do as well. But in order to salvage the presumed universality of great works of literature, we deny the existence of human beings as if their minds were neutral. People likely to read this article will all have had about the same education and belong to the same culture, a subculture of the United States.

To take but one idea that we are all probably going to presuppose as true, we demand nowadays psychological interpretation in terms of Freudian psychodynamics. We shall think that an interpretation of character which is intellectualistic, which does not take into account a person's unconscious motivation, his repressions, his tacit aspirations, is superficial. "Freudian" is to be sure a vague term; Freud's psychodynamics has been modified by his successors. But there is a residue of his teachings which is still accepted and forms a large part of our "apperceptive mass." To read most nineteenth-century novels today demands that we set such considerations aside, for if we want to read such books sympathetically, we have to look for values other than psychological realism. But just as we are delighted when Balzac or Dickens lights upon some psychological detail which fits in with our contemporary hypotheses, so we are delighted to find in the *Odyssey* that Odysseus's nurse and dog recognize him when not even his wife does. We then overlook all the other details which do not fit in. The program of realism which seemed shocking in Zola now seems self-evidently justified. Our culture is scientific and no one "in our set" has failed to take on the scientific attitude, if not all the details of any special science. I am not saying that realism is a *sine qua non* of every literary work. We can still read *The Rape of the Lock* with the greatest delight and need feel no compulsion to maintain that it has a deeper or higher kind of realism. Yet if we do resort to that sort of evasion, it is because we are of our time without knowing it.

There are certain features of a culture, or subculture, to be more accurate, which seem to be inescapably present in any evaluation. One is the sort of moral attitude that guides the behavior of fictional characters. When the nineteenth century demanded that good be rewarded and evil punished, it was because the great mass of even intelligent readers believed that the universe was so ordered that good really would be rewarded and evil punished. The last words of *Tess of the D'Urbervilles* were a genuine shock to most readers and could not have been written in 1800. Pessimism as a philosophy was unknown in the Occident before Schopenhauer. It was thus not a sentimental prudishness that caused men to withdraw in disgust from books that were "bitter," "immoral," "depressing," "sordid." The fact that we no longer use such adjectives when we criticize a book does not imply that we are any wiser in an absolute sense than were our grandparents. It implies, if that verb is not out of place, that we have been through two frightful wars and have been living in an earthquake area for now two generations. It has often been pointed out, and in a tone of surprise, that Jane Austen never mentions the Napoleonic Wars in her novels. The surprise is unwarranted. The fact is that one could live in the English countryside in those days and not think of the Napoleonic Wars except as something being carried on by the Army and Navy. Wars went on and so did life. That is no longer true. Our wars permeate our whole lives; I did not invent the term "total war." There are still plenty of novels written in which the events go on without the horror or cruelty or hypocrisy of war being mentioned. Murders and detection have taken its place. But there are still boys who have framed copies of Kipling's *If* hanging on their walls.

The dominant features of a culture will be reflected in literature whether an author realizes it or not. I imagine that most serious authors are aware of what they are doing and when they use, for instance, the vocabulary of the barracks, they know why. So too when they introduce, or fail to suppress, erotic scenes, both normal and abnormal, they are aware that their society no longer feels guilty about admitting the existence of such things. If one asks why this has come about, when only a generation or so ago it would have been unthinkable in English, the answer is easy. Psychologists have explored the Unconscious and know its importance. A man of my generation is at a disadvantage here. He can still be repelled by *From Here to Eternity*, to say nothing of *Tropic of Cancer*. *Fanny Hill* in my youth was sold under the counter. Even in college courses in Horace or Martial we were told to omit certain verses or whole poems. The result, honesty compels me to say, was that we increased our Latin vocabulary in our private rooms. It would be foolish for such people—I am talking of my contemporaries—to rage against the dirt, the monstrosities, the ugliness of modern fiction. For whatever a critic says either in praise or blame is in part autobiographical. Rationality is something that has all but disappeared from the arts. Having been put through horrors unequaled since the Thirty Years' War, we purge our souls of pity and terror by greater and greater horrors in art. The mutilations of the human figure in the sculpture of Henry Moore, in the paintings of Picasso, in the *anti-romans* of

Beckett or Genet, are no longer felt to be mutilations. The critic turns his attention away to the purely aesthetic aspects of such works, meaning by "aesthetic" the formal or non-human. But it should be observed that the ability to redirect our attention in this way probably indicates our indifference to human suffering. One is always indifferent to the usual. We no longer live in a world that gives humanity a central place. The physical-chemical world has become our focus. After all, have we not learned recently that whatever we are is an affair of the nucleic acids? I happen to think that the inference drawn by our artists is wrong. For, if the nucleic acids can produce a Shakespeare, the more power to them. The level of our human problems is well above that of chemistry. One simply cannot attribute to a cause or set of conditions all the traits of their effects.

A good bit of criticism consists in praising and blaming. I should like to suggest that there are other possibilities. One, and not the least important, is interpretation. A critic, if he knows enough, can spend his time looking at a work of art and noting what is there. We have too often assumed that we can see the whole thing at a glance, immediately. But we now know that our immediate experience is mediated by our whole past and that we are more likely to see what we are looking for than anything else. Though the drive towards looking for levels of meaning has not always reached the goal of clarity, yet the program was a good one. For at least it pointed out that things are not only what they seem. The trouble has been that we have too often assumed the primacy of the perceptual. But we now know that the perceptual is based on non-perceptual interests.

I have said nothing about that type of criticism which looks for an observance of the rules. This was very appealing to men who thought that class-characters were more important than individuality. And when all reasoning was supposed to be syllogistic, which demanded at least one universal proposition as premise, generalizations seemed essential. This compulsion has been weakened by the Romantic movement. The individual has come more and more prominently into the foreground, even in the sciences. The attempt to return to Classicism, inspired by Charles Maurras in France and by the Neo-Humanists in this country, fizzled out after World War II. It was ironical that Eliot's critical essays had more influence than his critical theories and his poems had more influence than either. The Romantic movement could not be blocked by the pundits. It satisfied a deeply felt need that went well beyond the supposed doctrines of

Rousseau. And as the regimentation of modern life became stronger and stronger, the need became greater and greater. The outbreak of all kinds of delinquencies, both silly and serious, was to be expected. There is no merit in being good under compulsion. There have been delinquents even in monasteries. These are truths that demand recognition if one is engaged in criticism. If, however, this is granted, then literature is an integral part of life both for the writer and for the critic. And when this is granted, the purely aesthetic point of view loses its privileged position. The critic can legitimately be asked to point out the relation between what is said in a book and the culture in which it was written. So far as it illuminates or reflects that culture, it will take on greater interest. But that does not mean that a book divorced from its culture is sick or unimportant. One can look at the conditions of writing as well as at what has been written.

My purpose in this brief paper has not been to simplify but the contrary. Aesthetic has been over-simplified even since Baumgarten wrote his famous book. In spite of the name, the discipline does not deal exclusively with perception, nor could it. We still unfortunately talk of the visual and auditory arts as if we thought that painting was only visual and music only auditory. And some writers have been known to insist that anything beyond the perceptual was an unwarranted detail in a work of art. The pathos of Purity is undoubtedly very great but it can be resisted. We can grant that one sees a painting and hears music without also admitting that they are purely visual and auditory. The unheard melodies of Keats's urn still tinkle and even some abstract paintings still look like real objects. It is the thickness of works of art that I am anxious to emphasize, a thickness that comes from their human ties. If they do not have these ties or if the ties are attenuated, then as far as I am concerned they are amusing toys. The problem of literary criticism cannot be solved unless we first have a clear idea of all that the word "literature" connotes.

Northrop Frye

CONTEXTS OF
LITERARY EVALUATION

I MUST BRING THE QUESTION OF LITERARY EVALUATION DOWN TO THE context of our own professional routine, and though I might rationalize this context as being existential, committed, and the like, even here all I can offer is an analogy that seems to me pedagogically instructive. The pursuit of values in criticism is like the pursuit of happiness in the American Constitution: one may have some sympathy with the stated aim, but one deplores the grammar. One cannot pursue happiness, because happiness is not a possible goal of activity: it is rather an emotional reaction to activity, a feeling we get from pursuing something else. The more genuine that something else is, the greater the chance of happiness: the more energetically we pursue happiness, the sooner we arrive at frustration. The more one says he is happy, the more quickly we get out of his way to prevent him from making us miserable.

So with the sense of value in the study of literature. One cannot pursue that study with the object of arriving at value judgments, because the only possible goal of study is knowledge. The sense of value is an individual, unpredictable, variable, incommunicable, indemonstrable, and mainly intuitive reaction to knowledge. In knowledge the context of the work of literature is literature; in value judgment, the context of the work of literature is the reader's experience. When knowledge is limited, the sense of value is naïve; when knowledge improves, the sense of value improves too, but it must wait upon knowledge for its improvement. When two value judgments conflict, nothing can resolve the conflict except greater knowledge.

The sense of value develops out of the struggle with one's cultural environment, and consists largely of acquiring an instinct for the different conventions of verbal expression. All verbal expression is conventionalized, but we quickly realize that some conventions are more acceptable to our social group than are others. In some societies, including our own until quite recent times, the different conventions were linked to different social classes, and high and low speech were at least symbolic of the conventions of lord and peasant respectively. Today we still have, despite the linguists, distinctions between standard and substandard speech, and a corresponding distinction, though one quite different in its application, between standard and substandard writing. The critic who fights his way through to some kind of intuitive feeling for what literary conventions are accepted in his society becomes a representative of the good taste of his age.

Thus value judgments carry with them, as part of their penumbra, so to speak, a sense of social acceptance. I remember a paper on Yeats by W. H. Auden, given in Detroit in 1947. He referred to Yeats' spiritualism in terms of its social overtones of lower middle-class credulity and drawn blinds in dingy suburban streets, and remarked that A. E. Housman's Stoicism, while it may have been no less nonsense, was at any rate nonsense that a gentleman could believe. There was of course an intentional touch of parody here, but actually Auden was putting an evaluating criticism into its proper, and its only proper, context. Every attempt to exalt taste over knowledge has behind it the feeling that the possessor of taste is certainly a gentleman, while the possessor of knowledge may be only a pedant.

The task of the evaluating critics, who review contemporary books and plays, is partly to prevent us from trying to read all the books or see all the plays. Their work is quite distinct from that of the literary scholar who is trying to organize our knowledge of our past culture, even though it is called by the same name and engaged in by many of the same people. The literary scholar has nothing to do with sifting out what it will be less rewarding to experience. He has value judgments of selectivity, just as any scholar in any field would have, but his canons of greater and lesser importance are related to the conditions of his specific research, not directly to the literary qualities of his material.

There is a vague notion that historical criticism is a scholarly establishment, and that all critical methods which are not simply branches of historical study, whether explicatory or archetypal, are antihistorical, and ought to be applauded or denounced as such. But, of course, every great writer who lived in a different time or cultural orbit from ourselves is a challenge to the assumptions on which our evaluative statements are made, and knowledge of his assumptions makes our own more flexible. The fundamental critical act, I have said elsewhere, is the act of recognition, seeing what is there, as distinct from merely seeing a Narcissus mirror of our own experience and social and moral prejudice. Recognition includes a good many things, including commentary and interpretation. It may be said—in fact it has been said by Mr. Krieger, and said very well—that it is not really possible to draw a line between interpretation and evaluation, and that the latter will always remain in criticism as a part of the general messiness of the human situation. This may often be true as regards the individual critic. Nevertheless there is a boundary line which in the course of time inexorably separates interpreting from evaluating. When a critic interprets, he is talking about his poet; when he evaluates, he is talking about himself, or, at most, about himself as a representative of his age.

Every age, left to itself, is incredibly narrow in its cultural range, and the critic, unless he is a greater genius than the world has yet seen, shares that narrowness in proportion to his confidence in his taste. Suppose we were to read something like this in an essay published, say, in the eighteen-twenties. "In reading Shakespeare we often feel how lofty and genuine are the touches of nature by which he refines our perceptions of the heroic and virtuous, and yet how ignobly he condescends to the grovelling passions of the lowest among his audience. We are particularly struck with this in reading the excellent edition by Doctor Bowdler, which for the first time has enabled us to distinguish what is immortal in our great poet from what the taste of his time compelled him to acquiesce in." End of false quote. We should see at once that that was not a statement about Shakespeare, but a statement about the anxieties of the eighteen-twenties.

Now let us suppose that an evaluating critic of our own age goes to work on Dickens. He will discover that melodrama, sentimentality, and humor bulk very large in Dickens. He feels that a critic of our time can accept the humor, but that the melodrama and sentimentality are an embarrassment. He has to pretend that melodrama and sentimentality are not as important as they seem, or that Dickens has a vitality which carries him along in spite of them. He will also realize that his own age sets a high value on irony, and disapproves of coincidence or manipulated happy endings in plots and of exaggerated purity in characters. So he will bring out everything in Dickens, real or fancied, that is darkly and ambiguously ironic, or hostile to Victorian social standards, and the coincidences and the pure heroines and the rest of it will be passed over—in short, bowdlerized. To interpret Dickens is first of all to accept Dickens's own terms as the conditions of the study: to evaluate Dickens is to set up our own terms, producing a hideous caricature of Dickens which soon becomes a most revealing and accurate caricature of ourselves, and of the anxieties of the nineteen-sixties.

As long as criticize means evaluate, the answer to the question: "Whom does the critic criticize?" seems at first a very easy one. The person the critic criticizes is, of course, the poet, whom the critic, in the traditional metaphor, judges. The drama critic attends a play and then writes a review judging it; if he is a literary scholar, then he reads the great poets in order to judge them too. Who would bother to be a critic unless one could be in the position of judging the greatest poets of the past? Alas, this carryover from judging to studying does not work, and the literary scholar, many bitter and frustrating years later, discovers that he is not judging the great poets at all. They judge him: every aspect of past culture shows up his ignorance, his blind spots, his provinciality, and his naïveté. When criticize means evaluate, the answer to the question "Whom does the critic criticize?" turns out to be, in scholarship, the critic himself. The only value judgment which is consistently and invariably useful to the scholarly critic is the judgment that his own writings, like the morals of a whore, are no better than they should be.

Of course literature, as an object of study, is a limitless reservoir of potential values. Think of how large American nineteenth-century writers bulk in our cultural imaginations today, and of how impoverished those imaginations would be if they did not include such figures as Ethan Brand or Billy Budd or Huckleberry Finn. Yet it is not so long ago that the question was frequently and seriously asked: "What on earth could you find to say about *American* literature?" There is in fact nothing in past literature that cannot become a source of imaginative illumination. One would say that few subjects could be duller or less rewarding than the handbooks studied by Miss Frances Yates in *The Art of Memory*, yet her study has all the mental exhilaration of the discovery of a fine new poet. But when value is totally generalized in this way, it becomes a superfluous conception.

Or rather, it is changed into the principle that there is value in the study of literature, which is an unobjectionable way of stating the relationship.

The experience of literature is not criticism, just as religious experience is not theology, and mental experience not psychology. In the experience of literature a great many things are felt, and can be said, which have no functional role to play in criticism. A student of literature may be aware of many things that he need not say as a critic, such as the fact that the poem he is discussing is a good poem. If he does say so, the statement forms part of his own personal rhetoric, and may be legitimate enough in that context. Naturally a reader of a work of criticism likes to feel that his author is a man of taste too, that he enjoys literature and is capable of the same kind of sensitivity and expertise that we demand from a good reviewer. But a writer's value sense can never be logically a part of a critical discussion: it can only be psychologically and rhetorically related to that discussion. The value sense is, as the phenomenological people say, pre-predicative.

The study of literature, then, produces a sense of the values of that study incidentally. The attempt to make criticism either begin or end in value judgments turns the subject wrong side out, and the frequency of these attempts accounts for the fact that more nonsense is written in literary criticism, especially on matters of theory, than in any other scholarly discipline, not excluding education. Fortunately, its practice is considerably better than its theory, even when its practice includes MLA papers and doctoral theses on the birthday odes of Colley Cibber. No one deplores more than I do the purblind perspectives of scholarly critics, or the fact that so much criticism is produced with so little intellectual energy that it has all to be done over again. Still, it is better not to adopt a critical approach which makes the writing of sense impossible, however lugubrious the result of better premises may often be. With the enormous increase of personnel required in the humanities, I foresee a time when demands that every scholar be productive may be reversed into efforts at scholarly contraception. This may lead to a growing awareness of the difference between the criticism which expands our understanding of literature and the criticism which merely reflects and repeats it.

In the meantime, the effort to reverse the critical machinery continues to be made, usually in some such terms as these: is not a value judgment implied in, say, choosing Chaucer rather than Lydgate for an undergraduate course? Surely if we were to elaborate a theory explaining *why* some writer is of the first magnitude, and another only of the tenth, we should be doing something far more significant than just carefully studying them both, because we should also be proving that it was less important to study the smaller man. I do not know of anybody who claims that a valid theory of this sort exists, but I have often been reproached for not devoting my energies to trying to work one out. The argument reminds one a little of that of Sir Thomas Browne that a theory of final causes, working through universal principles of design like the quincunx, would give us a master key to all the sciences.

It is also part of the great Northwest-Passage fallacy of criticism which always gets stuck in the ice of tautology. The greatest writers are—let me see—imaginative rather than fanciful, or possessed of high seriousness, or illustrative of the sharpest possible tension between id and superego. The critic invariably discovers these qualities in the writers he considers best, overlooking the fact that they are merely synonyms for his preferences. The circumambulation of this prickly pear can go on for centuries, as long as the terms used are brought up to date in each generation. Or one may draw up a list of categories that appeal to the sensibilities of the critic because they are fashionable in his age, and call them characteristic of all great literature of all periods. The effect of this is to canonize the taste of that age, and make it into a dogma binding on future generations. I. A. Richards made a parenthetical suggestion about such universal categories in *Practical Criticism*, but obviously soon realized, not only that the procedure involved was a circular one, but that, once again, such phrases as the "inexplicable oddity" of birth and death merely echoed the anxieties of the nineteen-twenties. For those who wish to persist with this or similar methods, a certain degree of paranoia will be found most helpful, if not essential.

It is because I believe in the value of literary scholarship that I doubt that value judgments have a genuine function in acquiring it. Those who try to subordinate knowledge to value judgments are similarly led, with a similar consistency, to doubt that genuine knowledge of literature is possible, or, if possible, desirable. There are many ways of expressing this doubt, or disapproval. One is the chorus that has for its refrain: "But literature is alive, and you're anatomizing a corpse." Such metaphors take us back to the vitalism that has long since disappeared from biology, and the scholarly critic is constantly being told that he is leaving out whatever the objector regards as the seat of the author's soul, whether his heart, his blood, his guts, or his testicles. The basis of this response is a fixation derived from adolescence, when the sense of social approval is so highly developed, and when it seems so utterly obvious that the end of reading is to assimilate everything into the two great dialectical categories of value judgment, which in my own adolescence were "swell" and "lousy." But it seems to me (if we must use these metaphors) that there is only one thing that can "kill" literature, and that is the stock response. The attempt of genuine criticism is to bring literature to "life" by annihilating stock responses, which of course are always value judgments, and which regularly confuse literature with life.

On the next level there is the notion that university deans and chairmen demand a certain amount of historical research from new recruits as part of a kind of hazing process, before one is allowed to start on one's proper evaluating work. This research is assumed to exist all on one level, and to be nearly exhausted, so that one is now forced to look for something like the Latin exercise books of Thomas Flatman or the washing bills of Shackerley Marmion. The appearance of every genuine work of literary scholarship knocks the bottom out of this notion, but it revives in each generation of graduate students. More sophisticated versions of the rejection of knowledge are, first, the helpless historical relativism which says that as Samuel Johnson or Coleridge made some of the mistakes likely to be made in their day, so we can only go on making a fresh set of mistakes, and can learn nothing from our predecessors. Second is the assumption that most interpretation, if at all subtle or difficult, is something that the author could not have understood, and hence has simply been imposed on him by the critic, a pretext for an activity begun in self-hypnosis and sustained by group hysteria. If any reader doubts that such a reaction exists, he has probably never written a book on Blake's Prophecies.

In short, the more consistently one conceives of criticism as the pursuit of values, the more firmly one becomes attached to that great sect of anti-intellectualism. At present it seems to be fashionable to take an aggressive stand in the undergraduate classroom, and demand to know what, after all, we are really trying to teach. It appears that we are concerned, as teachers, with the uniqueness of human beings, or with the fullness of humanity, or with the freedom to be aware, or with life itself, or with the committed ironies of consciousness, or with learning to be at home in the world, or in fact with anything at all, so long as it sounds vaguely impressive and is not reducible to treating literature as something to be taught and studied like anything else. Seek ye first the shadow, we are urged, and the mere substance will be added unto you, if for some reason you should want it. It seems to be in literature that the teacher is most strongly tempted to cooperate with the student's innate resistance to the learning process, make himself into an opaque substitute for his subject instead of a transparent medium of it, and thereby develop his charisma, which is Greek for ham. But as values cannot be demonstrated, the possession of them is realized only by their possessors, hence the more evangelical the sales pitch, the more esoteric the product. I would of course not deny that teaching is a different activity from scholarship, and that many assertions of value are relevant to the classroom that are not relevant to the learned journal. But I think that in literature, as in other subjects, the best students are those who respond to intellectual honesty, who distrust the high priori road, and who sense that there may be some connection between limited claims and unlimited rewards.

Eric Donald Hirsch, Jr.

PRIVILEGED CRITERIA IN
LITERARY EVALUATION

HOW WELL A LITERARY WORK FULFILLS PARTICULAR CRITERIA OF EX-
cellence is not easily decided, but is at least decidable. If critics
are able to agree upon their criteria, they can also agree, and often
do, in their specific evaluative judgments. More often, however,
critics find themselves applying different norms with the result that
some of the most vigorous debates in practical and theoretical criticism are those which concern the proper choice of criteria. But is
there any proper choice of criteria in literary evaluation? Is it possible to demonstrate the inherent superiority of one evaluative mode
over another? In short, do privileged literary criteria exist? If they
do not, it must follow that no truly definitive value judgment can be
pronounced upon any literary work.

When David Hume granted that no specific criteria of literary
judgment could be "fixed by reasonings *a priori*,"[1] he was able to
recommend instead an institutional criterion founded upon experience: a literary work should be deemed excellent which mankind
has long judged to be so, or which the intellectual aristocracy of the
present day judges to be so. Hume placed his confidence in the uni-
formity of human nature and the observable consensus among well-
educated men. Good judges could be depended upon to agree that
Addison is better than Bunyan.[2] Hume's pragmatic canon may be
called "institutional" because, like all institutions, its authority rests
upon social agreement. Just as legal pragmatists define correct judgment institutionally as the majority rule of the Supreme Court, Hume
implicitly defined it as the majority rule of the best judges. In Hume's
day the best judges could be recognized and accepted; implicitly they

could be institutionalized on the analogy of the Supreme Court, the French Academy, or the Pope.

Sheer authority has always played a role in literary judgment, but the institutions in which it has resided have become constantly more diffuse and weak. Aristotle's rules gave way to the Humean consensus, which, in turn, gave way to the modern fragmentation of all traditional jurisdictions. Yet anyone who questions traditional authority is thrown back upon his own standards of taste, just as Luther, in questioning papal authority, was thrown back upon his own inward judgment in matters of faith. For some centuries now we have all been literary protestants without Pope or priesthood. Prophets and sects we continue to have, like the other Protestants, but nothing resembling a Pope or a Supreme Court. Matthew Arnold's admiration for the French Academy was wistful and half-hearted, as though he foresaw the collapse of its authority in modern times. His idea of substituting an inward Academy in the minds and hearts of Englishmen was just another retreat into the pervasive literary protestantism.[3]

Coleridge, coming between Hume and Arnold, saw very clearly these analogies between the sources of authority in religion, in law, and in literature. Authority is normally derived from socially accepted institutions, and when the institutions are endangered, new grounds of authority have to be provided. In this perspective, Coleridge's literary theories have the same philosophical and social motivation as his writings upon church and state. For Coleridge, judicial authority in all cultural domains must henceforth be deduced by necessity from the nature of the cosmos and the human mind. The new, intrinsic system of authority thus derived would be independent of mere prophetic revelation on the one side and accidental social development on the other. Everywhere, perforce, the model of excellence would be the pattern of the God-infused cosmos: the unity of all in each; just as everywhere the model of disvalue would be the contrary of the divine plan: disconnection, dead and spiritless. Thus, in literary judgment, all criteria of excellence may be comprised in the principle of organic unity, the reconciliation of opposite and discordant qualities.

Coleridge's was the most significant attempt in criticism to erect a comprehensive philosophical substitute for the fallen edifice of literary authority. Mankind could no longer depend upon the dispersed and discredited Humean consensus; unless "the reviewers support their decisions by reference to fixed canons of criticism, previously established and deduced from the nature of man, reflecting minds will pronounce it arrogance in them thus to announce themselves to men of letters as the guides of their taste and judgment."[4] Every decision must show its credentials; predilection must give way to principle.

This great program failed (as all similar ones have) for two equally instructive reasons. First, Coleridge's great root principle, deduced from the nature of man and the cosmos, was impossibly general, so that he was frequently unable to correlate his particular evaluative criteria with his universal principle. Because much that he found excellent in literature could not be reduced to the cosmological archetype, he had the good sense (against his announced program) not to attempt the reduction. Second, he failed because the philosophical deduction of critical canons proved to be no more self-evident or self-confirming than the arbitrary canons of the petulant reviewers. The great underlying principle which had generated the new philosophical canons of criticism could not itself command adherence unless one happened to share Coleridge's belief in an organic, God-infused cosmos where each thing has a life of its own and we are all one life.[5] Coleridge's deduction required a prior commitment from the general reader which was no less arbitrary than the prior commitment to shared values required by the ordinary reviewer. In Coleridge's system, more—not less—reliance was placed upon a higher, *ab extra* revelation, and the new religion, upon which all depended, became merely one more sect among other literary sects. Despite Coleridge's grand, catholic effort, literary protestantism held its inevitable sway.

In our own, still more fragmented era, further efforts have been made to solve the problem which Coleridge so clearly perceived. Since there is no papacy in intellectual affairs, the definitive judgment of literary value will have to come from principle, not authority. And the principle will have to be one which can rightly claim a preferential status in relation to other evaluative principles. Thus, a great deal of effort in recent literary theory has been directed to the deduction of evaluative criteria which can be shown to have this privileged status. The throne of vanished authority will be occupied by a supreme jurisdiction mightier far than that which we have lost. Through it, we shall be able at last to make permanently valid judgments of literary value. No longer the nightmare of protestantism—graceless zealots fighting over modes of faith; ultimately we shall establish a new universal criticism founded upon the inherent nature of literature itself.

This modern strategy was the only one left which gave promise of success. In the absence of an instituted authority or a *consensus didacti*, the only possible way to secure a privileged status for evaluative criteria would be to deduce them from the nature of literature itself. Literature would have to be judged as literature, poetry as poetry, and not referred to some alien standard. Self-evidently, such a judgment would be more definitive than an evaluation based upon social utility, arbitrary rules, or personal taste. To judge literature as literature and not another thing would be to reach a determination independent of shifting opinions and tides of taste, for the judgment would be made upon intrinsic grounds. Other modes of evaluation would continue to be made on other premises, but they would remain merely relative judgments, dependent upon external and changeable value preferences. Intrinsic evaluation, on the other hand, would be permanent and secure, privileged and immutable, because the grounds of judgment would be derived from the very nature of the thing judged.

Aristotle had done the thing before, and, in his own way, so had Coleridge. But the motto "literature as literature" was in itself no protection against internecine warfare between those who adopted it. In fact, the most vigorous polemics in recent critical theory arose between the Chicago critics and the New Haven critics who shared the same revolutionary goal of deposing extrinsic scholarship in favor of intrinsic criticism; the Trotskyites were embattled against the Leninists over the true method of the revolution, and only the vigor of their conflict sufficed to mask the structural identity of their aim. No matter if Aristotle or if Coleridge was taken to be the true prophet of the revolution, its goal was conceived by both parties to be the criticism of "literature as literature."

Despite the important benefits which have accrued to us in the domain of interpretive analysis by virtue of this critical revolution, polemics and failure were its inevitable fruits in the domain of evaluation. For the goal of a definitive, literary evaluation of literature is actually a mirage masked by a tautology. The ideal of a privileged "literary" mode of evaluation is rendered hopeless by the impossibility of deducing genuinely privileged, literary criteria of evaluation. I make this statement categorically, because an analysis of the various types of evaluative principles which have evolved in the history of criticism reveals that such criteria have never been successfully formulated, and, in the nature of the case, never could be.

Broadly speaking, four principle modes of literary evaluation have evolved in the history of criticism, and in their basic structures these four modes would seem to exhaust the possibilities. Of course, any such scheme of classification will oversimplify the subject matter and will serve to indicate only the underlying logic of the problem rather than the richness of the various solutions that have been proposed. For in actuality, all good critics and theorists have adopted more than one of the four strategies. Thus, when I attach a particular historical name to one of them, I am suggesting a preponderant emphasis rather than formulating an adequate description. Nonetheless, each strategy retains its characteristic features, whether viewed in isolated purity or in admixture with others, so that if conclusions can be reached about the relative merits of each, it will be possible to decide which strategy, if any, occupies a privileged position.

The first type of evaluative theory I would call extrinsic, since it ruthlessly decides whether a work of literature is good or bad on the grounds of its external relationships. The great example is, of course, Plato. His line of argument is beautifully consistent and rigorous. A work of literature shall be judged good if and only if it is good for the state. What is good for the state is to be defined thus and thus, and what is bad thus and thus. Those elements in literature which conduce to bad effects should be censored or at least censured. Tolstoy is another of these ruthless extrinsic critics, and although very few men have had the courageous if not perverse rigor of a Plato or a Tolstoy, a number of very great critics, Johnson and Arnold for example, have practiced a measure of extrinsic evaluation. I. A. Richards once made the remark that if the extrinsic critics were to be lined up against the intrinsic ones, all the best brains would be found on the side of Plato.[6] That is a point to which I shall revert at the end of this paper.

The fountainhead of the second type of theory is Aristotle, the father of evaluation-through-the-genre. A work shall be judged good to the extent that it fulfills the intrinsic imperatives of the kind to which it belongs, and it shall be judged bad to the extent that it fails to fulfill those generic imperatives. Each thing shall be judged not in relation to the state or some other external standard, but in relation to the proper criteria of the subsuming species. Thus, as the Chicago theorists have insisted, the right way to judge a comic novel is not according to universal or external literary criteria, but according to the criteria specifically appropriate to comic novels.

The third type of theory, which might be called individualistic, is Aristotle pushed to the extreme of nominalistic skepticism. True, the proper way to judge a work is according to its own intrinsic imperatives, but these cannot be defined in advance by reference to a limited number of genres and sub-genres. Every new work is *sui generis*. One has only to look at the history of literature to discover that Aristotle's norms of tragedy do not accurately define the norms of Shakespearian tragedy. And, in fact, the norms of *Hamlet* are not even identical with those of *King Lear*. The only system of criteria genuinely intrinsic to a work is the one defined by the particular goals of the work itself. The only privileged criterion, therefore, is adequacy: how fully does the work accomplish what it is trying to do; how expressive is it of its own intent? The word "expressive" should remind us that the most considerable representative of the individualistic theory is Croce.

Finally, the fourth type of theory is a well-represented one which embraces a large number of writers in the history of criticism. I call it the broad-genre theory. With Aristotle in the middle and Croce on the far right, these more liberal intrinsic critics want to comprise all or most of what we call literature within a single comprehensive class having certain common attributes and excellences. Under this theory the Aristotelian principle is extended over a much wider domain, so that instead of positing that all tragedy aspires to arouse and purge our pity and fear, one posits that all literature aspires to instruct and delight, or to achieve complexity, or to express the dream of man. Sometimes the broad class literature is narrowed, for example, to poetry and non-poetry, so that Coleridge in his version of the broad-genre theory defines the attributes of poetry in such a way that it embraces some passages of prose and excludes some passages of verse. Other broad-genre theorists, notably those who pursue the discipline of aesthetics, expand the confines of the subsuming species to include not just all literature but all art. But in every case, theorists of this persuasion determine their criteria of evaluation according to the intrinsic, Aristotelian pattern. They posit a species: literature, poetry, art; they define the proper excellence of that species in a generally applicable way; and they evaluate individual works according to the degree they fulfill that proper excellence.

What we have, then, in the history of criticism are four basic strategies for formulating criteria, three claiming to be intrinsic, and one being unabashedly extrinsic. The three intrinsic procedures are, as I have suggested, Aristotelian in their skeletal structure, so that the fundamental conflict goes back, very appropriately, to Plato versus Aristotle. That awesome thought should not deter us, however, from attempting an adjudication between them on this narrow issue of literary evaluation. Very briefly, and reversing the previous sequence, I shall review some of the problems that beset each type of evaluative procedure.

The broad-genre type of theory was very forcefully and cogently criticized by the late Ronald Crane in his essay on Cleanth Brooks and critical monism.[7] By critical monism Crane meant, among other things, the iterative use of a single canon of evaluation for all works of literature. Crane argued that the universal application of a single criterion like irony or complexity inevitably ignored the primary aims and values which informed the work. Thus, on the universal criterion of irony, the greatest poem of the twentieth century is Einstein's $E = MC^2$.

To Crane's objections regarding the inappropriateness of such critical monism, it is possible to add another which is more central to the present analysis. Broad-genre evaluation proffers an implicit claim which it fails to make good. It claims a privileged status for its judgments because it evaluates literature as literature. Its criteria claim to be intrinsic on the assumption that all the works we call literature have in common certain implicit aims. Yet this assumption has never been successfully defended, and indeed it is false. The only occasion when a particular criterion such as beauty, complexity, paradoxicality, maturity, sincerity, etc., could be intrinsic to a work is when that quality is in fact an intrinsic aim of the work. And since no such quality is universally aimed at by all literary works, no such criterion could be universally intrinsic. I do not mean to imply, as Crane did, that there is something illegitimate in applying a single criterion to all literary works. On the contrary, I shall, in the end, defend its legitimacy. What I deny is the claim that such criteria are intrinsic, that they could have a privileged status. Broad-genre evaluation cannot do the job it pretends to do. Since its criteria are *not* self-grounded in literature, it cannot attain to the authoritative, intrinsic evaluations it proposed to give us.

The next kind of theory, the individualistic sort represented by Croce, is in fact the only kind of evaluation whose criteria are truly intrinsic. It asks simply, what is this work trying to achieve, and has it achieved it? Frequently, one hears the objection that such hypothetical evaluation is a delusion because we can never really know what a work was trying to achieve, only what it in fact did. This objection is invalid. It may be true that we are never certain what a work is trying to achieve, but our guess about its aim can be correct, and with enough evidence we can approach certainty. If absolute certainty were required in literary study, not a single interpretive statement in all existing exegeses could meet the requirement. The Crocean mode of evaluation is, in fact, very widely and successfully practiced. My criticism just now of broad-genre theories is an example of it. My objection was that these theories were trying to be intrinsic and were not succeeding, and I would think that any such Crocean judgment must be considered valid. The Crocean method of formulating criteria is, then, intrinsic. But do its criteria thereby gain privileged status? I think not, for here the so-called intentional fallacy achieves its limited applicability. What difference does it make how well an aim is achieved if it is not a valuable aim? Not even Croce, I think, would judge a work good which perfectly achieved some perverse or idiotic aim. So I conclude that although Croce's theory is the only one capable of providing truly intrinsic criteria, this theoretical purity is almost entirely irrelevant to serious criticism. If common sense tells us that many intrinsic failures are more valuable in our literature than many intrinsic successes, then intrinsic success is not going to be the privileged standard we have been seeking.

It was precisely this Crocean atomism which the Chicagoans, following Aristotle, sought to overcome when they formulated the genre theory of evaluation. In Aristotle's view, it did not matter at all that Euripides might have *wanted* to compose a plot requiring stage artifice and did this admirably, for in the genre tragedy, the best kind of plot resembles the one in *Oedipus Rex* which is more conducive to the proper pleasure of tragedy. Thus, the standard is not what the work was actually aiming at but what it should have been aiming at whether it knew it or not. This solves the Crocean problem by positing generic criteria which exclude silly or perverted aims. At the same time, it overcomes the insuperable problem of broad-genre theories by positing criteria specifically appropriate to the work at hand. A comic novel must not have a hero whose moral flaws are so egregious as to foreclose entirely the reader's sympathy and thus his ability to laugh. To achieve comedy, the work must obey the psychological demands essential to comedy. Thus, if an author were foolish enough to attempt a comedy having a hero who is morally repugnant, the result would be disgust, not laughter, and the author would fail in his aim. In this way it is possible to deduce generic criteria which are not dependent upon the aims which a

misguided or unenlightened author might actually have intended;
yet such criteria would nevertheless be intrinsic to his work since
they would govern the genre which subsumes the work.

It is a very neat trick, and I believe that this middle course between the Scylla of the Croceans and the Charybdis of the Coleridgeans represents the most considerable attempt yet made to solve
the problem of intrinsic and thus presumably privileged evaluation.
But for all their theoretical subtlety, the modern Aristotelians have
not sponsored very much significant evaluative criticism, partly because the theory itself is defective. For in brute fact, the modern
Aristotelians have attempted an impossibility. It cannot legitimately
be argued that the intrinsic aims of a work are different in any respect
from its actual aims as intended by its author. If a writer tries to
achieve laughter with a morally repugnant hero, he may not succeed
(I am not sure that he could not succeed) but his failure would not
lie in his refusal to conform to the ineluctable criteria of a subsump-
tive genre called comedy. His failure would lie in his having in-
compatible aims, or in having insufficient abilities to make them
compatible. On this point Croce has the best of the argument:

> We must leave writers and speakers free to define the sublime or the
> comic, the tragic or the humorous, on every occasion as they please
> and as may suit the end they have in view. . . . If such definitions be
> taken too seriously, there happens to them what Jean Paul Richter
> said of all the definitions of the comic: namely, that their sole merit
> is *to be themselves comic* and to produce in reality the fact which
> they vainly try to fix logically. And who will ever logically determine
> the dividing line between the comic and the non-comic, between
> laughter and smiles, between smiling and gravity, or cut the ever
> varying continuum into which life melts into clearly divided parts?[8]

If an actual aim of a comedy or any other kind of work does not
correspond to the generic model posited for it, then the mere model
cannot impose the aim; and if the aim of the work does correspond,
then the model is not needed to sanction or disclose it. The Chicago
theorists, when they enter the region of immediate practice, have
shown how difficult it is to be an orthodox Aristotelian in a world
that is in fact Crocean. Aristotle was wrong to suppose that human
productions can be classified in a definitive way like biological
species, or that works of art could have intrinsic goals different from
those actually aimed at by their human authors.

The supreme irony is that Aristotle is himself the source for a refutation of all these generic schemes of evaluation. The broad genre

theories like those of Coleridge and the New Critics, as well as the narrow genre theories of the Chicagoans, must assume the essential similarity of the members within the genre. For the Coleridgeans, all of literature is assumed to be unified by certain distinguishing traits, just as for the Chicagoans all comic novels are similarly unified. In other words, they assume that literature as a whole or some sub-genre of it has a definable essence or telos which can govern the formulation of criteria. But we may be permitted to be skeptical so long as that essence is not satisfactorily defined. According to Aristotle, the essence of any class is that system of characteristics which are shared by all its members, and which are not shared by things outside the class. Thus, a true class requires a set of distinguishing features which are inclusive within the class and exclusive outside it; it requires a differentia specifica. That, according to Aristotle, is the key to definition and to essence. But, in fact, nobody has ever so defined literature or any important genre within it. As Croce put the case: "If an empirical definition of universal validity be demanded, we can but submit this one: The sublime (or comic, tragic, humorous, etc.) is *everything* that is or shall be so *called* by those who have employed or shall employ these *words*."[9] Croce's nominalism would hold a fortiori for such words as "literary" or "literature," and his view is powerfully supported in the work of Wittgenstein.[10]

So much, then, for the intrinsic evaluation of literature and its three basic strategies. Useful and even indispensable as they are, they cannot attain to the privileged status which they implicitly claim. When they are intrinsic (i.e., Crocean) they do not usually proffer significant evaluations; when they do, they are not usually intrinsic. We are left, then, with extrinsic evaluation, that is, with criteria of judgment which are not grounded in the nature of literature. We are left with the mode of Plato, Tolstoy, and, in large part, of Sidney, Johnson, Shelley, Arnold, in fact with most of the criticism that is worth terming evaluation at all. For instance, the Coleridgean mode of criticism practiced by the New Critics is, for the most part, extrinsic, despite its pretense of being otherwise; criteria like complexity, maturity, richness, compression, tension, etc., are (except when they happen to coincide precisely with the author's intention) extrinsic criteria. Their sanction comes entirely from the religious, moral, and aesthetic standpoint which sponsors such criteria as estimable values.[11] They are not sanctioned by anything intrinsic to the nature of literature.

Yet that is precisely the reason these extrinsic criteria have been productive of significant criticism. They induce judgments of value which transcend the aims of individual works and thereby permit comparative evaluations which have reference to larger dimensions of life. It was only when the New Critics tried to exclude certain judgments as being "extrinsic" or "unliterary" that they went astray and unnecessarily inhibited the practice of criticism. For as soon as the adjective "literary" is given accurate content in a particular usage, it turns out that the New Critics have been as unliterary as Plato or Tolstoy. In their delusion has lain their strength. Similarly, the significant criticism of the Chicago school has been extrinsic criticism. Its most important critical effort, Booth's *The Rhetoric of Fiction*, is an excellent piece of moral-aesthetic extrinsic evaluation. That it claims, quite inaccurately, to be entirely Aristotelian and intrinsic in no way diminishes its importance as a persuasive and important work in the tradition of Plato.

Most evaluation worthy of the name, then, is extrinsic. And the criticism which has been most widely useful and esteemed has combined two kinds of extrinsic standards; it has adduced extrinsic criteria of technical excellence (as in Aristotle), and it has adduced extrinsic criteria concerning the benefit of literature to mankind (as in Plato). Even Aristotle argued platonically that good tragedy purges the audience of emotions which are deleterious to their happiness and to the good of the state. And even Plato, in *The Laws* and elsewhere, recognized that works of art can be well-made or ill-made, whether or not they are good for the state. But neither the Platonic nor Aristotelian kind of criterion, individually, or as is usual, complexly mixed together, can be deduced from the nature of literature. Both kinds of criterion are grounded in value-preferences which must make their own way in the world.

And in the modern world no single hierarchy of values is privileged. We lack the institutionalized authority or the genuinely widespread cultural consensus which could sponsor truly preferential criteria in literary criticism. Absolute evaluation requires an absolute; it requires a universal church. But the actual world of literary evaluation has been for some time now a protestant world where preferential criteria are in fact only the preferences of a sect. To hope for more absolute sanction is to pursue a will-o'-the-wisp.

Consciousness of this cultural fact can lead to a liberating clarity rather than to pure skepticism. The fact that no system of evaluative criteria can manage to sustain a claim to privilege does not imply that some system of values does not in reality deserve to sustain such a claim. Plato, for instance, could be right that the good of the state is the ultimate value to which all others are subordinated, and he might even be right in his conception of the good of the state. He might also be wrong. Mere men cannot pass that ultimate judgment with absolute certainty. Yet men are obliged to take a stand, and it is well to recognize that any pretense to "purely literary" literary criticism is simply to disguise one's stand even from oneself. For, if there is no privilege in literary evaluation, there is nevertheless objectivity and accuracy, and these reside entirely in the judged relationship between literature and the criteria we choose to apply to it. If our criterion is "maturity," and if we make clear what that criterion means, then our judgment of a work's maturity can be just as valid and absolute as a judgment drawn on the basis of some criterion for which we falsely claim a privileged status. The critic's choice of criteria depends upon the purposes he has in view and ultimately upon his own protestant inward light. But his evaluations upon those criteria can be absolutely accurate.

Thus, there is no valid reason to preserve any affection for the empty shibboleth "literature as literature." Its success in the world has been a measure only of its delusiveness, of its logical meaninglessness. No strategy of thought can ultimately protect the critic or the teacher from his responsibility to draw judgments about the value of literature within any context where it has for him significant value. And beyond this, the critic has a responsibility to knowledge itself: an obligation to know just what his criteria are, to know what he is doing and why.[12]

Notes

1. J. W. Lenz, ed., *On the Standard of Taste and Other Essays* (Indianapolis, 1965), p. 7.
2. *Ibid.*
3. *See* his essay "The Literary Influence of Academies."
4. J. Shawcross, ed., *Biographia Literaria* (2 vols., 1907), Vol. I, p. 44.
5. E. L. Griggs, ed., *Collected Letters of Samuel Taylor Coleridge—Volume II: 1801–1806* (Oxford, 1956), p. 864. (To W. Sotheby, Sept. 10, 1802: "Nature has her proper interest; & he will know what it is, who believes and feels, that every Thing has a Life of its own, & that we are all *one Life.*")

6. *Principles of Literary Criticism* (New York, 1925), p. 71.
7. "The Critical Monism of Cleanth Brooks," in *Critics and Criticism Ancient and Modern,* ed. R. S. Crane (Chicago, 1952), pp. 83–107.
8. B. Croce, *Aesthetic as Science of Expression and General Linguistic,* trans. D. Ainslie (rev. ed.; New York, 1922), p. 90, p. 92.
9. *Ibid.,* p. 90.
10. *See,* more particularly, the application to criticism of Wittgenstein's observations in M. Weitz, *"Hamlet" and the Philosophy of Literary Criticism* (Chicago, 1964).
11. For documentation of this point, see R. Langbaum, "The Function of Criticism Once More," in *Yale Review,* LIV (1965), pp. 205–18.
12. See Wayne Shumaker, *Elements of Critical Theory* (Berkeley, 1952). On this point I agree entirely with Professor Shumaker, who closes his book as follows: "Judgments rendered against any evaluative reference frame, no matter how trivial, will have something of the character of proved fact if only the reference frame is adequately acknowledged. Judgments rendered against concealed standards, however, will always appear arbitrary and, to those unconvinced by rhetoric or authority, meaningless."

METHODICAL VIEWPOINTS
OF LITERARY EVALUATION

Luc Benoist

LITERATURE AND TRADITION

IN ORDER TO UNDERSTAND A PHENOMENON AS VAST AS LITERATURE WE may assume a number of different attitudes: we can, for example, analyze its varied elements or adopt a more synthetic procedure and bring into focus its corresponding necessities. I shall, however, approach it here from a third angle, a more realistic and profound one which with the help of history takes us to the very sources of literature. Thus its necessities as well as its means will reveal themselves in a far simpler and obvious way.

If we retrace the history of universal literature, going back as far as we can into the past, we arrive at the point where we see this literature disappear, leaving us with oral literature—not merely oral, but poetic, rhythmic, and chanted—a literature of action as the term *chanson de gestes* suggests, signifying a literature intended to accompany and comment upon action. This active event even marks the vocabulary since the major part of its words have their origin in the verbal expression of the gestures of the crafts. In every sentence the key word, the one which fosters the others, is the verb. It is not without significance that the voice of the Holy Scriptures says: "In the beginning was the Word" (in French "*verbe*").

In those historic times the sacred texts were passed on from father to son, from master to pupil, were memorized, and were eventually recorded in writing. They were the traditional texts. Let us therefore examine the relations that were established between this literature and tradition in the spirit of our master René Guénon. It would be simplest to go back to the origin of the actual setting down of these texts. History, however, is rather obscure on this point, and I shall choose to replace history with logic and consider whether the link that exists between literature and culture is an essential and necessary one and, as a result, whether a cultivated people without literature does indeed exist.

It is obvious that such people (as well as civilizations) without literature do exist. And it is the ancient culture of illiterate people which will permit us to determine the necessary elements of an absolute literature, for any culture worthy of the name carries within itself an ideal of formal beauty and quality which can be felt and achieved by everyone, whatever his degree of development or social condition. In more general terms: the recognition of a culture, of which literature is but a congealed and late phenomenon among many others, will allow us to analyze its bases. These I would term as follows: (1) a structural permanence, (2) a universal symbolism, (3) a primacy of the spirit.

The most casual look at the wealth of ancient literature reveals its ritual and poetic character, the Vedas or the Bible, for example, but the same is true for the epic poems of Greece and Persia. Many of these works existed long before they were recorded on parchment or paper, and some of them were never actually written down. We must therefore widen our concept of literature to include oral literature which at one time was the literature of whole civilizations and nowadays is that of "illiterate" peoples.

"*La lettre tue et l'esprit vivifie*" means that the important thing in regard to literature is not the fact of its being recorded but of its having been inspired, that is to say, its ritual character. This can only come about through its religious and quasi-organic origin. An unwritten literature is much more solidly anchored in the ancestral memory of man than any other. It is part of his heritage, part of his nature. It has the power to civilize him profoundly. Between a civilized and a merely "literate" people there is as much difference as between "to be" and "to have" in the sense established by Gabriel Marcel. A people whose memory is rich in the highest poetry is more completely civilized than a people possessing nothing but libraries with unread books. The mere capacity to read does not imply the realization and the advantages of this capacity. A people without books uses poetry not as a superfluous and elegant distraction in the sense of the Marxist "superstructure" but as ceremony, as ritual, as well as a necessary accompaniment to the most important moments of life such as births, weddings, burials, or traditional seasonal celebrations. In short, this poetry which we tend to reduce to the marginal role of ornamentation in initiations and other rituals was, on the contrary, a fixing of the gestures of *life* itself, the source of the rituals and of *art*, a human game mimicking *life*, a divine game in substance.

When these traditional rites and this vital necessity no longer exercise the memory, our assurance of finding in books what we have not learned or what we have forgotten exhausts our memory and causes it to decay. Since all tradition is linked to memory, man is thus removed from his sources; he becomes uprooted without having left his country, his town, or even his house. He is an uprooted man intellectually, spiritually, as well as socially, for language even more than the soil is his homeland.

From the Hindu point of view, as we are informed by A. K. Coomaraswamy, a man is not considered a scholar unless he *knows by heart*.[1] That which he has to memorize from a book merely forms part of his information. A Western scholar, in contrast to this, is someone who knows where to find the knowledge he lacks. This is why what is called information takes on such importance today. A superficial and inhuman kind of knowledge makes modern man a slave to a mechanical system of information. It is the ignorant slavery of a scholarly robot.

The same principal difference which separates spoken from written literature separates poetry from prose. Poetry is meant to be spoken and prose to be read. The merit of oral literature is essentially to be poetic; its content is a message of mythical nature and its inspirational sources are spiritual. We might say therefore that traditional literature is originally a kind of cosmic poetry imitating, so to speak, the process of creation as such. And whenever literature seeks to "purify itself," it must return to this source.

The legends that have been preserved and passed on by this poetry are indeed the original tales of the creation of the earth and of man, eternal objects in the depth of the consciousness of the individual. Tradition is known to be based on hereditary filtration, on the transmission of an imminent principle of spirituality, superior to man, founded on a visible permanence in the basic structure of his being, and in a symbolic language espousing this same structure.

We need only cast a glance at the present literatures of our civilizations in order to realize how far removed they are from these old models. Today we could divide our literary styles into two major groups: (1) literature of *fact* which reports the facts of history, legend, tales, novels, memoirs, portraits, biographies, all of which essentially compose the weft of the literature of fiction or entertainment, and (2) literature of *action* which contains writing of a critical, polemical, or utopian nature as well as philosophical and moral treatises which, in their most recent state, constitute the category of a literature of commitment.

The only category which in a certain sense has kept its ancient character of direct speech is the theatre. It is the only literature which can simultaneously serve as entertainment, as the expression of conflict or of ideas, and remain poetic. It is not a coincidence that the theatre of today appears to us as the most promising of all the categories of writing, even if its potential is not being realized.

We shall, however, keep our attention focused on history. We find that in the course of time a degeneration has deformed original inspiration. The primacy of the spiritual which reigned, for example, in the Middle Ages was replaced in the sixteenth century, upon the advent of the Renaissance, by an aristocratic primacy of formal beauty. Then after the bourgeois revolution of 1789 the primacy of romantic expression answered the popular need for strong emotion and sentiment. Through a different reaction, however, Romanticism had preached a certain anti-intellectualism, had returned lyricism to the place it had lost, had given expression to those men of depth who respond to the secret impulses which generate the fundamental themes of love, struggle, and death.

Novalis and Hölderlin, later Nietzsche and Heidegger, drew attention not to the declamatory word but to the intimate voice, the interior monologue of which all literature is born. This renewed poetic impetus manifested itself in a recollection of former conditions, in an anticipation of the future achieved by means of a technique of concentration common to both the poet and the prophet. Exercises in ecstasy have made it possible to regain and understand the rites of Oriental religions, the methods of leaving the self which produce the highest state of lucidity. The importance of the body in the life of the spirit has been understood. The ancient bard was part of a brotherhood and he sang in his turn just as the artisan took his turn at the instrument of his particular trade. Identity, or at least equivalence, existed between the two professional initiations. The ancient gods on whose behalf the poets spoke represented deified human passions. For our forefathers' memory itself was a divinity and a power since it presided over the continuity of life and the identity of self. We can see that the Romantics were both right and wrong at the same time. The original language was a memory which expressed an activity that was both practical in its symbolism and poetic in its expression. The voice of the poet was true to the voice he had "heard" which came from beyond, even when it had the sound of his own voice. He modulated his song after an ancestral wave just as the loudspeaker sends a voice over the invisible waves of the radio.

But nowadays an industrialized and mechanized civilization removes our language further and further from its origin. The search for abstraction has cast off all human support. This spiritual decapitation has lowered the literary function to the level of the biological as we may see, for example, in writers of the naturalistic school. The irrational element of ancient spirituality has been transformed first into the psychic subconscious and then into the somatic and the physical. Nevertheless man was left with his ancestral yearnings. He found himself alienated, deprived, and, as a result, in revolt. His literature thrives on violence and despair because of his weakness and excessive logic. With its devaluation of expression it suffers from all the excesses. Or else, at the other extreme, it takes refuge in preciousness. It would be inappropriate to judge this literature from a spiritual point of view since it is precisely from an absence of spirituality that it was born. It has constantly managed to replace the religious personality first by the scholar, then by the hero, then by the politician, by the organizer, and, finally, by the salesman. We thus witness a disappearance of any kind of hierarchy, a return to an undifferentiated primordial condition which incidentally has been foreseen by tradition.

This evolution is perfectly evident in the development of language from the original gnomic poetry onward. From the inspired word, language has sunk in our own day to what a contemporary critic, Roland Barthes, has found justification in calling "the zero point of writing." It is the ideal of a language *without qualities*, like Musil's hero; that is to say, a language as abstract as mathematics, the anticipation of a homogeneous society, of a mass civilization reduced to the level of pure sensation comparable to atonal music which relates poetry to prose and ends by confusing them—prose having become poetic and poetry prosaic in a common indeterminate state.

The most objective among contemporary writers are satisfied to pause before the object or, as Francis Ponge puts it, to take "a biased look at things" (*"le parti pris des choses"*), things which moreover fade away under a closer analysis, under the pulverization of the thought which reveals our "reign of quantity."

The veneration of the object in the *nouveau roman* transforms the latter into an herbarium, a mineral collection, a silent album similar to the *mutus liber* of the alchemists even if without their secrecy. The novel *The Planetarium* by Nathalie Sarraute begins with a forty-page description of a doorknob. The author tells us, however, that the real subject of her novel is creation at the instant of its birth. The contemporary writer who most truly writes in this state of genesis is Ferdinand Céline, a poet of the new spoken language, but he has at least understood the traditional role of literature.

Nevertheless the positive and ponderable element in contemporary literature is precarious, volatile, and illusory if it is not transformed into transcendent humanity. This is particularly true since the modern novel is without a plot, this wonderful thread of time, a factor more vital to us than space as Marcel Proust has precisely observed. Proust furthermore expressed the last state of a purely intellectual literature by placing it above life in a famous line from his "*Temps retrouvé*": "Real life, life discovered and illuminated at last, consequently the only life truly lived, is literature," but it is a literature that has arrived at its ultimate calcification in exact opposition to the concept of a literature which is oral and vital.

We must now emphasize a phenomenon of the greatest importance: if literature can only express that which is outside and above things with the help of these things and their spoken images, it is because words correspond much more closely to the images which we have of things than to the things themselves. Literature is a vast masked ball. We express our sensations, our feelings, with the help of ideas rather than, as we tend to think, by the reverse process. Every expressed idea, however, is far from bringing enlightenment because the ideas themselves are in turn explained through the help of the objects, and thus one mystery is explained by means of another. As Claudel says, "the eye listens," and when nothing is there to talk to it, it looks without seeing and without understanding. For, as we are told by Théodule Ribot, we are only able to see what we know or imagine in advance. We are only able to see when we can interpret a scene with words burdened by their past, heavy with everything our ancestors have seen, lived, and thought with those words. We are compelled to encompass the world with the words of our ancestors, words which are the more significant the greater their age, the more marked by their long history. But because of a fatal generalization of vocabulary, because of a metaphoric extension of the real sense of the word, an organism which formerly served the movements of a living entity calcifies. Literature reabsorbs itself and descends to a formalism which belongs to the realm of the *précieux*, the *rhetoriqueurs*, the baroque, the euphuists, and the Gongorists. Literature is reduced, so to speak, to the "zero point of writing," as we have seen. This zero point belongs to a quasi-mathematical language which in its generality is a parody of metaphysics, a petrified metaphysics which shows its excess today. It is applied abusively to everything from the most instinctive, subconscious, and sensual language to the language of drugged minds with an indefiniteness which removes the boundary between the true and the false, between poetry and prose, lucidity and madness. This process renders all the more topical and acute the efforts in France of Lacan and Foucault to put literature on trial, for they have opened up a chasm between words and things as if at all times ideas were not superimposed upon them both, with knowledge being, as Plato tells us, merely a recollection or memory. Plato has also stated, returning to the idea of oral literature, that the man who occupies himself with "serious things" must not write but teach. We know that what he called serious things were not meant to be personal and human objects, but eternal truths, the real nature of the human being, the spiritual food of our immortal part which every wise man has to face seriously. Our mortal part may survive on bread alone, but it is by means of myth, the basic structure of things, that humanity is nourished. On the other hand, it perishes if we substitute the pseudo myths of race or of progress for our real myths.

If modern literature is still capable of producing works of value, it does so because of its ability to remain frequently faithful to its original inspiration in its attempts, today as in the past, to reproduce the facts and acts of man. Contrary to popular opinion, is it not the human activity in a work which becomes dated but rather its explanation, not the sequence of action but its psychological interpretation. What remains of lasting value is the pure action, the progress or the fall of the hero. In order to characterize this kind of novel, the Germans have created the word *Erziehungsroman*, the novel of education or development. I would describe such a work as *vocational* in the sense that the myth of the initiation of the artisan is also the history of a vocation, because the discovery in the most illustrious works of literature of the thread of these ancient rites would not be due to a sterile and distant survival, a dedicated plagiarism, but because these rites owe their sequence and their reason for being to the lives of men who experienced them. Rites and works of art derive from the same model. The initiations and mysteries of Eleusis retraced the daily labors of agrarian civilizations. The rites of Western trade guilds retrace the stages of work of the builder. The myths of

Genesis echo the everlasting nostalgia for a lost Paradise. The Platonic myths speak of man's double ambition which rends his body and soul.

It is not farfetched therefore to recognize in time-honored works a rather clear reflection of these aspirations. The treasure coveted by the hero of a narrative, symbol of happiness and celestial joy, takes diverse forms. It can be—stated quite clearly—Paradise itself, or an invisible sacred object such as the Grail, or a symbolic flower, the rose or lotus, or the love of a woman as real as she is symbolic like the betrothed of the fairy tales. In these works the hero, aided by supernatural intervention or by his own inspiration, struggles with his enemies, triumphs over obstacles, accomplishes difficult tasks, conquers his lost bride and achieves happiness. In its essence, that part of all written literature, including that of our own day, which survives the vicissitudes of fashion is only a fragment of this whole, limited to the quest, the triumph, or the fall.

Having said this much, it is easy to confirm the process of initiation in a variety of works of diverse nature, language, and date. The reader is asked to excuse those analogies which might seem to him elementary; I have preferred them to very unusual examples. In his *Paradise Lost* Milton depicts Satan, the first romantic hero, who has been hurled into an undifferentiated chaos together with the rebel angels and yet promises them their return to Paradise. But after the creation of man, Satan, jealous of man's happiness in Eden, succeeds in having Adam and Eve driven in turn from Paradise. Milton's poem stops with the Fall and does not relate the Redemption. The situation is quite different in Bunyan's *Pilgrim's Progress* whose hero moves from the city of perdition to the celestial city, as in Dante's voyage. The splendid analysis of the latter by René Guénon is too well-known to require recounting here.[2]

The *Legend of the Holy Grail* is also a tale of a spiritual ascension. It is a description of the life of medieval chivalry according to the Cistercian viewpoint. The hero Percival is a kind of knightly messiah who in the course of his adventures meets a sick and powerless sinner-king whose kingdom and whose people have been stricken with sterility. The king leads Percival into his castle where he takes part in a mysterious ritual procession in which young women clad in white carry a spear repulsively covered with blood, a trencher, and a precious vase encrusted with stones: this is the famous Grail. After many trials and a religious initiation he conquers the Grail and brings life to the bewitched kingdom.

A less well-known example, although the Peking Opera has produced it on the stage, is the Chinese novel *Si Yeou Ki*, the voyage to the Occident. It concerns a Chinese monk's quest for some sacred Buddhist texts in India. The novel transfigures the historical narrative. It tells of how the hero, Hiuan Tsang, protected against all hostile and infernal forces by a superhuman delegate of Taoism, the Monkey-King Souen Hing Tchö, succeeds in bringing back to China the authentic sermon texts of the Buddha.

Paradise, the Holy Grail, the contents of the sacred books of the Lesser Vehicle,[3] are the themes of direct and illuminating narratives the nature of which needs no exegesis. Nor need we linger over the mysterious alchemical texts in which the search for gold may simultaneously conceal the acquisition of material wealth and the Philosopher's Stone, that supernatural substance which, according to the Vedas, is immortal.

We have seen that the most spectacular elements in these quests consist of voyages, trials, and combats, and that frequently the narratives do not go beyond such preliminaries as these or the separation of couples which we find in the beginning of every love novel. The true battle is the one between good and evil, vice and virtue, the one which brought fame to Hercules after his victory over the monsters which ravaged the universe. The Spaniard Prudentius has represented this struggle between good and evil in his *Psychomachy* where these psychological entities have donned the breastplate and taken on the arms of the warriors. This eternal struggle between good and evil can be found simplified and adapted to modern taste in the detective story. Chesterton has given us a masterpiece of metaphysics in his *A Man Named Thursday*, in which at the end we recognize beneath the mask of Mr. Sunday, chief of police and gang leader at the same time, the mysterious powers of God the creator.

Yet the struggle can be assumed without obvious reward, as a mere trial. This is the case in the most venerated book of India, the *Bhagavad-Gita*. This fragment of the *Mahabharata* tells of the struggle for supreme power which confronts two branches of the same family: on the one side the five sons of Pandu with Arjuna at their head, and on the other side their uncle Duryodhana and his ninety-nine brothers. In front of the two armies which are lined up for battle Arjuna is led on his chariot by Krishna disguised as a relative of the line of Yadu. The dialogue which flows between them forms the heart of the poem. Arjuna seems to weaken in this fratricidal battle and his soul is beset by despair. He cannot reconcile himself to striking out against men of his own blood, but Krishna persuades him that to refrain from doing so would be a crime against his vocation as well as his honor and would still not prevent the battle. He tells him, "The truly wise man sees struggle in repose and repose in struggle."

The same lesson is taught by the novels of chivalry although the action may seem absurdly gratuitous to us. But it is precisely this gratuitousness which constitutes its nobility. This attitude, mingled with courtly love, appears in Moslem Spain in the midst of an Arab civilization influenced by secret societies. The chivalrous cult of womanhood which later dominates all classic French literature shows its true colors here as action and as sacrifice. To win the heart of his lady, the lover becomes the accomplished warrior and the inspired poet, thereby imitating Mejnoun who fell in love with Leilah at first glance. The Sufis regarded him as the model soul who, by abnegation and sacrifice, obtains in death the kiss of God.

By way of Andalusia this poetry took over the entire Occident, and in the eleventh century the poets of Provence were inspired by it and lent it their themes, their images, and their rhythms. Love, they considered, was the mover of all action and the principle of every kind of merit. The feeling which consecrates it is *joy*, knowledge through rapture, a state of grace and of harmony with the world, of intoxication with its beauty. Such is the secret of the initiated Sufi whose vocabulary the poets have adopted.

Not all heroes are that fortunate, however; witness the protagonist of the *Roman de la Rose*. It is true that it is the story of a dream, and that the poet upon awakening can easily console himself for not having been able to pick the flower of his desire. The theme of the search for the beloved is very often paralleled, especially in tales of wonder and imagination, by the theme of pursuit which is embodied in the Westerns of our own day. A king promises his daughter to the one who accomplishes a predetermined exploit, usually impossible without supernatural aid. This daughter is often the helper and accomplice of the would-be fiancé. Such is the case in the story of Jason whom Medea helps in his perilous adventures. The same is true in other tales with the theme of the ogre's daughter and the young man—tales with which we are familiar from well-known versions such as *La belle au bois dormant* and *Peau d'âne*.[4] Instead of having to search for a treasure or a bride, the hero is obliged to become himself after having been transformed into an animal, the transformation serving as a symbol for his degradation to subhuman levels. Sometimes he loses only a special faculty or a part of his human body, such as his voice, his sight, his beauty, or his intelligence. He might be in search of his heart or the light, an allusion to the enlightenment of the initiated. The *Golden Ass* of Apuleius, for example, has his real face restored by eating rose petals and is thereby initiated into the mysteries of Eleusis.

In the *Arabian Nights* the metamorphoses are countless. I single out *The Porter and the Three Ladies of Baghdad* because it touches on an interesting theme: the magicians' duel. A sorceress who restores to his original human form one of the heroes who had been transformed into a monkey, enters into combat with the ifrit, the originator of this transformation, and by dint of opposed metamorphoses and increasing power kills her opponent. In *A Midsummer Nights' Dream* Shakespeare gave Bottom an ass's head. Goethe in *Faust* makes use of the myths of rejuvenation and the acquisition of secret knowledge, the same myths which our modern scientists pursue nowadays.

Life is more or less a successful apprenticeship, and it is not surprising that many notable works have made use of the apprenticeship symbol. In *Wilhelm Meister* Goethe's hero is the apprentice of death and of immortality, like the initiates of secret societies. Wilhelm can fulfill himself neither as poet nor actor but only in the active life of his trade as carpenter which is also the trade of The Architect of The Universe. Novalis' hero is a miner who in the practice of his trade discovers miraculous metals which ripen in the bosom of the earth like alchemical fruit. *Der grüne Heinrich* by Gottfried Keller is another novel of education as is Joyce's *Ulysses* in which the interior monologue, this poetic form of prose, allows the author to use a succession of styles like technical exercises, thereby himself becoming the artisan-hero of his book. Finally, Proust's work is also the novel of a vocation. His characters, like the victims of Arabian sorcerers, transform themselves into each other. They are subject to intermittences of the body as the author is to intermittences of the heart, to eclipses of memory, the illusions of passion, the deceptions of intelligence, the infatuation of desire, and finally the nothingness of the world which disappears beneath his quest as in Balzac's *Le Peau de chagrin*, to mention a truly beautiful book.

Travel, and especially the voyage to Utopia, forms an important part of writings of multiple meaning in which the persistent desire for the return to the Lost Paradise and the nostalgia for Eden is invariably hidden. I shall not at this point engage in a study of the

Platonic myths which are well known and have often been explored, but I cannot omit Atlantis, be it of real or mythical nature, nor the other miraculous cities such as *The City of God* by Saint Augustine, *Thélème* by Rabelais, *Utopia* by Thomas More, *Leviathan* by Hobbes, not to mention those of Saint-Simon, Fourier, Prudhon, Cabet, or Marx.

The myth of the desert island which furnished Defoe with his masterpiece is an admirable and simple theme. Shakespeare in *The Tempest* adheres to the notion of the restoration of a lost order on an enchanted island, regained from the savage anarchy of Caliban by the Sorcerer-Duke Prospero, whose name evokes prosperity in general. He delivers the celestial spirit Ariel and introduces a reign of the harmony of music and the rhythm of the sea in his kingdom.

These novels, poems, epics, and tales have not always received serious treatment but have rather been handled with a kind of humor which lends them the cruel mark of bitter truth. This is true for Rabelais who in his *Pantagruel* mocks the chivalrous idea with gross buffoonery. His Third Book shows Pantagruel carrying a colony of Utopians to Dipsody. Panurge constantly questions the opportuneness of his marriage concerning which he asks advice of an enormous number of ridiculous people and in desperation decides to consult the oracle of the Divine Bottle. His voyage continues in a Ulyssian circuit until he arrives before Bacbuc, priestess of the Divine Bottle. Despite the elaborate ritual Rabelais wrote a handbook of humanism, as we recognize from the famous formula he adopts: "Science without conscience is but destruction of the soul." Cervantes' great novel stems from the same spirit of positive criticism and humanistic ideals. Swift, on the other hand, is harsher, and his painful pessimism borders on madness. His descent to the underworld is without return.

The more time elapses and the more literature in its evolution departs from its origins, the more it loses its original clarity. The logical and brief structure of the real narration carried within itself a certain amount of credibility which composed its charming naïveté. The literary narratives, however, conceal under their borrowed tinsel the pure, unadulterated lines of the archaic theme.

Now that we have discussed the nature of literature, following traditional norms as well as natural evolution towards specialization and progressive quantification, the reader might expect to foresee its future forms and directions. This would be quite a presumptuous undertaking on our part. This is all the more true if, as we believe, the traditional rules are absolute models, in which case they are imposed on everyone, and no one can anathematize his own time without ridiculously setting himself up as the judge of Providence. As Léon Bloy has said so admirably, "For a believer everything that happens is admirable!"

It is possible, however, to determine the consequences of the traditional rules. And within the narrow limits of individual freedom it is advisable for everyone in literature as well as in other subjects to avoid two equally extreme positions: the dogma of a calcified pseudo tradition and the anarchy of a pseudo liberty without limits which is of interest to the observer only because the bankruptcy of its partisans allows us to determine the natural limits of our liberties.

That is the reason for the expiration of all dogma after a relatively short term. Only such work is possible which attaches to an interior reform adapted by nature to our heritage and compatible with our nature rather than hostile to it. This is the best way to surmount the stratification of classes which steadily increases in our civilization and hinders the development of a popular literature. In short, we must eliminate the difference which arises between two often confused notions, individual culture and collective civilization, produced things and accepted ideas, a monastic culture and an ant-hill civilization, a spiritual culture and a mechanical civilization.

Centuries of history stand between these two conceptions, and the tension which has developed between them has enabled a new romanticism to arise. Between the death of classical civilization and the void of the mechanical one, we have seen a competition of human progress arise. Are we to decide which is the road to salvation? Is it the relativity of civilizations rather than the universality of cultures? Or is it the bitter universality of our civilization rather than the relativity of culture? We need to regain the original unity of human culture. Or, to express it less dramatically, we need to search the fields of biology and psychology for arguments against a generalized mathematization. Our conscience revolts at the idea of the electronic brain. The fact is that our satisfactions are not of an intellectual nature alone but are at the same time biological, vital, subjective, as well as aesthetic and sentimental—desires which are satisfied by literature.

In our time science has for many of us replaced Providence, for those among us in any case who worship her without knowing her, which is indeed the only way of worshiping science. And she in turn worships a God unknown even to her priests. We are nevertheless not among those who at the close of the last century had declared her bankrupt. We shall be satisfied to have the scientists themselves show us the limits and barriers that they have temporarily encountered. Investigations on the atomic level have led us to question the concept of the immutability of natural laws. We know that certain phenomena do not conform to the laws of symmetrical reciprocity. In fact, it has long been suspected that asymmetry may be a law of existence of living things. Thanks to nuclear physics, it would appear that these two thresholds of indetermination provide us with a numerable symbol of our liberty, and this glimmer of light suggests that there is hope for the humanization of a science which has sore need of it. Biology appears on many counts to be in opposition to physics and protects us from complete mathematization of culture. The same is true of ethnography which recognizes a solid spiritual basis for the most scorned ancient civilizations.

These considerations, however, should be of no concern to literature if the limits of its proper domain are precisely defined, and these lie elsewhere. It must rid itself of everything which is of interest to other techniques and other arts, everything which can be seen, heard, or touched, and it must withdraw into its own intangible kingdom where nothing can follow it, the interior, invisible, and spiritual domain which has ever been its own. The constant mediator between consciousness and reason is the supernatural and informal spirituality which creates it. Tradition does not speak only one language but masters them all. The true language is not semantic but semeiological, not a grammar but an inspired word, and some of the most significant writers of our century, Proust, Céline, Miller, Musil, produced works which are a synthesis of all the genres: memoirs, essays, moral or sociological portrait sketches, journalistic accounts, and things observed. Tradition is a surrealism, true in its aim and in its inspiration. It is a culture which is older than civilization. Surrealism, the singular and final form of romanticism, has glorified instinctive inspiration perhaps too exclusively. By means of surrealism, the romantic revolution reached its apogee with Camus' l'Homme Revolté. This aperture into another world, aided by hallucinogenic drugs, was opened by the adherents of le grand jeu.[5] But this surrealism has, in fact, produced nothing of value in literature, and its principles remain more legitimate than its works which too frequently deserve the hard judgment of one of its writers who considered "the conversations not only unworthy of having been written but even of having been heard."

Another attempt to direct culture toward civilization was made by existentialism, a movement with a better reputation which produced better results; but between the two institutions there is language, that is to say literature. Can technique, which governs existential man of the new breed, convert materially civilized man into a spiritually cultivated being? Must we not recognize here a paradox and a utopian situation?

The return to tradition is a return to original principles. Biology has demonstrated that the most powerful energy is found in the germ and in all beginnings in general. This is the secret of the return to childhood and of the immortality drugs of the Chinese tradition. At the point of origin the possibilities are limitless, but the passage of time and the increasing development of forms reduce the number of possibilities, close many paths of development, reduce the role of chance. In order to acquire new energy we must place ourselves at the point of departure. We must, as in the ancient initiations, rise up from hell to find rebirth, destroy the reign of quantity by seeking quality. What have others done—Proust, Céline, Miller—but recount and relive their childhood?

But simultaneously a return to origins is to rediscover the sacred domain, since the profane individual is only a degraded believer and not a total atheist. This return to a sacred state, however, must be governed by the conditions it imposes, by ancient and precise rules.

This intangible sacred domain still exists. If its name and appearance have changed, it has nevertheless not disappeared. It has progressively restricted itself to certain places, certain periods, certain celebrations, certain individuals, to an inwardness of man, to his soul, to poetry. The interiorization of the sacred realm has progressed at a pace proportionate to the dominance of the world by rationalism. Certainly it is easy to believe that man only values a subjectivity which has been vaunted by psychoanalysis. Despite appearances, it is the same phenomenon. What changes are the words, the supporting and transferring metaphors, while the goals remain unaffected. The essential is concealed within the dynamism of the idea and not in the static word.

The task of contemporary literature is to find an expression of a new spirituality or, rather, a new form of an eternal spirituality which is itself constant. Beyond theology, psychology, ethnology, and sociology each individual strives to attain this common center. René Guénon alone has long ago described its nature, and this quest constitutes a posthumous triumph for him. During the search for this universal sacredness, the name of "primitive Christianity," that is, natural Christianity, has been applied to it. Religion is not the parasite so abused by the rationalists but the enduring concept of humanity glorified by art, literature, and theology. The work of art is a ritual of beauty, the symbol of pure being, which has the merit of not mutilating man in his development. The same is true of literature which is a common language gathering men of the new civilization, a night-school for new savages. It must be able to speak the languages of all its members, their dialects, their jargon, their slang, and their nonsense, provided that beyond this short-lived union the heart can be reached. The genuinely civilized man must rid himself of his own culture in order to render himself susceptible to all possibilities. The present role of literature is to civilize existence.

Poetry, above all, will show the way. It requires no logic foreign to itself. The poet sees the invisible. His memory is that of the collective subconscious. He divines that which is hidden and, more particularly, that aspect of the future which is already present in the thought of today. He adopts the spiritual exercises of Eastern religions which facilitate the recollection of former lives. This memory of the past is achieved by a control of breathing, the soul of life. The concentration induced by the holding of one's breath develops this memory.

Tradition thus conceived and revealed reigns above and beyond all form. Esoterism, the means and the explanation of this tradition, attempts to by-pass all cultures in an effort to attain universal constants and arrive at a position of command over tomorrow's civilization, regardless of the form it may assume.

[Translated from the French by Manya Mauner]

Notes

1. A. K. Coomaraswamy, "The Bugbear of Literacy," in *Asia and the Americas*, February, 1944.
2. René Guénon, *L'ésoterisme de Dante*, 3rd ed. (Paris, 1946).
3. "Lesser Vehicle" is a synonym for Hinayana-Buddhism.
4. Tales of Charles Perrault. Cf. Gédéon Huet, *Les contes populaires* (Paris 1923). After Perrault's time the term "Fairies and Ogres" occurs; cf. Andrew

Lang in his introduction to *Perrault's Popular Tales* (Oxford, 1888), p. XXXV.

5. *"Le grand jeu"* refers to a complete set of Tarot cards used not for a card game but as a collection of esoteric wisdom and tradition. Cf. the book of Arthur Edward Waite, *The Pictorial Key to the Tarot* (New York, 1959). In France predicting the future is sometimes called *"le grand jeu,"* especially when Tarot cards are used. In the above context the term is used as it was by a small group of French prewar writers among whom the most prominent was René Daumal, author of *Mont Analogue*. They used this term as the title of a journal of which only a few numbers appeared. René Daumal and his friends were much influenced by the remarkable initiate Gurdjieff who sought by means of drugs and certain esoteric rites to go beyond the literary stage which for him was only a means and not an end.

Walter Hinderer

LITERARY VALUE JUDGMENTS
AND VALUE COGNITION

IN THIS ESSAY—WHICH COULD WELL BE SUBTITLED "SOME PROPAEDEUTIC
Observations on Anthropological Aesthetics"[1]—I deal with what is in
many ways a curious problem and, despite the apparent "unscientific
nature of the topic,"[2] I propose to keep it experimental in character but without limiting myself solely to the experimental approach. Yet what, in terms of "literary value judgments," does the
word "unscientific" mean? It dismisses a topic as dubious because it
has no place in science. But the remarkable thing about this topic
is not only that it has a place among the presuppositions[3] and principles of a science which discredits it, but that it is applied, consciously or unconsciously, in scientific practice. Walter Müller-Seidel
has found a formula for this: "Editing and interpretation are interrelated in the same way as interpretation and evaluation."[4] For every
thorough interpretation, in displaying the methods of literary scholarship, demonstrates the value of its object. Moreover, it is in the nature
of the aesthetically valuable that it and it alone provides a high
interpretative yield:[5] indeed, for reasons to appear later on, there is
no ceiling to interpretation.[6] Wilhelm Emrich, drawing on Friedrich
Schlegel, has spoken of a "continuum of reflection." According to
René Wellek and Austin Warren, the impossibility of interpretation
inherent in a literary work of art is explained as follows: "The
'materials' of literary works of art are, on one level, words, on another
level, human behavior experience, and on another, human ideas and
attitudes. All of these, including language, exist outside the work of
art, in other modes; but in a successful poem or novel they are pulled
into polyphonic relations by the dynamics of aesthetic purpose."[7]

The "continuum of reflection," the multivalence of the work of art, the integration of the various parts of the whole work,[8] the "imaginative integration" and "amount (and diversity) of material integrated,"[9] all form part of a very complex interrelationship, and it is necessary to analyze this interrelationship in order to establish the principles of a theory of literary value judgment.[10]

Let us first examine the misgivings prompted by the topic "literary evaluation." Is this discrepancy between science and its presupposition really attributable solely to science and not in some degree to the presupposition itself? There must be reasons why such a perceptive analyst as Northrop Frye finds it necessary, in his *Anatomy of Criticism*,[11] to comment on value judgments as follows: "Value-judgements are subjective in the sense that they can be indirectly but not directly communicated. When they are fashionable or generally accepted, they look objective, but that is all."

Is that really all? Have we not just said that, in terms of both value and evaluation, every interpretation must necessarily have preferred its object to other objects before it can set the whole hermeneutic apparatus in motion and apply it to the object found valuable or worth valuing? Would it not be futile, must it not appear ridiculous, to gear such efforts to an inadequate object? Since Hugo Kuhn's concept of "reduced interpretation"[12] it has been taken for granted that worthless literary works may also be appropriately dealt with, although with only a few simple tools rather than a large-scale apparatus. But what of scholarly editions? Is anything at all to be gained from devoting years of effort and extensive machinery to producing elaborate and costly historical-critical editions of works by third-rate authors? Must not the editor first inquire into the value of the object of his efforts?

We see how this curious problem of valuing tempts us to ask questions, but does that mean that the problem per se is "questionable"? Northrop Frye gives a straightforward answer: "Value-judgements are founded on the study of literature; the study of literature can never be founded on value-judgements."[13] This sounds apodictic, no doubt deliberately, although what is intended to be apodictic reverses the facts. But Frye's answer is not a frivolous one; it is just as firmly based on logical reasoning as are the answers of René Wellek and Austin Warren,[14] for example, or of Walter Müller-Seidel, Wilhelm Emrich, and Max Wehrli. Frye's polemical attitude[15] toward the subject of literary evaluation is founded on an insight shared with other scholars: namely, that judgments based on taste are subjective, arbitrary, and fundamentally banal. For him, "Good taste follows and is developed by the study of literature; its precision results from knowledge, but does not produce knowledge."[16] Our aim is not to discuss the misconceptions of Frye's polemic but merely to bear in mind that he adopts a position which amounts to the commonplace: *De gustibus non est disputandum*. But this commonplace has a history of reasons to ignore which would be, to say the least, irresponsible. This history has as its premise a correct observation: that taste judgments are based only on subjective experience, not objective cognition. However, this fact—i.e., that taste judgments proceed from an emotional experience brought to consciousness by the functions of the intellect—is clearly indicated by the compound noun itself, "taste judgments." Now, if the powers of intellect bring to consciousness the feeling of value, this does not necessarily mean that value feeling is corrigible by the intellect; the only thing that is corrigible is the judgment which proceeded from the value feeling. From this we see that Frye, in his interpretation of an essentially correct partial aspect, has not been sufficiently precise or done adequate justice to the process of value cognition. Nevertheless, this imprecise statement makes it clear that in fact the Janus-headed problem of evaluation cannot be put down merely to science: it also inheres in the thing itself, to which Immanuel Kant has given the following universally valid definition in his *Kritik der Urteilskraft*:[17]

> Now the concepts in a judgement constitute its content (what belongs to the cognition of the Object). But the judgement of taste is not determinable by means of concepts. Hence it can only have its ground in the subjective formal condition of a judgement in general. The subjective condition of all judgements is the judging faculty itself, or judgement. . . . Taste, then, as a subjective power of judgement, contains a principle of subsumption, not of intuitions under *concepts*, but of the *faculty* of intuitions or presentations, i.e., of the imagination, under the *faculty* of concepts, i.e., the understanding, so far as the former *in its freedom* accords with the latter in its *conformity to law*.

With this definition Kant, the brilliant analyst of the human intellectual apparatus, has categorized the problem of value as a peripheral phenomenon of the theory of cognition. In the light of the *Kritik der Urteilskraft*, are *any* value-theory considerations permissible? Is it worth-while to devote ourselves to an object which forces human cognition from a position of unequivocal objectivity into subjectivity, degrades it, so to speak, to the status of servant of an untrustworthy mistress? It is questions like these that show us the chief misconception in the history of reasons that led to negative answers, since such questions imply a pragmatic point of departure which, seen from the standpoint of the phenomenon of value judgments, is false.

A feeling of value is a response to an object, to a work of art. Hence in discussing literary evaluation we must include not only the linguistic work but also the person reading or listening to it—indeed, where possible, the creator of it. A feeling of value is embedded in a complex relationship between the act structures of the creator and the recipient and the multistratified nature of the art object serving as the medium between them. An analysis of the personal act structures that are geared toward certain strata in the linguistic work, that respond to this work of art, will always uncover the innate legitimacy of such a work which, as Käte Hamburger has demonstrated in her book, *Die Logik der Dichtung,*[18] enjoys its own mode of existence.

I

In every discussion of values, the object of value judgments remains untouched. No one questions the existence of valuable objects, or the existence of a gradation of valuable objects. So, whereas the fact of valuable objects, the existence of values, remains undisputed, doubts focus merely on the feasibility of value cognition. In his *Kritik der Urteilskraft,* Immanuel Kant has already demonstrated the impossibility of value cognition on a conceptual basis. The intellect depends on the "free play of emotional forces" which proceeds from a complex relationship of acts set in motion in the recipient by the work of art. The subjectivity of the acts entails relativity of judgment, a relativity that is deplored and forms the basis for the discussions of values. Unquestionably aesthetic value is not an absolute value inasmuch as it only manifests itself in the reaction of the beholder or the recipient, i.e., in the personal domain. However, in recognizing that value judgments are relative we cannot conclude that values are relative too, but merely that value judgments are subjective. On the contrary: the relativism of value judgments and value ideas proves that values are objective. False judgments and intuitions of an object can only be corrected if there is a correct and permanently valid judgment or a correct and permanently valid intuition of an object. The work of art per se remains, as we have said, unaffected by the failure of our value judgments. An incorrect value feeling misses the mark; but some value judgments find their mark. The relativity of value judgments merely proves, therefore, that subjective judgments are conjoined with the person, that mistaken judgments—of which there is no dearth in the history of literature—are always the fault of the person.

Now some people are, as we know, endowed with more subtle organs with which to judge works of art, just as some people are endowed with better sensory organs. We take it for granted that color sense presupposes a soundly functioning organ. Why should it be otherwise with the organ designed for value feelings? This is why Max Scheler and Nicolai Hartmann have spoken analogously of "value blindness." Just as the universal validity of a mathematical proposition does not necessarily imply that everyone can understand it, "but merely that everyone who understands it must agree with it,"[19] so the universal validity of aesthetic values does not necessarily mean that evidence of it is felt by everyone. Aesthetic values demand an adequate attitude, a trained or reliably functioning organ. Moreover, the fact that the history of literature contains, albeit tacitly, a firm gradation of valuable works of art is an indication that aesthetic values transcend historicity.

These are claims which we shall shortly try to substantiate in more detail; but for the time being it seems clear that all doubtful attitudes toward value judgments are based not only on misconceptions but on pre-judgments, or better, pre-feelings. It follows that correct value judgments are not a matter of luck but of the adequacy of communication with the object itself. The value-feeling organ must not be encumbered with pre-judgments, pre-feelings, or arbitrarily formed opinions if it wishes to address itself adequately to the object—a process that is by no means always easy, especially in appraising contemporary art, for the human being is in part—an external but not uninfluential part—a historical creature, embedded in a whole cluster of behavior compulsions that stem from his environment. The multiplicity of human potentiality can exhibit every typology of life form,[20] occupation and rank, social stratum and social change, psychological attitude,[21] historical[22] and world-view image, philosophical system,[23] method of scholarship in the natural sciences and the arts, human thought form, level of consciousness,[24] and possibilities of expression—all from the most diverse perspectives.

These perspectives demonstrate clearly that man is a multistratified creature occupying a position in a broad scale of interrelationships. This multistratification reappears in the "culture objectivations" by which man seeks to realize himself as a being, precisely
because, in every aspect of the being-side of his existence, he lives in
a "state of unknownness." As Karl Mannheim reminds us in his
lecture "*Seele und Kultur*,"[25] Kant realized that for man "not only
the surrounding world but we ourselves are merely manifestations
and in the final analysis incomprehensible, since all we get to see is
the shining reflection of our nature." Among these culture objectivations, by which man, through complex arrangements of interrelationships, through material-shaping energies, expresses this "shining
reflection of his nature," are works of art. The spiritual values "shining forth" in such works of art are part of the potentiality of human
nature. The Beautiful, the True, and the Good are the three highest
values or ideas of Occidental tradition. The mingling of these values,
particularly in the concept of *Kalokagathie*,[26] has brought a good deal
of confusion into aesthetic discussions, a confusion with an old and
pragmatic tradition. In an age such as the Enlightenment, which was
chiefly concerned with an educational program for the bourgeois
class, literature had a practical function, a single function, placing
the reason-oriented doctrine of virtue above all aesthetic values. Likewise in the Middle High German classical period, the "System of the
Virtues" of an elite[27] stands well to the fore. But in addition to moral
philosophy, which clearly seems bent on triumphing over aesthetics,
in addition to Christian ethics and secular systems of virtues, there
exists a further source for the coalescence of the ethical and aesthetic
spheres: that of rhetoric.

In an interesting work[28] Klaus Dockhorn has demonstrated how the
skeleton of "pragma–pathos–ethos," of presentation of "facts–character–passion," flowed into the various poetics, maintaining itself
there until the time of Lessing, Schiller,[29] and the Romantics. At
least since Cicero and Quintilian, the aim of rhetoric has been to
ultilize the subject of a speech to convince (*probare*), and to utilize
the passions to move (*movere*) the emotions. Yet we see that behind
the basic concept of rhetoric there stands an anthropological view.
Rhetoric, whose goal is influence, aims its arts of persuasion at all
three human faculties: at the intellect (*probare*), at the imagination (*conciliare*), and at the emotions (*movere*). The person wishing
to use such means effectively must be not only a master of these

talents but also an artist, since he must generate those faculties in his audience by means of his oratory. Yet what happens when this consummate skill falls into the wrong hands and serves a wrongful cause? We see why the primary attitude demanded of an orator is virtue. Cicero says in *De Oratore*:[30] "For should we wish to teach eloquence to those who lack these virtues, we would not make orators of them: instead we would be placing weapons in the hands of madmen."

These views were echoed in poetics, in aesthetic programs and writings, and still wield their influence today. Hermann Broch, who ridiculed the aesthetic outlook of *l'art pour l'art* and dubbed "the goddess of beauty" a "goddess of kitsch,"[31] regarded "the problem of art as such" as an "ethical" problem.[32] Like Plato, he placed art in the service of a higher purpose. Yet Hegel really does the same thing in describing the beautiful as a miracle of the past that the reflection level of the present can no longer produce.[33] But despite this covert feeling of the philosopher's superiority to art, Hegel in his *Ästhetik* saw with surprising clarity certain problems of interest to us here. Whereas Schiller in his "Kallias" letters to Körner defined "beauty" rather unfortunately as "freedom in manifestation,"[34] Hegel defined it as the "sensuous shining forth of the idea."[35] Like Kant, he differentiates the beauty-discriminating organ quite clearly from the faculty of scholarly thought: "Beauty in art offers itself to the *sense*, sensibility, intuition, imagination, it has a different domain from thought, and the grasp of its activity and its products demands a different organ from that demanded by scholarly thought."[36]

Where, then, is this organ located, and what are its properties? All we know is that it is anchored in the realm of feeling. But the behavior structures of value feeling, as we know since Max Scheler,[37] vary according to intended values, value levels, and value types, so that we must distinguish between an intentional "*feeling of something*" and "*all mere states of feeling*."[38] There is such a thing as a "primordial intentional feeling"[39] where the act of feeling is geared to the sensation of feeling. Sensory states such as pain and desire are felt and, in being felt, are transmitted to the centers of consciousness. The manner in which this process takes place in a person's various strata is described by Erich Rothacker in his book, *Die Schichten der Persönlichkeit*,[40] by means of an example. In feeling such values as "pleasant, beautiful, good," "feeling acquires a cognitive function in addition to its intentional nature."[41] Feeling is directed in this case toward something objective: i.e., values. This movement can, accord-

ing to circumstances, issue either from the self toward the object, or
from the object toward the self, a movement "in which something is
given to me and 'becomes manifest.'" It is to this phenomenon that
Hegel referred when, in referring to the beautiful, he spoke of the
"sensuous shining forth of the idea."[42] Max Scheler, however, has defined this phenomenon much more precisely from the aspect of
value-feeling behavior structures. Value feeling stands in the same
relationship to its value correlative "as the 'idea' to its object."[43] In
other words, this relationship is an intentional one. I shall shortly give
more concrete form to this somewhat abstract-sounding statement
in a closer examination of human value feelings.

II

The acknowledgment of the three human bases of organization—
physis, psyche, and nous—is an old one. We have phenomenology to
thank for the insight that the higher strata rest on the foundations of
the lower. From these various strata proceed the various faculties.
Idea and intuition presuppose the existence of sensory organs. The
mark of the human being is his intellectual potentiality, which enables him to rise above the limitations of his environment. By virtue
of this potentiality man is "open to the world," has "world."[44] A basic
trait of the human spirit is the ability to separate nature and existence
(cognition of nature and form), to abstract and ideacize. Man can not
only recognize objects existing in the sphere of the non-self; he can
also make objects of his own physiological and psychic make-up, his
psychic experiences and vital functions. The various strata are so
closely related, however, that in feeling acts and thought acts—
where the higher faculties are in turn "founded" on the lower—they
all invariably participate simultaneously; a very acute perception is
required to distinguish one act structure from another and to define,
say, the causality sequence of each.

For the lowest level of the responsive act, Konrad Lorenz,[45] the
researcher in the field of behavior and animal psychology, has discovered that man also possesses innate release mechanisms to which
certain types of behavior respond. The receptive correlative of such
release mechanisms is geared particularly to characteristics of expression. "In this way the most astonishing objects acquire quite
remarkable, highly specific values of feeling and emotion inasmuch

as *human* attributes are, so to speak, 'experienced on' them."[46] Impressions of nature, faces of animals, are thus automatically humanized. The essential element in this process is that we cannot exclude this "humanization" of objects from our consciousness. This is because our reaction to certain traits is automatic, a reaction at which our reason makes us smile but which we cannot obliterate. According to Lorenz, such release mechanisms are also the basis for our "aesthetic and ethical value senses."[47] Aesthetic scales of relationship are "tailored" to "certain proportional characteristics of the human body."[48] He demonstrates this to be a matter of innate reaction processes by pointing out that the whole kitsch industry consistently makes use of "the form- and relationship-characteristics" to which our mechanism responds. Lorenz ascribes the aesthetic appeal of what primitive tastes regard as "beautiful" to "a 'perception' of numerical harmony."[49] In other words, the principle that is exploited by fashion and advertising is that of the "golden section." In ethics the motifs that prompt an emotional response in us are likewise relatively few. Here, too, the experience takes place automatically: we cannot blot it out, even when reason tells us we should reject the manner of presentation as being of low caliber.

What conclusions can we draw from this for our problem? From the innate release mechanism, which reacts to very simple sensory (or imagined sensory) relationship traits, we see an interweaving in all responses of ethical and aesthetic reactions. We also see that reason cannot obliterate these reactions but can merely correct them later. All this is empirical proof of our discovery that in act structures, as they occur in aesthetic evaluation within the cluster of value feelings, the higher levels rest on the foundations of the lower strata or faculties. To speak of a special organ of value feeling is not meaningful inasmuch as the value act takes place on all strata. The process begins with the relationship traits to which the release mechanism responds; this leads to the aesthetic emotional state at which, almost simultaneously, the act of feeling is directed and proclaims itself in our intellect as judgment. Moreover, we see here how unreliable is the concept of "the beautiful"; all it really does is describe the receptive correlative of the release mechanism which, as we know, is the unreliable step in the value act. So Hermann Broch is right to describe the "goddess of beauty" in art as the "goddess of kitsch." But Broch's other observation—that without "a dash of kitsch"[50] no art can succeed—also seems correct, because even the highest step of the value act cannot exist without the lowest. At this point, however, we find a further characteristic that argues against the definition of the aesthetically valuable as "the beautiful." All art, especially the linguistic work of art, represents a plurality of values as far as the art remains within the human sphere. "Beauty value" is only a very external part of such value presentations and by no means their most important. Consequently it may sometimes be absent. It will not even be missed.

Aesthetic value is founded on a plurality of values and hence, even when beauty value is present in a particular work, is on a higher level than beauty value. Traditional aesthetics has completely failed to recognize this fact, and the result of this fundamental misconception is a whole cluster of false deductions.[51] What is true of the beautiful seems, if we slightly extend Nicolai Hartmann's exposition in his *Ethik*,[52] to be true of the good, which is subordinated to ethical value. In his *Tractatus Logico-Philosophicus*,[53] Ludwig Wittgenstein has given precise formulation to this fact: "It is clear that ethics cannot be expressed. Ethics is transcendental. (Ethics and aesthetics are one.)"

The "truth criterion" of the aesthetic and the ethical is evidence,[54] and evidence neither is produced by nor proceeds from concepts. In his *Strukturanalyse der Erkenntnistheorie*,[55] Karl Mannheim has described evidence as the "psychological truth criterion" and has distinguished it on the one hand from the ontological truth criterion, which regards as true every proposition corresponding to reality, or to being, and on the other from the formal or logical truth criterion, which regards as true every proposition conceived with logical necessity. Accordingly, value feelings or value insights are evidential in character; they occur in a series of feeling acts, which we may simply call value acts. It is important to note, however, that the higher value acts of the aesthetic and the ethical are always mere by-products: in other words, they can be achieved only via the intention of other, i.e., extra-aesthetic or extra-ethical value objects. Hence what we call aesthetic value, to which our value feeling responds positively, is constituted not through direct intention (not even in the case of the writer or the artist) of a certain aesthetic value but rather through the sum of all the inherent extra-aesthetic values and value responses.

In the history of aesthetics and literary criticism we continually find, side by side with the idea of "the beautiful," an emphasis on the secondary tendencies, the various values of action, of passions and emotions such as fear and pity, of materials, topics, and world images.

This is due, as we have said, to the complex interrelationship of acts in the analysis of which single components are often taken for the whole and the value object approached with preconceived opinions or pre-judgments that have been preformed by arbitrary conceptions and sentiments. Accordingly, value feelings which are later precipitated in judgment in a more or less faithful reflection of the emotions can represent only specific responses to individual strata and values in the work of art or be preformed by certain expectations. The value feeling which is adequate to its object and which, as it were, surrenders to it in the "free play of the emotional forces," unaffected by the external and internal conditions that would falsify the relationship, spontaneously embraces all the structures, strata, and value potentialities or valences inherent in the art object. Value feeling responds, so to speak, to the totality of the relationship traits, a totality that consciousness can only approach step by step and never simultaneously. Interpretation, which proceeds necessarily from value feeling, must therefore, according to conceptual analysis, continually return to its point of departure: value feeling. Hence interpretation is an appeal to the evidence,[56] an evidence, moreover, of the aesthetic value in value feeling.

A sense of value that is not intact, that has remained, as it were, in the forecourt of the release mechanism, can result in a kitsch outlook which may even focus on what is in fact an artistically valuable object. Hermann Broch was the first to point to the problem of the "kitsch person."[57] Ludwig Giesz devoted a whole chapter to this in his remarkable study, *Phänomenologie des Kitsches—Ein Beitrag zur anthropologischen Ästhetik*.[58] Although the problem of kitsch enables us to draw important conclusions on aesthetic value and literary evaluation in general, this is not the place to explore this matter further.

III

Literary value judgments are only possible when we are given appropriate value objects. To try to apply value judgments to the *memento mori*, for instance, of Old High German literature would be an odd project. Generally speaking, pure philology manages to get along without value judgments. It does not require a subtle sensory apparatus. But within the scope of "literary works of art," are there not cases where value feelings would be inadequate? The question is wrongly put; for value feelings always indicate the value level of the object as well. They decide automatically, i.e., spontaneously, on the gradation. But to speak of a gradation in itself gives rise to new problems. Doesn't an ode by Hölderlin rank higher than a poem by Conrad Ferdinand Meyer? This question is also wrongly put. As soon as a work of art achieves aesthetic value, distinctions on this value level are no longer possible, just as we cannot compare species—i.e., play off drama against the novel or both against poetry and vice versa.

Literature, even aesthetically valuable literature, is written by human beings for human beings. As Karl Mannheim has seen, even culture objectivations exist in a social context. Inasmuch as literature represents a creation for human beings it responds to a human need, in the process of which the needs, like the need-satisfying creations, correspond to anthropological strata. Conversely, this stratification is matched by a similar one in the literary work. These needs were met by literature when still at the oral stage, in fairy tales, myths and mythologems, and in the various saga forms. All values in literature, therefore, are also values responding to human needs, although this is not to say that these values are identical with literary values, to which, dissociating the aesthetic aspect from "the beautiful,"[59] we have given the general term aesthetic value. As Hermann Broch says,[60] the artist is concerned merely with "spying on the object, . . . ferreting out the laws by which the object operates," and hence, by our extension, with the intention of extra-aesthetic values. Hence literary-aesthetic value is, so to speak, "the ripe fruit that, after a lucky strike, falls into the lap [of the poet]."[61] It is true, of course, that from the general aspect of needs and extra-aesthetic values, literature, like other fields of art, contains a good deal of unripe fruit. But this is in the nature of things; for not every writer (and not every writer in every work), any more than every reader, listener, or viewer, can sustain his freedom from the extra-literary compulsions of needs and social behavior. In common with the viewer and the recipient, the creator is affected by contemporary taste and governing needs. The gamut of needs extends all the way from the desire for entertainment, for adventure, for the colorful diversity of events, for emotional upheaval, for the "pleasant," the "charming," the "delightful," for vicarious experience, to religious and spiritual needs, to worship, culture, and *Weltanschauung*.

Corresponding to every fulfillment of these desires and needs is a reaction according to the psychological pattern of desire/aversion with which the motivating mechanism on the lower level responds to the fulfilled or unfulfilled motivating goal. In the case of the intention of spiritual values, however, we do better to speak of needs rather than motivating goals, although higher needs rest on the foundations of the lower, or in other words are, as Max Scheler has shown, sublimated motivating goals in which the motivating energies for the attainment of higher values are given a new function.[62] The class of values stands in correlation to wantings, strivings, and needs; hence, with Scheler[63] and Nicolai Hartmann,[64] we distinguish between material values, factual values, vitality values, and pleasure values on the lower levels, and moral, aesthetic, and noetic values on the highest, the spiritual level.

These lower and higher literary values find their corresponding value responses in such types of feeling states as the charming, the fascinating, the capricious, the pleasant, the touching, the idyllic, the comical, the humorous, the sublime, the elegiac, the grotesque, the fantastic. In the history of poetics and aesthetics, these feeling values or modes of sensibility are erroneously interpreted as value genera,[65] as varieties of the aesthetic aspect. These in turn fan out into subspecies and entail many definitions of eras, trends, and styles. Schiller, in *Über naive und sentimentalische Dichtung*, was one of those who also used this method to differentiate between elegy, idyl, and satire. Such concepts as the delightful, the graceful, the pleasant, became typical concepts of literary rococo.[66] We use such terms as melodrama, comic epics, and comic novels. For reasons already demonstrated by Lessing and Schiller, the sublime and the tragic are feeling values that are most adequately achieved by tragedy. We could go on citing examples indefinitely. The time has come for a typology of the *artes poeticae*[67] to clarify these relationships historically, but we can already say that these feeling values are no more adequate for the definition of species, eras, and styles than concepts of extraaesthetic values are adequate for the definition of aesthetic value. Nevertheless, we can see from such values of mood or state that they are tied to particular topics, to certain necessary subject matter, and to a particular manner of presentation.[68] Specific values of mood or state demand specific subject matter—the "objective correlative," as it were, of these values—while specific subject matter in turn demands specific form. This reciprocity between subject matter, form, and feeling state or feeling value was discussed by Goethe and Schiller in their correspondence.[69] In a letter to Goethe dated 15

September, 1797, Schiller observed that the concepts of species and subspecies were to be categorized in this way: "It would be an excellent thing if you were to develop your ideas on choice of subject matter for poetry and the plastic arts with Meyer. This substance partakes of the very essence of Art, and its direct and simple application to true works of art would make it highly pragmatic and appealing." Schiller speaks of "the absolute determinateness of the object," and continues: "If we add to this proposition the further one that the definition of an object must always occur through means proper to an art species, that this definition must be consummated within the special limits of any one art species, we would have, I fancy, a criterion sufficient to protect us from being led astray in our choice of objects."

Since a close, mutually constituting reciprocity exists between form and object, it is possible to deduce concepts of species from formal and thematic-objective definitions, but with the proviso that these be supplemented by the various ways of feeling; for a constituting correlation exists likewise between way or genre of feeling and the object plus its adequate form. Yet when we use a feeling quality such as "graceful" to describe a literary object, we are describing not the aesthetic value but merely a value of feeling. Feeling values, of course, also vary according to the level of each. But low feeling values such as the graceful, the delightful, and, more particularly, the touching, prove that even as extra-aesthetic values they testify in some measure to aesthetic value, especially inasmuch as it is harder for them to achieve aesthetic value and they continually run the risk of sinking into the shallows of kitsch. On the other hand, such higher genres of feeling as the sublime, the tragic, are boring or comical in effect if they fail to achieve aesthetic value, to strike the "pregnant note," in Schiller's phrase—that is, fail in the adequate formal penetration of the subject matter.[70] Furthermore, apart from such failures, we must always, in evaluating literary works, be guided by the potentialities in a particular species' scope, bearing in mind that this scope is determined by subject matter, hence form and feeling. We cannot compare operettas with operas or operas with oratorios, popular novels with novels of the highest literary quality, philosophical poetry and epigrams with lyric poetry, or a rococo epyllion by Wieland with Goethe's *Faust*. Species also possess specific hallmarks and categories. All this seems very obvious, yet often enough the history of value judgments and false judgments seems to prove the contrary.

Now that general conditions have been further clarified, we can turn to the processes involved in the receiving of objects of literary merit. In order to make this more readily understandable, let us take an example that is simple and familiar and whose value is beyond dispute: the poem *Wanderers Nachtlied*,[71] which Goethe wrote on September 6, 1780.

IV

Über allen Gipfeln
Ist Ruh,
In allen Wipfeln
Spürest du
Kaum einen Hauch;
Die Vögelein schweigen im Walde.
Warte nur, balde
*Ruhest du auch.**

We will not attempt any interpretation here but will merely use the poem for demonstration purposes. Regardless of whether we read the lines or say them slowly to ourselves, we are immediately "tuned in," we experience an existential state of harmony, a state of feeling that lifts us out of whatever other state we happen to have been in. The poet had the power to transpose us into a mood or state of which he himself was conscious and which he could not capture conceptually. What quality of feelings do we experience in this state? It is a state of calm, of relaxation.[72] This calm emanates from Nature, and the beholder is embraced by it, becomes almost identical with it. As with the poet, so with the reader or listener, reverberations from this calm of Nature extend into the state of eternal rest intimated by the poet, a kind of fulfilled tranquility.[73] The poet achieves this effect

---

*O'er all the hill-tops
Is quiet now,
In all the tree-tops
Hearest thou
Hardly a breath;
The birds are asleep in the trees:
Wait; soon like these
Thou too shalt rest.

English rendering by H. W. Longfellow as in *An Anthology of World Poetry*, ed. Mark Van Doren (New York, 1936). [*Transl.*]

by a specific arrangement of words: the nouns name the subjects, the verbs denote the lack of activity, although in one case—the word *Ruh*—even the noun denotes lack of activity. Moreover, the word *Hauch* conveys not so much a noun-subject as a mood. Analysts of the verbal material have pointed to the effects of sound, to the acoustic phenomena. The governing meter is basically iambic. Lines 4, 5, 7, and 8 begin not with anacruses but with stresses breaking the regular starting rhythm. The final stress is particularly marked and this, also in rhythmical terms, brings the poem to an emphatic conclusion. Then we note that the individual sections of the poem (four altogether) are separated by increasingly strong caesuras. The first caesura, between lines 2 and 3, is marked only by a comma; the second, between lines 5 and 6, by a semicolon; and the third, between lines 6 and 7, by a period. Between the caesuras the lines are closely knit by enjambments, only the third section consisting of a single and hence exceptionally lone line (6).

This is enough to show us the many different ways in which the individual sections are knit together to form a metrical, grammatical, and logical unity, and how truly indissoluble is the unity they form. Wolfgang Binder[74] has given us an impressive demonstration of the similar subtle formal and material processes traceable in Hölderlin's short odes. If we applied this method to our poem we could explore the coordination of the sections all the way into the most minute elements of the language and bring to the surface the poem's step-like construction. All this would merely go to show how complex and subtle this seemingly simple work of art really is. Further, it has different layers. One of these is, of course, that of the verbal material which the poet has structured in this complex manner so that what is in fact incommunicable—beyond concepts—is communicated to our emotions. In his *Maximen und Reflexionen*[75] Goethe himself describes art as "the communicator of the inexpressible." This "inexpressible" eludes the grasp of even the most skillful analysis of form, which can lead only to the threshold where conceptual power of cognition ends and cognition of feeling—evidence—begins.

But is not this outermost layer of the poem—its verbal material—in itself something very non-objective? In this poem by Goethe, the experience of Nature, the objects of Nature, and the culminating thought, are all conveyed to us by material that has itself already been preformed by meanings. Goethe liberates these words from their everyday framework of meaning, giving them a new function through new coordination. It is nevertheless amazing that these simple letters (abstract signs for anyone unfamiliar with the language) should produce such an effect.

To explain this we must look to a second layer which, however, would not be present without the outermost layer. In terms of material this layer is no longer *in* the poem but in the inner realm of the listener or reader, or better, the recipient. The words trigger stimuli in our sensory organs, produce sound-forms and aural images from which our imagination picks up meaning-signs and then signals these on to the appropriate centers. In this process, acts of feeling and awareness are coordinated. Just as a record player reproduces music, the tone arm palpating the structure stamped into the record and passing the contents on to the loudspeaker, so our emotional intellectual apparatus reproduces the implanted contents of the poem and their qualities of meaning. Everything—our intuitions, perceptions, emotional values—is reproduced *in* us, which proves how greatly the work of art (in our example, the poem) depends on the person reading or hearing it. Every work of art is subject to this reciprocity, a state which in turn should ideally be supplemented by the creator of the work; for what has reoccurred in us through and in the poem has already occurred earlier in the poet. So we see that the poem communicates to us the poet's ways of experiencing and feeling, and these have to contain something of universal validity for them to be able to speak to us at all.[76]

Käte Hamburger[77] has convincingly defined the lyric species as existential on the basis that a lyrical "I" is always the speaker in the poem and that the poem has no fiction levels in the sense of a novel or a play, but merely one unmistakable voice. Nevertheless, lyric poetry, like all forms of artistic literature, has a symbolic rather than real mode of existence. The art object as such has no place in any context of reality: it cannot "be," it merely "means."[78] The *Gipfel*, *Wipfel*, and *Vögelein* in our poem are in no sense real mountaintops, treetops, and birds: they have only a vicarious function, they only "mean." Whereas actual objects "mean" no more than what they "are," art objects point beyond themselves, their direction being toward the object side and toward the conceptualizing sense that created—we may even say, structured—the art object.

It is this indissoluble "two-sidedness of object and meaning" that constitutes the symbol structure, the logic, of art.[79] It is only because literary art "means" something that we can "discover the meaning," i.e., interpret it. Kant's philosophy can be explained by a commentary, but it can never be interpreted because, as we have seen, interpretability requires the symbolic mode of existence. Kant's philosophy has a different logical structure from that of artistic literature; yet, as Roman Ingarden has shown in his penetrating analysis,[80] it is in the stratum of meaning of literary art that aesthetic values have their origin.

Now in a verbal work of art there are many associations of meaning originating in the plurality of strata, and the result is an accumulation of meanings. According to their symbolic structure, these meanings are actually function values which imbue the factual content with meaning but at the same time point and extend well beyond it. Käte Hamburger speaks here of "the variable tension between the meaning and what is meant."[81] Although what is meant in the factual contents includes this content, the latter occupies but a small space within the scope of meaning. This is because of the artistic "I's" creative act that supplies the form and structures the material and layers of the work. The direction of meaning, the sense-giving function, always points from the lower to the higher layer relationships, although at the pinnacle it does not come to an end but remains on principle open, never finding fulfillment in a factual content however the latter may be constituted. The "terminal meaning"—although strictly speaking there is no termination—is our experience of aesthetic value, which "shines forth"[82] in the complex relationship between poetry and poetry-recipient without materializing. Ingarden saw this climax as a "revelation of metaphysical qualities,"[83] and indeed it does lie beyond real existence structure. In the history of aesthetics this is also a frequently defined phenomenon but one that even Walter Benjamin[84] associates with the idea of "beauty": "the essential law of beauty is demonstrated in that beauty appears as such only through a veil." We say: aesthetic value does not shed its veil, it appears in value feeling, the sole authority capable of experiencing it.

The "unveiling of metaphysical qualities"[85]—Roman Ingarden looks at the phenomenon from the various strata—naturally begins with the work's object stratum, although the other strata are also involved. Ingarden[86] proposes dividing the strata in literary works of art as follows: 1) stratum of word-sounds and the sound-forms built on them occupying a higher level, 2) stratum of units of meaning on various levels, 3) stratum of a diversity of schematized views, view-continua, and view-series, 4) stratum of objects represented and their vicissitudes.

This series may be rearranged. What is important for us to realize from this theory of strata is that "characteristic value qualities"[87] are formed in each stratum. It appears to be a mark of high-caliber artistic literature in particular that it "must harbor a diversity of *different* aesthetically valuable qualities which, when combined, inevitably constitute a special, polyphonically formed harmony."[88] This recalls the statement of René Wellek and Austin Warren[89] quoted at the beginning of this essay. However, multivalence[90] is not a sufficiently reliable mark of aesthetic worth; for in the case of lyric poetry, let us say, where the quality of stratification is reduced by limitations of subject matter, such a criterion would overlook this species' specific-existential mode of existence which, as we have seen, originates in the poet's scope of utterance.

V

In describing value acts we lean chiefly on the works of Nicolai Hartmann,[91] whose *Ästhetik* has gone almost unnoticed by scholarly research,[92] and on Max Scheler's[93] and Moritz Geiger's[94] studies. We have seen in the course of this essay that the complexity of the art object finds response in a complex structure of acts. The elements of intuition, idea, pleasure, and evaluation are to be differentiated in this structure. In applying himself to the art object—in our case a poem—the art recipient is lifted out of, emancipated from, the real associations in which he existed as a person: he forgets the world around him, is "transported," becomes a "savorer of delight." Yet simultaneously with this there occurs an active and passive participation of every human faculty, a process almost analogous to the creative one. In his essay *"Goethe und die Naturwissenschaften,"*[95] Gottfried Benn has described it as follows: "It is a productive thinking . . . , a wide-ranging, perspective awareness of associations and origins, a submerging of thought in the object and an osmosis of the object in the envisaging spirit."

This "characteristic of inner re-creation"[96] accomplished spontaneously by our emotional and intellectual apparatus is linked to the "play of emotional forces" released in the recipient by poetry and to "imagination." But we must distinguish between the act of enjoyment and the act of evaluation. For the agreeable sensuous state, the feeling of pleasure released by the object, the enjoyment that is already more consciously savoring the sensuous state, and the value feeling (later to become a value judgment) then to be found in both act structures: these are all subsequent act elements that respond to the impressions received through the sensory organs. The reception of the sensory foreground or outermost layer of poetry must be completed for the act structures we have described to become effective and to be able to absorb the value qualities of the various layers. It must be emphasized that it is not the sensory organs but the subsequent act structures that convey these value qualities. In our example such value qualities were, for instance, the experience of a total state of existence, of (as has been said) a fulfilled tranquility. Subsequent act structures, while being founded on the structures of sensory cognition, operate independently of them.

Let us simplify matters by extracting two serially coordinated acts from this complex relationship between work of art and listener or reader: the responsive act and the re-creative,[97] but without overlooking the fact that these acts engender the phenomena of pleasure, enjoyment, and value judgment in free interplay. Schiller observed these relationships correctly in his twentieth letter, "Über die ästhetische Erziehung des Menschen," and described them in his concepts as follows: "Man cannot pass directly from perception to thought; he must take one step back because only by eliminating one determinant can the opposite one come into play. He must therefore, in order to exchange passivity for independent activity, a passive determinant for an active one, momentarily rid himself of all determinants and pass through a pure and simple state of pure and simple determinability." Schiller believes that on its way from perception to thought the mind passes through "a middle mood in which sensuousness and reason are simultaneously active." He has therefore also called this the "'free mood." Nietzsche describes this in Der Wille zur Macht[98] as the "aesthetic state" that "possesses a superabundance of means of communication simultaneously with an extreme susceptibility to stimuli and signs." The "aesthetic state" reacts directly to the symbolic mode of existence. It is this state that produces the adequate relationship to the "manifest nature"[99] of this symbolic mode of existence, embracing those unreal elements which the latter "makes manifest."[100] In the aesthetic state, pleasure and delight are the aesthetically value-indicative emotional elements which then find expression in value judgments. Although enjoyment has a passive component, it can still never deny its "I"-participation, its active component. To do so would entail surrender to the object, a typical mark of the kitsch person. Enjoyment—and this is a further interesting aspect of this act structure—is superimposed also over the extra-aesthetic value feelings that respond to the various layers. Hartmann substantiates this by saying: "All affirmative value feelings have an element of pleasure: the everyday ones associated with things and facts, as well as the vital and ethical ones."[101] For this reason alone, a value feeling cannot be entirely absorbed by extra-aesthetic values; besides, these latter, as Hartmann has convincingly shown,[102] are always merely the basis for aesthetic values, regardless of how high the level they occupy (e.g., ethical and noetic values). One-sided interpretations[103] which seek aesthetic value not only in world images, world views, cultural and cognitive values, conceptions of virtue, and social and political ideas, but also in erotic or "entertainment" effects, etc., are the very ones which show that the aesthetic state is often interrupted and falsified by specific trends. It is true that all these trends or intended extra-aesthetic values occur in specific strata of poetic writing, but their symbolic mode of existence should be enough to prove that these values of meaning extend beyond factual content, that they point upward to something that is beyond materialization. We experience it in the "aesthetic state," in our value feelings, as something which "shines forth," becomes evident, in the work of art.

The inadequate attitude that fails to perceive the "logic of literary art" results in the whole cluster of mistaken attitudes that range from self-indulgence to the enjoyment of extra-aesthetic values all the way to the intoxicating ecstasy in which art becomes a drug. It would seem that discussion of literary value judgments should really come to an end once the basic facts have been perceived from both sides—from the "logic of literary art" and from the adequate act structures. It follows almost as a matter of course that we join Nicolai Hartmann[104] in requiring from partners in poetry "an inner liberation from pleasure in the practical value of the contents of the object, and a liberation from the mood value of oneself, the subject."

[*Translated from the German by Leila Vennewitz*]

Notes

1. Throughout this essay "aesthetics" is to be understood in a purely general sense; that is, as entirely dissociated from beauty and as an overall concept for everything pertaining to art. Hence the phrase "the beautiful" is also suspect here, although for reasons quite different from Bertolt Brecht's. Cf. e.g., "Forderungen an eine neue Kritik," in *Gesammelte Werke* (Frankfurt, 1967), Vol. 18, p. 113 ff. [The reader is reminded that usage of the term "anthropological" sometimes differs in German and in English. However, since English usage is on occasion more akin to the German one, there seems to be no reason not to allow the word to stand in the English title here. *Transl.*]

2. An illusion to the subtitle of Walter Müller-Seidel's very stimulating book, *Probleme der literarischen Wertung—Über die Wissenschaftlichkeit eines unwissenschaftlichen Themas* (Stuttgart, 1965).

3. See also Müller-Seidel, *Probleme*, p. 183.

4. *Ibid.*, p. 184.

5. Cf. Max Wehrli, *Probleme der literarischen Wertung*, quoted in Müller-Seidel, *Probleme*, p. 21. See also Max Wehrli, *Wert und Unwert in der Dichtung* (Cologne, 1965).

6. W. Emrich, "Das Problem der Wertung und Rangordnung literarischer Werke," *Archiv für das Studium der neueren Sprachen und Literaturen*, Vol. 200 (1964).

7. R. Wellek and A. Warren, *Theory of Literature* (New York, 1956), p. 241.

8. Cf. Herman Meyer's excellent essays, "Von der Freiheit des Erzählers" (e.g., p. 6 ff.) and "Zum Problem der epischen Integration" (e.g., p. 14 ff.), in *Zarte Empirie* (Stuttgart, 1963); also Müller-Seidel, *Probleme*, pp. 85–119, and S. C. Pepper, *The Basis of Criticism in the Arts* (Cambridge, 1946), pp. 74–95.

9. Wellek and Warren, *Theory of Literature*, p. 243, and Pepper, *Basis of Criticism*, p. 79.

10. René Wellek makes a similar demand in *Concepts of Criticism* (New Haven, 1965), p. 20: "We must return to the task of building a literary theory, a system of principles, a theory of values which will necessarily draw on the criticism of concrete works of art and will constantly invoke the assistance of literary history."

11. N. Frye, *Anatomy of Criticism: Four Essays* (Princeton, 1957), p. 20.

12. Cf. H. Kuhn, "Versuch über Interpretation schlechter Gedichte," in *Konkrete Vernunft* (Bonn, 1958); quoted also by Müller-Seidel, *Probleme*, p. 22.

13. Frye, *Anatomy of Criticism*, p. 20.

14. Wellek and Warren, *Theory of Literature*, p. 241; see also n. 5 and n. 6.

15. Frye, *Anatomy of Criticism*, pp. 3–29.

16. *Ibid.*, p. 27.

17. I. Kant, *Kritik der Urteilskraft*, §35: "The principle of taste is the subjective principle of the general power of judgement." English transl. by J. C. Mere-

dith, in *Kant's Critique of Aesthetic Judgement* (Oxford, 1911), pp. 142–
43. Excursions into metalogic and metamethodology cannot affect these ex-
positions; cf. E. Olson, "Die dialektischen Grundlagen des kritischen
Pluralismus," in *Über Formalismus—Diskussion eines ästhetischen Begriffs*
(Frankfurt, 1966), pp. 9–54.

18. K. Hamburger, *Die Logik der Dichtung* (Stuttgart, 1957).
19. N. Hartmann, *Ästhetik* (Berlin, 1953), p. 363.
20. W. Flitner, *Die Geschichte der abendländischen Lebensformen* (Munich,
    1967).
21. K. Jaspers, *Psychologie der Weltanschauungen* (Berlin, 1954).
22. F. Stern, *The Varieties of History* (Cleveland, 1956).
23. A. Dempf, *Selbstkritik der Philosophie* (Vienna, 1947).
24. Cf. e.g., B. Snell, *Die Entdeckung des Geistes—Studien zur Entstehung des
    europäischen Denkens* (Hamburg, 1955).
25. K. Mannheim, *Wissenssoziologie*, selections from the work introduced and
    edited by Kurt H. Wolff (Berlin-Neuwied, 1964), p. 71. [For translation
    source of *aufscheinen*, see n. 35. *Transl.*]
26. For Schiller, see K. Hamburger's essay, "Schillers Fragment 'Der Menschen-
    feind' und die Idee der Kalokagathie," in *Philosophie der Dichter—Novalis,
    Schiller, Rilke* (Stuttgart, 1966), pp. 83–128.
27. G. Ehrismann's view is opposed by E. R. Curtius' discourse, "The 'Chivalric
    System of the Virtues,'" in *European Literature and the Latin Middle Ages*,
    trans. Willard R. Trask, Bollingen Series XXXVI (New York, 1953), pp.
    519–37.
28. K. Dockhorn, "Die Rhetorik als Quelle des vorromantischen Irrationalismus
    in der Literatur—und Geistesgeschichte," in *Nachrichten von der Akademie
    der Wissenschaften in Göttingen aus dem Jahre 1949, Philologisch-His-
    torische Klasse* (Göttingen, 1949), pp. 109–50.
29. For Schiller and rhetoric, cf. Meyer, "Schillers philosophische Rhetorik," in
    Zarte Empirie, pp. 337–89; P. Böckmann, "Gedanke, Wort und Tat in
    Schillers Dramen," in *Jahrbuch der deutschen Schillergesellschaft*, Vol. 4
    (1960), espec. p. 12 ff.; E. M. Wilkinson, "Zur Sprache und Struktur der
    ästhetischen Briefe," in *Akzente*, Vol. 6 (1959), espec. pp. 402 ff., 413 ff.
30. Cicero, *De Oratore*, Book III, 14, 55; *quarum virtutum expertibus si dicendi
    copiam tradiderimus, non eos quidem oratores effecerimus, sed furentibus
    quaedam arma dederimus.*
31. H. Broch, *Dichten und Erkennen* (Zürich, 1955), Vol. 1, p. 303.
32. *Ibid.*, p. 314.
33. G. W. F. Hegel, *Ästhetik* (2nd ed.; Frankfurt, 1955), Vol. 1, p. 22.
34. F. Jonas, ed., *Schillers Briefe—Kritische Gesamtausgabe* (7 vols.; Stuttgart,
    n.d.), Vol. 3, pp. 245, 246.
35. Hegel, *Ästhetik*, p. 117.
36. *Ibid.*, p. 17.
37. M. Scheler, *Der Formalismus in der Ethik und die materiale Wertethik* (4th
    ed.; Bern, 1954).
38. *Ibid.*, p. 268.
39. *Ibid.*, p. 269.
40. E. Rothacker, *Die Schichten der Persönlichkeit* (6th ed.; Bonn, 1965),
    p. 171 ff.
41. Scheler, *Formalismus*, p. 271.
42. We find a variation in Friedrich Theodor Vischer: "The beautiful, then, is
    the idea in the form of restricted manifestation. It is a sensuous single unit
    that is manifest as the pure expression of the idea so that there is nothing
    in this idea that does not appear sensuous, nor does anything sensuous

appear that is not the pure expression of the idea." In *Ästhetik oder Wissenschaft des Schönen* (2d ed.; Munich, 1922), 1st vol., *Die Metaphysik des Schönen*, p. 52.

43. Scheler, *Formalismus*, p. 272.
44. Cf. also Scheler, *Die Stellung des Menschen im Kosmos* (Munich, 1949), espec. pp. 37–57.
45. K. Lorenz, *Über tierisches und menschliches Verhalten—Aus dem Werdegang der Verhaltenslehre* (Munich, 1966), Vol. 2, espec. pp. 156–99.
46. *Ibid.*, p. 158.
47. *Ibid.*, p. 161.
48. *Ibid.*
49. *Ibid.*
50. Broch, *Dichten und Erkennen*, p. 344.
51. For Schiller, see Hamburger, "Schillers Fragment 'Der Menschenfeind, . . .'"; this, of course, is where the whole range of aestheticians belongs, from Hegel, Solger, Vischer, and Schopenhauer down to Nicolai Hartmann and Hermann Broch.
52. N. Hartmann, *Ethik* (3d ed.; Berlin, 1949), pp. 251 ff. and 288 ff. English trans. by Stanton Coit, *Ethics* (3 vols.; London, 1950–51).
53. L. Wittgenstein, *Tractatus Logico-Philosophicus* (English-German version; London, 1955), No. 6, p. 421.
54. Cf. P. Szondi: "Evidence, however, is the adequate criterion to which philosophical cognition must subordinate itself." "Zur Erkenntnisproblematik in der Literaturwissenschaft," in *Die Neue Rundschau*, Vol. 73 (1962), p. 164.
55. Mannheim, *Wissenssoziologie*, p. 236.
56. See n. 54.
57. Broch, *Dichten und Erkennen*, p. 295 ff.
58. L. Giesz, *Phänomenologie des Kitsches—Ein Beitrag zur anthropologischen Ästhetik* (Heidelberg, 1960), pp. 68–75.
59. In his *Kritik der Urteilskraft* (English trans., pp. 41–2) Kant speaks of the "analytic of the beautiful," the "analytic of aesthetic judgement," and regards aesthetic judgment as that one "whose determining ground *cannot be other than subjective.*" That which formerly belonged to the field of theory of cognition was then identified unequivocally in Hegel (*Ästhetik*, p. 5 ff.) by the concept of "the beautiful." In the Introduction to his *Ästhetik* (*oder Wissenschaft*, p. 1), Vischer writes: "Aesthetics is the science of the beautiful." Later, in Hartmann's *Ästhetik* (p. 42), a distinction is made, but aesthetics is still held to be a science of the perception "of the beautiful object." Aesthetic value is regarded by Hartmann as the beautiful per se (e.g., p. 329).
60. Broch, *Dichten und Erkennen*, p. 304.
61. *Ibid.*
62. Scheler, *Die Stellung*, espec. pp. 62 ff.
63. Scheler, *Der Formalismus*, pp. 120–25.
64. See Hartmann, *Ästhetik*, pp. 328 ff., and *Ethik*, pp. 269 ff.
65. Hartmann also, as already mentioned, succumbs to this error (*Ästhetik*, p. 328), because he still associates the aesthetic with the concept of "beauty."
66. Cf. e.g., A. Anger, *Literarisches Rokoko* (Stuttgart, 1962), Vol. 25.
67. I hope to be able shortly to present a comparative collection of this kind as applying to literature in the German language.
68. See also Hartmann (*Ästhetik*, p. 14), who, like Schiller and Goethe before him, has emphasized that not every genre of form is possible in every subject matter, but "only a certain genre of form in certain subject matter."

69. Cf. also G. Lukács, "Der Briefwechsel zwischen Schiller und Goethe," in *Goethe im XX. Jahrhundert*, ed. Hans Mayer (Hamburg, 1967), espec. p. 383 ff.

70. See also Hartmann, *Ästhetik*, p. 402.

71. E. Staiger has called it "one of the purest examples of the lyric style," in *Grundbegriffe der Poetik* (6th ed.; Zürich, 1963), p. 13.

72. E. M. Wilkinson gives a similar interpretation in "Goethe's Poetry," in *German Life and Letters*, N.S. 2 (1949), pp. 319–29.

73. Cf. E. Trunz in the commentary to the Hamburg edition of Goethe's works (6th ed.; Hamburg, 1962), Vol. 1, p. 477.

74. W. Binder, "Hölderlins Odenstrophe," in *Hölderlin-Jahrbuch* (Tübingen, 1952), pp. 85–110.

75. Goethe, *Maximen und Reflexionen*, Aphorism 729.

76. For the complex of problems concerning the "public" and the "private," see Müller-Seidel, *Probleme*, pp. 41–58.

77. Hamburger, *Die Logik*, espec. the chapter, "Die Beschaffenheit des lyrischen Ich," pp. 162–208.

78. *Ibid.*, pp. 246 ff.

79. *Ibid.*, p. 246.

80. R. Ingarden, *Das literarische Kunstwerk* (2d ed.; Tübingen, 1960), p. 26.

81. Hamburger, *Die Logik*, p. 247.

82. In the sphere of "the beautiful," the *Scheincharakter* (quality of "shining forth" [cf. n. 35], of "manifestation") of the aesthetic has evoked a number of problems: cf. the interesting correspondence between Emil Staiger and Martin Heidegger, published in E. Staiger, *Die Kunst der Interpretation* (Zürich, 1955), pp. 34–49, on the interpretation of *lucet* and *videtur* in Mörike's poem, "Auf eine Lampe."

83. Ingarden, *Kunstwerk*, p. 314.

84. W. Benjamin, "Goethes Wahlverwandtschaften," in *Goethe im XX. Jahrhundert*, p. 234.

85. Ingarden, *Kunstwerk*, pp. 317 f.

86. *Ibid.*, p. 26.

87. *Ibid.*, p. 27.

88. *Ibid.*, p. 319. Strictly speaking, the "aesthetically valuable qualities" mentioned by Ingarden actually refer to extra-aesthetic values.

89. Wellek-Warren, *Theory of Literature*, p. 241.

90. See also G. Boas, *A Primer for Critics* (Baltimore, 1937), p. 136 (*Wingless Pegasus*, rev. ed.; Baltimore, 1950).

91. Hartmann, *Ethik* and *Ästhetik*.

92. The name is not even mentioned in the very informative work by K. E. Gilbert and H. Kuhn, *A History of Esthetics* (Bloomington, 1954).

93. See Scheler, *Der Formalismus*; also *Vom Umsturz der Werte* (4th ed.; Bern, 1955), pp. 30–163; *Schriften aus dem Nachlass* (Bern, 1957), Vol. 1, pp. 326–339; *Die Wissensformen und die Gesellschaft* (2d ed.; Bern, 1960), pp. 17–51 and pp. 282–358.

94. M. Geiger, "Zur Phänomenologie des ästhetischen Genusses," in *Jahrbuch für Philosophie und phänomenologische Forschung*, Vol. 1, Part 2 (2d ed.; Halle, 1922), pp. 567–684; and *Zugänge zur Ästhetik* (Leipzig, 1928).

95. G. Benn, "Goethe und die Naturwissenschaften," in *Goethe im XX. Jahrhundert*, p. 409.

96. See Hartmann, *Ästhetik*, p. 15 f.

97. *Ibid.*, p. 17.

98. Aphorism 809, from *Nietzsches Werke*, Vol. X (Leipzig, n.d.), p. 65.

99. Friedrich Schlegel says in an *Athenäum* fragment: "Poetic manifestation

[cf. n. 82] is the play of ideas, and play is a manifestation of actions,"
Schlegel, *Kritische Schriften*, ed. Wolfdietrich Rasch (Munich, 1956), p. 35.
100. Cf. Hartmann, *Ästhetik*, p. 34 ff.
101. *Ibid.*, p. 74.
102. *Ibid.*, espec. pp. 342–62.
103. It is interesting to note that Russian formalism also recognized the primacy
of aesthetic structure. In V. Erlich, *Russian Formalism*, ed. Cornelis H. van
Schooneveld, Leiden University (The Hague, 1955), p. 159, Mr. Erlich
quotes the following view held by Zhirmunskij: "In literary art, the elements of so-called content have no independent existence and are not
exempt from the general laws of esthetic structure; they serve as a poetic
'theme,' an artistic 'motif' or image, and in this capacity participate in the
esthetic effect to which the work of literature is geared."
104. Hartmann, *Ästhetik*, p. 74.

Roman Ingarden

THE PHYSICALISTIC THEORY
OF LANGUAGE
AND THE WORK OF LITERATURE

THE PHYSICALISTIC THEORY OF LANGUAGE DOES NOT, STRICTLY SPEAKING, belong to the theory of art and is not part of aesthetics. However, questions about the nature of language, and about the physicalistic concept of language especially, are important ingredients of contemporary philosophy. This latter theory is not an isolated phenomenon of the twentieth century. As we know, there is a certain interplay of philosophy, science, art, and so on in every cultural epoch. Thus, towards the end of the nineteenth century we can see a relationship between, for instance, impressionism and Bergsonism, as in their treatment of the dimension of time. Certain works of literature are also related: Marcel Proust's novel in France, and Thomas Mann's *Magic Mountain* in Germany, and so on. There are analogous situations in the twentieth century. You can see it beginning with post-impressionist painting which led to abstract art. In literature, too, there was Dada in France, and there were other, similar attempts at creating a kind of "abstract" literature—that is, at tracing the work of art back to a mere combination of sounds or to a combination of verbal sounds.

There is also a tendency in philosophy to build up the physicalistic theory of language. But this theory is merely one element in a much broader stream of philosophy and in the treatment of a much larger group of problems. And those who started on those problems probably had no idea that they would one day declare language to be a physical entity. The sequence of events that led from twentieth-century positivism to so-called neo-positivism may be enlightening. The first steps in that direction were very honorable in intention. It was postulated that science, and philosophy too, were infallible. Not exactly Papal infallibility, but an infallibility of science, nevertheless: mistakes, errors, false theories must not occur, they must be eliminated, thrown overboard as so much unnecessary ballast, so much nonsense that must on no account be allowed to interfere with the development of science. Those were very grand claims. There was no *real* claim to infallibility, it must be understood, but the dominion of error was to be strictly limited, so that the best possible conditions could obtain for a responsible science and, most especially, for a responsible philosophy. And for this purpose, these individuals envisioned (not for the first time in the history of philosophy) an ideal, a model that had to be followed throughout all the sciences, throughout all of man's knowledge. This model was, of course, the science of mathematics with its supposed strict exactitude, its deductive systems, where everything is in a manner of speaking certain. This ideal was to be realized, if possible, in every science. And out of this ideal a slogan was developed which was so loudly proclaimed in the nineteen-thirties that special congresses of scientists and philosophers were organized to subscribe to it. It was the slogan of so-called unified science, which means that an attempt was made to reduce *all* sciences to *one* science, to weld *all* knowledge into *one* science. These individuals tried to create a certain basic science— an idea which had been tried before, to be sure. For instance, Franz Brentano had previously tried to create a basic philosophical science, namely descriptive psychology. But now, strange to say, although everyone had the highest regard for the ideal of mathematical exactitude, they did not choose mathematics as the basic science but physics instead. Physics was to be the basic foundation of everything else. Why? I suspect that the reasons were not merely of a methodological-cognitive nature, but that there were other reasons to which I shall refer later. There was some hesitation at first as to what exactly this basic science should be—but the decision went to physics.

This gave rise to certain—sometimes tacitly understood—principles, certain canons, dogmas, codes of behavior. Important among those was a very definite concept of objectivity, meaning objectivity of perception, or rather, objectivity towards the results of perception. There are different versions of objectivity and not all are couched in terms derived from cognitive theory, but here we are considering just such a version. And what was considered "objective" in that case? Objective were those results of perception which could be obtained while the perceiving subject was in a completely passive state. Every activity on the part of the perceiving person was suspect, dangerous; it could easily become a source of error. Only that which is found, which is given, is objective—this is the basic tenet of Positivism. Only that which is given while one remains completely passive is "objective." As soon as any kind of thought processes, deductions, inferences, functions enter the picture, there is the danger of non-objectivity. Activity is the basis for the possibility of error. Unfortunately, it was Descartes who gave the first impetus in this direction. He said: "If anything has misled us even once, we must no longer believe in it; it has thus become doubtful and whatever is doubtful is not part of science. Only that which can be ascertained without any doubt is part of science."

It is a fine principle. You know how far it got Descartes. But in the twentieth century we have not yet reached Descartes with this principle. There was still a second question that had to be answered, namely: what exactly is that which is simply and passively given? We were told that only sense impressions are passively given. Everything beyond pure sense impression is somehow suspect and cannot be objective but must be subjective.

Then there was another principle that appeared highly commendable at first. The philosophers were mainly to blame for it, but they were not alone. Phrases had been pronounced, and concepts were being used that were not clear, that were dark and difficult. This lack of clarity, too, was considered a phenomenon of non-objectivity: "Only that can be unclear which we have not succeeded in clarifying. Lack of clarity is our own fault." As a result it was postulated that: "All unclear theories, i.e., all theories which are not covered by the category of the objectively given, shall be rejected. We no longer want to consider them, we withdraw from them." There are still certain theories, it was said, which cannot be proved at all, because they transcend, and must transcend, the realm of that which can or could be given. Well, let's toss them out! These were, for instance, Carnap's famous "pseudo problems."

Yes, this is all very fine. Husserl, too, has said: When anything is essentially unperceivable, then it is the Kantian Thing As Such, so let's toss it out. It is not part of reality, not part of the perceivable. Therefore: toss it out! In this respect, Carnap says exactly the same thing.

Ah, but all that did not lead to good results after all. If something is unclear, the easy thing is, of course, to say: "We will have nothing to do with this, there is something fishy here, it is not good, let's toss it out. We withdraw from it. We withdraw from all the more difficult problems, we will have nothing to do with them." Of course it is much easier to deal only with things that are easy, that are clear. Instead of looking where the values are in a work of literature, or what makes the work beautiful or ugly, it is much easier to say: "Oh, those are complicated things, those are mysteries, we don't want to touch them, we will leave that out; we shall turn our attention to something else." And so one turns, for instance, to statistics: how many words are there in one sentence, and how many sentences of three words occur in a work of literature? And then one can make a very nice statistical table and, from these statistics, go on to beautiful mathematical laws. This is, of course, much easier than working out a difficult analysis of the foundation of values in a work of art. It is boring to make statistical calculations, but there are many who say: "Fine, now I can accomplish something, I will discover all sorts of truths."

Many, many years ago, when I was a student in L'vov, my teacher, Professor Jan Lukasievicz, who later became a famous logician, had written a short essay "On Science," which unfortunately was published only in Polish. He says there: "One can find very precise relationships, such as mathematical relations, functional relations, which have no scientific meaning at all and are thus not part of science." He took a Polish poem and showed that relations *did* exist between certain words, and that it was possible to write a formula relative to the function of those words in the various verses. A very fine discovery—but, as Lukasievicz said at the time: This is not part of science; this is merely a game.

The good principle not to accept anything unclear turned into something not so good: you were to pay no attention to anything that was not clear, confining yourself to that which seemed clear and which usually turned out to be basically banal. The result was that the problematic of large areas of philosophy became badly impoverished. But the principle remained very fashionable.

But these principles, so noble at the outset, have led to somewhat peculiar results, for instance, in the philosophical interpretation of mathematics. The mathematician regards "intuition" as a source of error. To find essential connections between the ultimate elements of a mathematical multiplicity (*Mannigfaltigkeit*—variety?), i.e., primitive, original connections, we cannot use our sense of smell, nor can we see or hear these connections; we must somehow discover them by means of special intellectual acts of perception. And of course there are dangers; we can make ten different mistakes on the way, we can fall into error. This is true, of course, but it does not mean that we always have to make mistakes. And neither does it mean that we should abandon in advance all intellectual efforts to understand something which at first appears unclear. And since intuition had been discarded in mathematics, and any appeal to intuition was being viewed with disfavor, the problem of the validity of axioms had become incapable of solution. One would have to give up the idea that the validity of axioms differs in any way from that of the sentences that follow axioms. Those sentences have been developed deductively and therefore, if the axioms are true, the rest must be true without fail. Actually, the sentences are different in respect to their validity from the axioms which cannot themselves be deduced from anything. But then it was said: there is no fundamental difference! In a deductive system we can take any sentence and make it an axiom. It is like a net that you can knot and hang up anywhere. If not this, then something else, it will all hold together anyway. You simply turn another sentence into an axiom. The choice of axioms is optional, but their foundation—if I may say so—does not exist *ex principio*. Therefore, every axiom is without foundation, it is a convention— you want the facts to be according to the demand of the axiom and that is all.

I once asked Professor Lesniewski, a colleague of mine: "Tell me, what exactly is an axiom in mathematics, according to your definition?" He answered: "Don't you know that? It is a sentence expressed by the letter *a*, and as for this *a*, I write it any way I like." That was the prevailing view.

There followed the so-called formalization in mathematics. The idea came up that we should express an axiom by first taking meaningless signs and then arranging them side by side in such a way that from their arrangement—from the sheer form of these first formulas— the meaning of the primal basic ideas would emerge. Strictly speaking, the axiom says nothing, it is meaningless, and so are its various elements; only this formal arrangement exists. And this was to be true, not only of the single axiom, but of the entire system of axioms: a definite arrangement of a finite number of symbols, meaningless in themselves, was to determine the supposed meaning of whatever else might arise in the axioms. The "meaning" of a sign in the system of axioms is nothing but its position within that sign system. Of course, this kind of system is not geometry; it is merely a formal or formalized system. And the principles on which such a formalistic system is constructed, or arranged, are subject to will. I can play it in such a way that I arrange everything, and after I have had my second cup of coffee, I can make a different arrangement—but I must stay strictly within the rules of the game; that is the only condition.

Then we have, for instance, the principles of logic. There are two kinds of logical concepts or logical signs: there are the constant, the "logical" constants, and there are the variables. The logical constants are, for instance: "and," "or," "if—then." At first, all this is meaningless and must be defined. "And" has a logical function; it can be placed between two other symbols, P and Q. Its "meaning" is determined by the fact that we say the whole compound sentence is true if the two variables, P and Q, are true; it is not true if one or both variables are false. This is a definite scheme. There are four formulas which among them determine the meaning of "and," of "or," of "vel," and of "if—then," with the help of these meaningless signs. And there is something else still to be considered: this "true" and "false" in the demonstration formulas, what does it mean? The logicians will tell you:

> We pay no attention to the question of what it means; that question is part of psychology or cognitive theory. We don't care at all what it means. We only know that there are two values, such as F and V or 0 and 1; that there is a two-value system in which we can create such definitions of "and," "or," and so on. But if we have a three-value system, then we take three values: 0, ½ and 1, or "true," "false," and "possible." What does it mean? It doesn't mean anything. These are simply three different elements—let us call them that—in a system.

And another thing: these constants, "and" etc., are defined through the "values" that have been attributed to the "compound sentences." Now, if I make a sentence, I write it this way: "P and Q." The word "and" is now determined by the formula in the above-mentioned table. What then, are they, this "P" and this "Q"? They are "variables"—to be exact they are "sentence-variables." Variables are not "P" and are not "Q," but it is difficult to say just what a variable is; it is a difficult mathematical problem. And so the logicians found a very nice way of overcoming this difficulty by saying: a variable is nothing else but an "empty space" where one can insert whatever one wishes, whatever is available in the system. If I say "P and Q," then it is merely an accident that I wrote "P and Q"; I could have inserted something else—for instance a bird. It is also possible to put nothing into these spaces, but they have the peculiarity that something can be "inserted" there, according to certain, chosen rules. When I write a relation, I write "R"—that is the chosen relation. Then, let us say "X" and "Y" in the formula XRY are empty spaces where we may now insert two parrots or some other thing; anything that can stand in relation to anything else. This "R" can stand for sameness, for difference, for similarity, for whatever you like.

But now things begin to get worse. For we need a general theory of relation and I have just written out a scheme, such as XRY: this is a two-fold relation between two elements "X" and "Y," which can be inserted here, and there is a "constant," for instance, sameness. But if I am making a *general* theory of relation and then get involved in twofold, threefold, etc., relationships, then I will have to insert a *variable* in place of this special relation: "R." This "R" is not constant either; it is a variable; "P" and "Q" are also variables. *The entire sentence (formula) consists of nothing but empty spaces*: there is nothing left, nothing but empty space. And yet there is no emptiness, for we now have three such empty spaces and they are not equivalent. The empty spaces "P" and "Q" are, after all, different from the empty space "R"; something different must be inserted there. Now there are different definitions of what can be inserted in place of this empty space—"definitions" of these variables.

Well, if I have a "human" ordinary language, I simply write down the definition and say: here in this "definition" we may not insert a parrot, only numbers may be inserted here, and they must be numbers from between 0 and 1, let us say; then everything is fine. And there is a definition for "R," a definition for what I may insert: here I may insert only something that has the structure of a relation, not something that is an element, or part of a relation. In order to know all this, we must now build up a theory of the structure of relations. This would have to be clarified. But there we say: "Ah well, that is another of those complicated things. Who knows what kind of difficulties may arise from this?" And so we omit the analysis of the essence of a relation, and perhaps we will be satisfied with some easy or easy-to-make definition. I say: all well and good—if you give the definition for the three empty spaces and say that they shall be arranged thus and so, then I am satisfied. But I would postulate: it is a different arrangement from the kind you find in geometry, where the "R" must stand left of "Y" and right of "X." In that case the result would be geometry, and I do not want geometry. I want a structure, some kind of basic structure of a logical sentence. A logical sentence or "sentence function" is precisely a relation between two variables and one constant. This works out very nicely when I can use a fully meaningful language—when I am not only allowed to use it, but when I also admit that such a language exists.

Instantly, we are involved in something tricky, something dangerous. In order to be able to define this very precise structure of a logical relation, I must use a language that has been taken from so-called everyday language; that is, where certain words are used that are not defined at all, not unequivocally defined, words that carry in themselves all the dirt of everyday language. This language must be used in order to define the above-mentioned relationship in the strictest sense. But the *definiens* is dirty, unclear, equivocal. What am I to do now? I have no other language—the language of mathematics has not yet been created, the language of logic has not yet been created, it is in the process of becoming. This is a very dangerous and disagreeable situation—you might call it a very serious and valuable situation and I will not contradict you. In valuable logistic essays, such as Lukasievicz's introduction of his new system of symbols, the ordinary Polish, German, or English language must be used. And there again all the faults of everyday language—so often discussed—get into the way of a science that wishes to be extremely exact. So they say: "Oh, we don't mind that at all, this is the meta-language which is being utilized; and this meta-language has not yet been defined. But the language that has been defined in this way is relatively alright." Or else, one does without any linguistic explanation of symbols and sticks with the above-mentioned formula and operates with that.

Yes, but you might say: there is no other language except that which consists of meaningless symbols, for that was what we started out with. How are we to work with that? We have nothing but meaningless signs. How are we to define these signs, these variables, and these constants? By further meaningless signs? Alright, fine, in that case let us add "A," "B," "C," and "D" to our "X" and "Y"—these, too, are meaningless signs. But if they are meaningless, then we cannot obtain the meaning from them which we are supposed to obtain. All I know is that such and such a large number of signs must be added to these existing signs—supposedly in order to define them. The first thing is the sign language and this "A," "B," "C," "D" is the meta-language. And now, if I want to know what "A," "B," "C," and "D" are, I must form a meta-meta-language which again consists of meaningless signs, for, according to this concept, there is no other language than one consisting of physical things, placed side by side. This is very consistent. But the entire operation does not lead to our goal. For, just as I did not know before what the variable "X" stood for, so I still do not know what it is, what is taking shape in the method here described. I only know that a long train of meta-meta-meta . . . language is somehow hidden behind it. These are all physical entities, placed alongside each other.

One may ask: is this really serious? Is this the way it is really done: that I am to write, let us say: o and o and then 1, and then o again and 1 and another 1, etc. Maybe I have now done it wrong. Why? What exactly guides me to do it right?

Suppose I have my mind on something else and don't know how to go about defining the word "and." If I ask myself: what does "and" really mean in the sentence "Peter has gone to sleep and his friend is glad"? Is the whole thing true or not? When can it be true? Let us say it is true when Peter has gone to sleep and when his friend is glad. I must visualize this situation and thus try to understand what "and" really is. When does "and" have the function that the whole will be true altogether? Well, when the various parts are in such and such a relation. How will I know that? I know it through meaningful language, by applying meaningful language to reality, when I understand what it means that my friend has gone to sleep. And so I take a peek. Is he really sleeping, or is he not sleeping? If he is not sleeping, then the statement is false. If he sleeps, then it is true. In other words, I can do it, not by writing down some signs without thinking, but by being guided by a meaning which I know beforehand, although I cannot define it because "and" is an original logical category. But this much I must understand in order to be able to write this supposedly quite arbitrary formula. In other words: in reality you do not place meaningless sign after meaningless sign in geometric order, expecting the meaning to emerge from this order. On the contrary, you are guided in advance by meaning. This meaning is smuggled into the formula and we say: it is correct, it fits, this is the way things really are.

One may argue: is it really true that "if—then" has this meaning, that "if P, then Q" is true in three cases and false in one case? Is this really true? And the people who do not believe in the so-called material implication might say: "Ah, but that is false, in real language it means something else entirely. And a sentence in which the premise and the conclusion are false is not true at all—I simply won't believe it." So now there develops an argument between two people who both have, shall we say, an intuitive sense of "if—then" and who would like to make the formula fit this intuitive sense. You cannot possibly work at the blackboard with all these formulas if you do not understand *beforehand* what "and," "if—then," mean.

I have thus tried to show that the Physicalistic Theory of Language can only be constructed, that in fact any practical system can be built up only if one already has a language, which is what the Physicalistic Theory of Language denies. No, it cannot be done any other way, for, when you try to do it the other way, you get only some beautiful signs, mere marks, chalk marks, nothing else.

Of course I know—and I will admit as much to the representatives of the Physicalistic Theory of Language—that it is very hard to say just what an expression means. And it is very difficult to clarify the meaning of "and," of "or," and so on. There are many different theories about the essence of meaning or the meaning of linguistic products, theories from various camps: theories by psychologists, by language-philosophers, by linguists, by logicians. And I could not really and responsibly say that all these theories are without fault, without obscurities, without difficulties. I myself am a student of Husserl and of course I am tainted by Husserl's theory of language, his first theory, dating from the period of his "Logical Examinations." I, too, tried to build a theory, and he formed a new one soon afterwards; this is what has tainted me. But if I were to free myself, I could not swear to it that this theory is exactly flawless—I am ready to admit as much. I merely say that the Physicalistic Theory of Language does not satisfy me. The question remains as to what exactly the meaning of a sentence is, whether it is really verifiable, whether this is an operation, or a game of chess. And the difficulties that exist cannot be solved, I believe; they cannot be eliminated by working from the Physicalistic viewpoint. And they are also contradicted by the facts. The facts are those objective bodies and events with which we deal all the time when we talk to each other, or when we read something. And I don't know if any of my esteemed readers have ever taken this attitude while reading: that they watched certain peculiar lines—one cannot call them signs—appear on the blackboard; and that they looked at these lines and did nothing else. Nobody does this. This is not the way we read what is being written.

We have to do with something quite different, something that is not one-sided and not physical—something that is, somehow, two-sided; on the one hand there is sound, the sound of speech, or the written sign; and on the other hand there is just something else which permits me to reach something entirely different now through the linguistic product, namely: reality. For instance, if I say that there are 50 people in a lecture hall, I do not deal with a group of sounds but with something else, something different from mere sound, which now permits me—to do what? Well, to go into the hall and to see whether it is true that there really are 50 people. This linguistic product has already taken me beyond the linguistic product. This linguistic product is made in such a way that it guides me; I go beyond the product and see that to which it points, which I can recognize with its help. These are facts which I must clarify. I must work on the question of how all this is possible.

Let me continue: when I have words to begin with, the word-sound itself takes me beyond this unique individual drawing, the unique individual sound-material. This is why the strict Physicalists had to modify their position a bit, at least in Poland. They said: these are not mere drawings, they are drawings which are of *equal* form. If I write "dog" twice, I do it in such a way that the two drawings have the same form, and these two equally formed signs taken together are an element of language. With this explanation they were going well beyond the purely physical; they came to the *type*, and, thus, to that which is actually meant by the word "dog." The English language has one *word*, one English *word*, "dog," and of course this word can be spoken several times according to this example, but this "dog," this type of sound is not something physical. You may wish to call it an "abstraction" and I will be happy to agree—at any rate, it is not something physical.

Therefore, the very premise of Physicalistic Theory, namely that I am dealing with physical objects, is false. I am dealing with types, with types of sound or types of drawing which are, somehow, general in nature. Why and how did we get to these physical things? Well, because there now are various very beautiful, frequently admired cognitive and metaphysical principles. There is, first of all, the principle—this is no longer language-theory but, if you like, metaphysics—that "only material things exist," or that "there are material things and there are other things which depend on material things, namely the so-called ideas, experiences of consciousness, etc." In other words, a man is either a radical materialist or he is a modified materialist who says: there exists this strangely psychological element, this matter of consciousness, but it is based on the physical, it is a kind of repercussion, an after-image of the physical. Well, alright. Then there is a second principle: "Only that exists which is strictly individual, strictly unique. Nothing exists that is not individual." Of all things and all phenomena there exists, so to say, only *one* copy, each one is "unique," there is nothing general. Well, if we assume this, we soon run into trouble because of sound types. The physical part, obviously, the physical sound is individual. There are, of course, the so-called common features: one thing is white and another thing is white—this gives us two white things and the "white" of these two white things consists of two different products. There is no *white as such*. And when we state that they are both white—well, then we compare them and say: yes, yes, they are similar—these are Hume's famous Circles of Similarity. But just what it means that they are similar—we do not say "identical" but "similar"—this again, is a very difficult question. And so we reduce the question of similarity in a very simple way: "Ah, you don't know what 'similar' means? Similar means two things which are partly identical and partly non-identical." Thus similarity is reduced to identity, identity in the sense of "being-identical," and correlated to "being non-identical." Anything that is, somehow, both, is similar, we are told. Whether this is true or not is a point one might argue. I believe that it is false, but suit yourselves. It is really very hard to say what "similar" means if it is not identical and non-identical at the same time.

There are Circles of Similarity—and there are circles or classes of identically the same *quale*. What is this identically same quale, in respect to which all elements belong to one class? If we say that there is such an identical quale which is not individual, well then this is something that makes the Physicalist's hair stand on end: that is Plato, that is metaphysics, two worlds. Horrors! But if you throw away the identical quale you can no longer create classes of identically equal elements. Then you must somehow throw many individual single objects helter-skelter into a bag and what you will find in there depends entirely on chance. So much for those metaphysical convictions,—far removed from the theory of language—that only the physical or the psychophysical exists, or that only the individual entity exists, while everything else that is not individual does not exist—these convictions have led to the Physicalistic Theory of Language.

And there is still another big problem: how does one learn a language? If language is nothing but a multiplicity of meaningless things which are somehow identical in form, then the thing is simple:

one need but listen or look and that will be enough. Or one might have to "study" the same rows of signs while at the same time acquiring and practicing certain psychophysical modes of behavior with whose help one will then react automatically to every new row of written signs. The understanding of language products is supposed to consist of such automatic reactions. But the trouble is that the whole thing does not result in any language after all. For, in both cases—whether they are to be mere physical (bodily) modes of behavior, or psychophysical, automatic reactions—they must be guided or regulated by something other than the mere visual perception of visual "signs," if they are not to be utterly arbitrary and accidental. In other words, we must be given directions on how to react to the repeatedly given visual shape. If these directions are given through meaningful linguistic products, then we again have—contrary to the general Physicalistic Theory of Language—admitted the existence of a language that is something more and something other than a multiplicity of physical objects. But if these instructions are given through purely physical "signs" that are perceptible to our senses (let us assume we have chosen drum rolls), then we are confined in a circle of purely sensual products in which no meaning and no linguistic understanding can occur.

But one might say: language must have both *meaning* and *sound*, word-sound which is typical or written signs which are typical. It is being done with those machines that can "read." For this purpose, types are produced—individually unchangeable signs to which the machine reacts. But then it becomes difficult. The typical sound can be grasped in a certain sense through hearing, but in order to grasp it truly one must be attuned to it. And the same goes for writing: if I am attuned to the typical, then I can also "see" it in a certain sense; my sight can be a great help to me. But what am I now to do with the meaning of language which can be neither seen nor heard? You say that is very simple. How do you teach children to understand a language? We don't know this precisely, we cannot say exactly how small children learn a language, because they cannot tell us until they speak, and once they speak the whole business is over. But then you can say: "How do we learn a foreign language? How, for instance, can I learn Norwegian? Well, I go into a store and point to a sausage, and the merchant gives it to me. After I have indicated my wish he will tell me the Norwegian word for sausage. For the first time I hear the word *pölse*; aha, that "means" sausage—this is the first confrontation between the sound and the thing, between the name and that which it names. Now, if I do this ten times I have practiced it and so there arises—we are told—the "association" between the name, that is, the sound, and the named thing. An association; we know that from psychology: when you have A, you somehow automatically also have B—the one calls forth the other, and there are laws for this. Thus, the way to learn a language is by drill, by establishing associations between sounds or signs and the things that are named. Things can be seen and sounds can be heard and so it all fits together nicely.

Since I am an adult and already know how to speak a language, I know that the sausage is the object which is "named" by means of the sound which I have heard from my merchant. But how can the child know that "sausage" is not a name describing the *sound*? For, in an association, the parts which may or may not appear together are equally positioned—it is a *symmetrical* relation. On the other hand, the relation between a name and that which is named is by no means symmetrical. The name "sausage" designates that which is named, the thing, the sausage—but the thing does *not* designate the name. And, strangely enough, the children understand that "sausage" is not the name of the sound "sausage," but the sound "sausage" is a name for the thing, for the sausage.

Add to this yet another theory: the theory of apperception. It is said that in apperception only the individual thing is given. The individual sign is perceived together with the individual thing; and now we have this sign in tenfold repetition, ten pairs of individually perceived things, and in this way a "general" name emerges. This is not a proper name like John Doe, but it is the word "sausage" or "table," and this does not refer only to this thing which has been shown, but also to other things which are individually quite different from the first thing. Now, how are we to explain this "flexibility" of the sign, that it can be used to describe not merely the given individual thing—when we are always, after all, shown the individual thing *as* an individual thing. This again is based on some sort of false theory of perception. It is not true that we perceive certain individual things, individual characteristics at first; strangely enough we begin by perceiving the typical in the thing we see. I have seen, let us say, a certain group of gentlemen ten times, but if you ask me how an individual gentleman looks, I would not be able to tell you. I would say only that there were so and so many men. I have grasped that fact. There is such a thing as a general character of a human being, and it is this general character which I perceive. Under the aspect of this gen-

eral character I perceive the thing in question, and at first I do not see
the individual character features. Only after years of experience do
I reach the point where I can say: now I know what this person
looks like. Only now can I grasp him in his individual features.

Thus, the starting point is not the perception of the individual thing
or the individual sign, but at best here is what happens at first sight:
I have a sign here; it is typical and I combine it somehow with the
typical aspects of that which I perceive, and this is why I can now
say that the word "table" can be used for this table and for any
table. Table-ness has somehow become associated with the word
"table."

But this does not yet explain why the name refers to the table and
the table does not refer to the name. This is a new function, a mysterious function: the intentional function, the intention which is
carried out in the act of naming. The word is "directed at" something
else, which the word itself is not, namely at a thing. A thing can at
best remind me of its name, but the thing is not directed, it does not
refer to the word, the purely physical thing has no intentional function. Words have this function, this special directedness, this pointing-
to-something.

But then there is a very remarkable fact known by those readers
who have small children. Language does not consist of names alone,
not even of names in various syntactic forms. There are, in addition,
those peculiar words which the logicians call "logical constants."
There are the so-called functors, or functioning words, as A. Pfaender
once called them. Words like "and," "or," "if—then," the copula "is,"
and so on. These words form a very special group, which Pfaender
called "pure functioning" words. There are a great many "little
words" which, among other things, facilitate inflection. And here we
stand before a strange fact: one day, while talking to my three-year-
old granddaughter, I suddenly hear her use the word "nevertheless"
in a correct context. "He was wrong, nevertheless." According to the
generally recognized empiricist concept we understand words as a
result of a previous corresponding sense-perception. But where does
a child experience the sense-perception of that which is meant by the
word "nevertheless"? There are several such words; "all the same,"
"still," "on the contrary," "however," "but," none of which are names
in the way in which the word "sausage" is the name of a thing.
Neither are they names of things which stand in various relations to
each other, such as equality. Where does the child take the sense-
impression that corresponds to such a word, to such a functor, to

"and," "however," "although," "nevertheless"? The child has a comparatively small vocabulary. And, interestingly enough, no one has told her what "nevertheless" means. How did she learn this? Of course she had heard her parents and me say the word, but that is not enough. She has to know, after all, in what kind of situation the word can be used. She must somehow have discovered the meaning of the word without any previous experience of the thing thus named, for this thing does not really exist. I don't want to construct a positive theory, but I know this: the business of learning a language is somehow different from the way in which the empiricist psychologists and others will have us believe. Language is *not* learned through perception of the individual things, because, first of all, the general names could not be created in this way, and, second, because there are many essential, structural, syntactic elements of language that cannot be grasped through perception but that are still understood and must be understood if any complicated linguistic products are to be created and used.

The Physicalistic Theory of Language cannot satisfy us as a theory because the difficulties connected with it make it impossible to adhere to. Besides, we must ask: what did the mathematicians gain with their formalized systems in which everything is made to consist of meaningless signs? They had thought: we formalize mathematical systems in order to eliminate intuition and explicit deductions; we want to replace all factual connections and relations with visually perceptible formulas. Then all you have to do is see whether the formulas are written correctly according to the rules. If we did not make any mistakes there, all is well—unless perception has misled me; that is, unless I am a victim of deception or someone has made a "typographical error"; but such an error can always be visually recognized and corrected, just as a proofreader corrects a printed galley proof. This would really be extremely helpful: instead of thinking, instead of performing difficult thought processes, one would only have to look at the sense-perceptible sign-formula with attentive eyes! But how can we verify these formalized systems? Do we use machines which scan the formula to see whether everything is correct in a purely photographic way? No, what we need now are "models," theories that are mathematically meaningful and which refer to certain intuitively grasped facts. Thus an abstract theory can be reduced back to elementary arithmetic or to Euclidian geometry or to some other model based on factually meaningful premises. This is the practical and the only way of checking a formalized system to see if everything is right. You do not check the non-formalized systems against formalized systems: you have to do it the other way around. That is the present stand of mathematics. Thus, basically, nothing has been gained. And, besides, the systems have not even been formed according to the Physicalistic rules. For again and again we have smuggled in meaning; again and again we have used various definitions constructed in normal everyday language, and, of course, this has introduced various misinterpretations which are contained in this language. And this, of course, brings with it the danger that the formalized system under consideration is by no means correct, because there is always the possibility that the definitions are not exact. Then we must return to the subject matter at hand to see, with the help of concrete examples, whether everything is correct or not.

And now let me come back to literature. What do I get when I hear a work of poetry in a language I do not understand at all; when, in other words, I am dependent on the mere sound-material alone? By coincidence I experienced such a situation recently in Oslo. I was at a meeting where the poems of a well-known poet were read and discussed. During the whole meeting I understood only a few words. Do I now have the slightest idea of those lyric poems that were being read aloud that night? None whatsoever! I have an idea of how the actress recited the verses; I could hear that in a purely phonetic way. But from these mere sounds I could not even tell what the Norwegian language really sounds like, for I cannot distinguish between the emotion expressed in sound by the lady who read those verses, and the material itself. Nor can I differentiate between the language melody or language pattern which is typical for the Norwegian language, and the melody of the recital as such. The lady may have read the texts in such a way that the Norwegian language melody was preserved or, conversely, in a way that ran counter to the typical melody—she might have broken the normal rhythm in order to show that this was exactly the sort of poem, the sort of verse that had quite a different melody and which would not fit into the melody of the Norwegian language as commonly spoken. But I could not grasp this; for me it was merely a stream of sounds with peculiar pauses from time to time. I don't even know what these pauses meant, whether they were simply moments of silence or whether they fulfilled a semantic or syntactic function. If I take the attitude that this is not merely senseless chatter but a real, spoken message, then I think, while hearing such a pause: aha, this is probably a period in the sentence; this is the separation between two sentences, or perhaps the actress has made some sort of artificial stop for effect. This, too, I cannot know. In short, the meaning does not exist for me. The subject that is being talked about and the statements that are being made about this subject do not exist. All kinds of phantasmagoria which I could set in motion through this poem do not exist, the poem I have just heard does not produce any flights of fancy. And even the plain sound-ensemble of the original Norwegian language does not exist. There is merely a stream of sounds among which I cannot even distinguish one word from another.

Is this sort of thing a literary work? a poem? a work of art? Or, if you prefer, a speech? Well, for me it is none of these things. There is no trace of the language, no trace of the literary work of art, not a trace of the world which is presented here, not a trace of the meta-physical qualities which are somehow shown. All this does not exist. It is exactly as if I were in a jungle and had come upon a colony of parrots making nothing but a loud racket in my ears. And just be-cause I have experienced such things as that Norwegian poetry read-ing, I cannot reduce the literary work of art to its basic sounds. Nor can I reduce it to mere language, as the formalists do. They, at least, allow quite a lot to remain in their theory; they admit that language has both sound and meaning—you might say that they see it as a kind of organism. But even that cannot satisfy me—not even in a mathe-matical treatise. I cannot be satisfied with merely understanding the meaning and not getting to that about which this meaning speaks, namely to a special fictional or non-fictional world that should arise there for me. According to my feeling and experience, I relate to the human beings presented in a work of art: they are not real people, but *depicted* human beings; I relate to various acquaintances I have made in that special world to which I can return whenever I wish. And I live with these people, I am somehow moved by them, or I hate them, and I say: this is simply unbearable. I become attached to these depicted people, to that depicted world—that is what inter-ests me in the whole business, the rest is merely a means towards reaching this experience.

Thus, I simply cannot accept the formalistic theory of language and literature because it contradicts my experience. You may now say: "Well, yes, you may be right, there are such experiences and one must give in to them. But what is being experienced? Does that which one experiences exist? Do the people who are depicted exist? No, they are not really existing persons, real people are encountered only in real life and in real surroundings." And then I must answer:

of course, they are not realities. They are not autonomously existing objects; they are, if you like, fictions. But there are such fictions—and this is the core of the matter. It is something I can relate to. And if I were now to think: "There are no depicted worlds, they do not exist in any sense; all these fictions that have been created in European literature for the last 3,000 years, and many other fictions, do not exist at all"—well, then I simply lose all of human civilization. There is nothing left but the people who love or do not love each other, who kill each other, and who do not even have anything over which they could fight one another.

What is the manner of existence of these fictions? How is it possible that these non-existent, non-real objects can move me, that they can delight me or awaken hatred in me? That is a problem, I admit. But it is a problem worth considering, worth clarifying. Let us not say right away: "It is so difficult that we do not want to work on it, we would rather work on signs and numbers, which is much easier." Yes, unfortunately it is true that it is hard to say just how these fictions exist and in what sense they belong to our world, how it is possible that something non-existent can somehow transform me when I am in touch with it. That is the problem, that is the problem of civilization, its existence and its role. And I cannot renounce the possibility of somehow coming to grips with this problem, if I can find the approach to it, and of somehow, in no matter how small a way, making it clear to myself.

[*Translated from the German by Maria Pelikan*]

Mario Jacoby

THE ANALYTICAL PSYCHOLOGY OF
C. G. JUNG AND THE
PROBLEM OF LITERARY EVALUATION

I

WHEN A PSYCHOLOGIST IS INVITED TO DISCUSS A PROBLEM IN THE FIELD of literary criticism, he must ask himself first of all what points of contact exist between that discipline and his own. What do psychology and the study of literature have in common? Literary criticism analyzes, interprets, and evaluates works of art; psychology tries to throw light on the nature of the human mind and its functions. But every literary composition owes its existence to the creative effort of a human being with special gifts for this particular endeavor. Thus, the poet's human qualities—as far as they affect the creation of his work—become part and parcel of the literary researcher's concern.

Conversely, the literary product itself provides insights into the basic human condition and its problems which do lie in the psychologist's field of interest. Therefore, no serious attempt at understanding literature can be made without an examination of certain psychological aspects. Psychology, for its part, has, since the beginning of our century, received some completely new impulses towards the exploration of man's creative imagination.

Sigmund Freud was the first man who tried to unlock the unconscious depth-dimensions of the human soul and to study its laws. Freud, the physician, was led towards these utterly unprecedented explorations by the mental anguish of his so-called neurotic patients.

He discovered that anxieties, compulsions, and hysterical states are expressions of mental conflicts. The adult no longer remembers these conflicts which he experienced in early childhood. He has forgotten, or rather repressed them from his consciousness. But, strange to say, they live on for years and years; they are hidden, but their force is undiminished. They exert "in altered dress twice as much stress."

The therapy Freud devised for these states is called psychoanalysis. It consists of recalling the unconscious conflicts into the patient's consciousness where he can deal with them. To achieve this, Freud used the so-called free association method: the patient had to tell the analyst everything and anything that came into his mind, even if it was embarrassing or seemed to make no sense; he was to exercise no criticism, make no conscious choice of what he would say. The free play of ideas brought to light memories and fantasies, and often the spontaneous account of a dream. Thus, Freud's interest was directed towards the exploration of fantasy and of dreams. The dream became his *via regia*—his royal highway to the unconscious mind. The year 1900, when Freud's book, *The Interpretation of Dreams* was first published, is considered the birth date of modern depth psychology.

Freud developed a theory for the understanding of dreams which were incomprehensible to the scientists of the time: the dream we remember is merely a façade, the product of a compromise between a latent, often offensively sexual wish, and its defense by the ego. There is a censor at work, even at night while we dream; it prevents the instinctual wish from emerging undisguised, in order to keep it repressed as completely as possible.

The language of dreams is so strange, incomprehensible, and symbolic because the censor sees to the distortion of the actual dream-thought. The interpreter must uncover the unconscious, latent dream-wish by means of free, uncensored ideas. According to Freud, the unconscious is the seat of powerful drives, most especially of a sexual nature, which demand gratification. The unconscious mind functions by the so-called pleasure principle; it strives for maximum pleasure, just as an infant does. Opposite the pleasure principle stands the reality principle which demands that we adapt ourselves to the requirements of civilization, a task we can accomplish only with considerable renunciation of instinctual wishes. The person who thinks and acts in a reasonable manner and does nothing but "strive for what is *useful* and guard himself against damage"[1] obeys the reality principle. Both principles are at work in us; and our ego, as the representative of the reality principle, sees to it that our instincts are modified and adapted to reality, to the restrictions of civilization.

But there exists a certain enclave, according to Freud, in the mental landscape of the human adult which remains subject to the pleasure principle: the realm of imagination and daydreams. Imagination is like an "area set aside for reservation in its original state and for protection from the changes brought about by civilization."[2] This gives man a chance to withdraw from the harsh demands of reality and from the sense of displeasure they produce, and to build his imaginary castles in Spain—his "pleasure palaces." Fantasy is one of our methods for making life bearable in the face of reality. Freud sees the working of our imagination as an illusionary-hallucinatory misreading of reality, a detour around the concrete demands of life, which is why, throughout his work, he puts a negative value on imagination. But, at the same time, he calls it the "raw material of literary production. The poet, by means of certain transformations, disguises and omissions, creates those situations in his daydreams which he puts into his stories, novels and plays. The hero of every daydream is always the dreamer's own person."[3]

The study of daydreams and fantasy thus automatically leads Freud into the realm of literary creativity. In his view the poet's "creations, works of art, were the imaginary satisfactions of unconscious wishes, just as dreams are; and like them they were in the nature of compromises, since they too were forced to avoid any open conflict with the forces of repression."[4] In contrast to religion which "limits the search for truth because it inhibits thought," he considered art "almost always harmless and beneficient; art does not try to be anything other than illusion."[5] Freud devoted his life's work to the search for truth and to the fight against those illusions which make us misunderstand or ignore reality.

In this sense he also applied his psychoanalytical methods to religion: he unmasked it as imaginary wish-fulfillment, and thus devaluated it. On the other hand, he was full of spontaneous and unstinting admiration for poets and literature. Undeniably, the works of Shakespeare, Dostoyevsky, or Nietzsche are fraught with intuitive insight into the labyrinthine depths of the soul. Freud says: "and we may well heave a sigh of relief at the thought that it is nevertheless vouchsafed to a few to salvage without effort from the whirlpool of their own feelings the deepest truths toward which the rest of us have to find our way through tormenting uncertainty and with restless groping."[6] In a roundabout way, Freud would concede a certain share in the reality principle to the poet or writer:

> Art brings about a reconciliation between the two principles in a peculiar way. An artist is originally a man who turns away from reality because he cannot come to terms with the renunciation of instinctual satisfaction which it at first demands, and who allows his erotic and ambitious wishes full play in the life of phantasy. He finds the way back to reality, however, from this world of phantasy by making use of special gifts to mould his phantasies into truths of a new kind, which are valued by men as precious reflections of reality. Thus in a certain fashion he actually becomes the hero, the king, the creator, or the favourite he desired to be, without following the long roundabout path of making alterations in the external world. But he can only achieve this because that dissatisfaction which results from the replacement of the pleasure principle by the reality principle, is itself a part of reality.[7]

Thus Freud assigns a legitimate standing to the poet from which the value-categories of psychoanalysis will not attempt to displace him. But his work is made the object of psychoanalytical interpretation. It resembles the dream in that it, too, is based on imaginary fulfillment of unconscious wishes. Therefore, the methods of dream interpretation can be applied to the interpretation of a work of literature. The work as such is not valued; instead, the psychoanalyst regards it as a façade behind which to search for the latent instinctual wishes of the author. The work of art is reduced to a manifestation of the author's personal experiences. "A strong experience in the present awakens in the creative writer a memory of an earlier experience (usually belonging to his childhood) from which there now proceeds a wish which finds its fulfillment in the creative work."[8] Freud's teachings gave rise to a flood of psychoanalytical interpretations of literary works, all trying to dredge up into the light the human, all too human secrets of their authors.

But Freud himself knew that these psychoanalytical interpretations could not really explain the mystery of artistic creation. He admits that "before the problem of the creative artist, analysis must, alas, lay down its arms."[9] For, the method by which the writer converts unconscious desires into a work of art is "his innermost secret, the essential 'ars poetica.'"[10]

One of the main reasons why Freud's collaborator, C. G. Jung, soon decided to go his own way was Freud's narrow view of the human imagination, his assumption that it was nothing more than an expression of unconscious instinctual wishes. Freud's discoveries enabled psychology to penetrate hitherto unknown continents. The unconscious life of the mind, which until then had been accessible only to the intuition, was now to be scientifically explored; its laws were to be discovered. Freud constructed the tools he needed for this difficult task out of the naturalistic-mechanistic ideas of his time. The phenomena of the unconscious mind, dreams and spontaneous fantasies, were to be causally related to the sex instinct. Thus, in the last analysis, psychological phenomena were to be reduced to biological manifestations. Freud's method therefore did not run counter to the naturalistic views of his time. But the contents of his causal chain were a shock to the hypocritical morality of his stuffy contemporaries, badly though they needed to be scientifically enlightened as to the meaning and importance of sexuality. And so Freud circumscribed the workings of man's imagination, so rich in images and ideas, with scientific models and theorems to which—with little variation—he clung all his life. C. G. Jung reports that Freud said to him one day: "My dear Jung, promise me never to abandon the sexual theory. That is the most essential thing of all. You see, we must make a dogma of it, an unshakable bulwark."[11] For Jung, this remark was "the thing that struck at the heart of our friendship."[12] Scientific truth was for him "a hypothesis which might be adequate for the moment but was not to be preserved as an article of faith for all time."[13] He felt that the newly discovered region of the unconscious mind had not been nearly enough explored to establish general, unshakable laws about it. He could not help but feel that such causal reductions necessarily narrowed our view and made it impossible for us to do full justice to the complex phenomenon of the unconscious part of the human soul.

Both Freud and Jung had noticed how often dreams and spontaneous fantasies resemble motifs from mythology, from fairy tales, and from folklore. Both began to study mythology around 1910. Freud, however, warned Jung, in one of his letters, not to stay away too long in those tropical regions of the occult; it was necessary to govern at home.[14] To his co-worker, Sandor Ferenzi, Freud wrote: "his own investigations have carried him far into the realm of mythology, which he wants to open up with the key of the libido theory. However agreeable all that may be, I nevertheless bade him to return in good time to the neuroses. There is the motherland where we have first to fortify our dominion against everything and everybody."[15]

But Jung's main concern was not the interpretation of myths by means of established theories that derived from the treatment of neuroses. He wanted to penetrate more deeply and without preconceived ideas into the unconscious life of the mind. The unconscious mind is, by definition, hidden from our consciousness; there is no direct access to it. Myths, fairy tales, and visions are spontaneous manifestations from which we can deduce unconscious psychic activity. Jung does not see them as epiphenomena of the realm of impulse, but as original, intrinsically human creations of the unconscious. He was astonished at the enormous variety of images and motifs that emerged through dreams and fantasy. Jung describes his practical approach: "I had often observed patients whose dreams pointed to a rich store of fantasy-material. . . . The variety defies description. I can only say that there is probably no motif in any known mythology that does not at some time appear in these configurations. If there was any conscious knowledge of mythological motifs worth mentioning in my patients, it is left far behind by the ingenuities of creative fantasy. In general, my patients had only a minimal knowledge of mythology."[16]

From these experiences Jung thought he might deduce certain general unconscious laws for the functioning of the human imagination. Primal ideas or archetypes seem to lie dormant in the mind. Under certain conditions, these archetypes can be actualized in a thousand different ways. They are alive in myths, rites, fairy tales, and in the religious ideas of every epoch, and they are forever being newly created in men's dreams and fantasies today. They must be based on some common mental activity. It was this activity which Jung set out to explore: "The existence of these unconscious regulators—I sometimes refer to them as "dominants" because of their mode of functioning—seemed to me so important that I based upon it my hypothesis of an impersonal collective unconscious."[17]

Jung differentiates between the personal unconscious which contains "the forgotten, the repressed, the subliminally perceived, thought and felt,"[18] and a deeper layer of the psyche which he regards as the creative primal ground of man's mental life. In the collective unconscious, there are dynamic contents at work which Jung called *dominants, primal images,* and, later, *archetypes.* The word archetype is derived from the Greek *archetypon,* that which was made first: the primal image, the original form, the model. The *ideae principales* of Augustinus originally inspired Jung to choose the name of archetype which has more or less the same meaning. According to Augustinus, the *ideae principales* are eternal, changeless, contained in the divine wisdom. The archetype is one of the most difficult and more frequently misunderstood concepts in Jung's psychology. During his lifetime Jung himself changed and differentiated his archetype concept as his researches progressed. In this connection I would like to mention his essay "On the Nature of the Psyche" in volume 8 of his *Collected Works*. His clearest and most inclusive ideas on the archetype are formulated there.

It is important to keep in mind a differentiation in the concept of the archetype: Jung makes a distinction between the "archetype as such" and archetypal images and ideas. The archetype as such is the unconscious disposition, the abstract pattern of images and ideas. It is not perceivable, but remains "a hypothetical and irrepresentable model."[19] Since its existence cannot be proved directly but only through its manifestations, the archetype must remain a hypothesis for the scientist. It effects the patterns of images and ideas in myths, fairy tales, visions, dreams, and fantasies. These patterns, which *are* perceptible to our consciousness, are the archetypal images and ideas. They are produced by the "archetype as such." At the same time they point to its hidden activity.

Although the "archetype as such" is, scientifically speaking, a hypothesis, it manifests itself to the subjective experience in very convincing ways. Every idea that ever fascinated or inspired mankind, and every idea that has driven men into fanaticism and mass hysteria was and is archetypal in nature. In the history of religion and philosophy it is easy to find those archetypal configurations that constitute the "spirit" of a particular epoch. In this respect, too, I would like to refer the reader to Jung's many writings in which he shows the relation between archetypal configurations and human consciousness, both in modern times and in the most ancient realms of human thought.

In examining the relation between literature and psychology the following is important: the "archetypal images" which Jung mentions in his work are equivalent to what we commonly refer to as symbols. The word *symbol* comes from the Greek *symballein* which literally means "to throw together." A symbolon in ancient Greece was a fragment of a cube or of some other object which could be fitted back together with the other half of the object. Friends would each take one such half to seal a friendship that often extended to every member of their respective families. The pieces were used as means of identification and were handed down through the generations in each family. If two halves fitted together to make a whole, the bearer of the fragment was legitimately identified and made welcome.

From this original concrete meaning, the symbolon came to stand for a contract or agreement in the legal field. In the aesthetic sphere, it came to mean what in German is aptly called *Sinnbild* (i.e., a "sense image" or "image of meaning"). An image becomes a symbol when he who looks at it sees in it a meaning beyond that which it depicts. This meaning swings within the image, shines through it. An image that strikes us as a living symbol points beyond itself and appears rich in meaning. For Jung, a symbol is the "best possible description, or formula of a relatively unknown fact . . . which cannot conceivably, therefore, be more clearly or characteristically represented."[20] Goethe, too, gave thought to the symbol. He wrote: "This is truly symbolic: when the specific represents the general, not as a dream or a shadow, but as the living and immediate experience of the unfathomable."[21] Goethe sees the unfathomable as being accessible to experience through symbols. In the language of the psychologist the "unfathomable" would be the abstract "archetype as such," the unconscious ground and condition for every act. As original, primal image, primal word, primal idea, it can be sensed and experienced through its image-pattern, the symbols. Gerhard Hauptmann says, in this context: "Poetry evokes out of words the resonance of the primordial word."[22]

Let us hear one more voice on this subject. Fritz Strich, the contemporary historian of literature, writes: "The symbol in literature is a specific case that has general validity, an image that coincides with the primal image, a phenomenon at one with the arch-phenomenon; it is that which persists through every change, it is unity in variety, the idea behind the appearance. For, that which can be called the idea of a work of literature is the general validity of the incidents it describes, its eternal truth, the primal image within its images."[23]

The psychologist must recognize that such experience of symbols is real, even while the archetype as such, manifesting itself in this experience, remains unperceivable. But it remains a hypothesis which adequately explains the realm of psychologic experiences. It is especially in respect to the symbol-concept that we can see how enormously Jung's work has extended and deepened psychological knowledge. Freud, too, speaks of symbols. But in his view they invariably serve to mask the sexual realm and its activity. In short, Freud always reduces the "unfathomable" to something known, namely sexuality and its organs. But if the symbols that occur in works of literature are always interpreted and reduced in this manner, they always lead to the author's personal sexual wishes and their sublimation. Such results may be accurate in many cases, but in the last analysis they remain of marginal interest both for the psychology of creativity and for the study of literature. This is why Jung says: "Whether something is a symbol or not depends first of all on the way in which our consciousness approaches it."[24] In other words: It is quite possible for our consciousness to remain closed to the wealth of meaning contained in a symbol and to reduce its meaning to some well-worn, generally known facts. When this happens, the symbol loses its depth, it no longer points to the "unfathomable," to that which transcends consciousness; it becomes a mere sign. In Jung's view a symbol is alive only "when it is the best and highest possible expression of something divined but not yet known even to the observer."[25]

Jung's particular endeavor is to make consciousness receptive to symbols in order to strike a possible chord of meaningful experience. He sees neurosis largely as "the suffering of a soul which has not discovered its meaning."[26] The ultimate purpose of translating symbolic images into the language of psychology, the "interpretation" of dreams and fantasies, which can at best be only partially successful, is to open the subject's consciousness to the events in his own unconscious mind.

Jung ascribes great importance to these "Relations between the Ego and the Unconscious,"[27] and for the following reasons: his psychotherapeutic experience made him regard the entire psyche, which includes both the conscious and unconscious part of the mind, as a self-regulating system striving for wholeness. This means that the unconscious activity manifested in dreams and fantasies contributes to the psyche's equilibrium in a compensatory manner. Modern experimental dream researchers have impressively corroborated this thesis of Jung's.[28] Our consciousness can be compared to the eye whose field of vision includes only a tiny part of the universe. Consciousness differentiates and decides according to space and time, causality, value, and so on. Out of all possibilities it chooses those which appear important for its particular life-experience and for the necessary life-adaptation. It sets its own direction, gives its own directives. Thus, contents and possibilities that do not lie in the chosen direction never enter the field of our consciousness. Therefore, consciousness is always more or less one-sided. There is a danger that this one-sidedness may become absolute, possibly leading to an unhealthy narrowing of the conscious mind, to a sense of emptiness and meaninglessness. The splitting-off of consciousness from its sources is, according to Jung, the cause of many neuroses; and man's "self-estrangement," so often mentioned in these days, is also based on the same thing. Jung says: "The more one-sided his conscious attitude is, and the further it deviates from the optimum, the greater becomes the possibility that vivid dreams with a strongly contrasting but purposive content will appear as an expression of the self-regulation of the psyche."[29] This is why he regarded the notation and understanding of dreams and fantasies as therapy of the first order.

The theory of compensation and the hypothesis of the collective unconscious led to new lines of inquiry about the handling and understanding of dream symbols. Jung inquired into the possibilities of new experience, new insights and attitudes as revealed and divined through symbols in dream and fantasy, which help us overcome stagnation of consciousness and achieve self-realization. The natural drive towards wholeness in the household of the soul is really, when seen in temporal sequence, nothing else but the vital urge towards self-realization, the psychic necessity of what Jung called the process of individuation.

In order to gain a better understanding of archetypal images in dreams and fantasies, Jung worked out a method which he called the method of amplification. "In Jung's method of amplification, the various dream motifs are enriched through analogous, meaning-related material which consists of images, symbols, sagas, myths, etc. The dream motifs are thus shown in every nuance of their possible meanings, and in all their various aspects, until their meaning becomes utterly clear. Then, each element of meaning which has been granted by this method is linked to the next element and so on until the entire chain of dream motifs has been laid bare and can be verified as a united whole."[30] This method, which can be used for the better understanding of all collective symbols, does not reduce—it expands. The parallels taken from myths, fairy tales, religious history are a kind of philogenetic association; they stem from a collective memory on which, in the final analysis, our entire culture is based. They direct the mind towards man's essential being as it has been created, shaped, and reshaped in the course of the millenia, and as it continues to echo in our soul. "Creation, change—the eternal pastime of the eternal mind"—Goethe's words may well describe the way our psyche works.

We have seen that Jung set a very high value on human imagination. The unconscious is creative, and this makes its irrational picture-language extremely valuable. All his life Jung defended its importance against the one-sided overvaluation of rational thinking. The unconscious regulators, the archetypes, make the human imagination possible. They are the seeds from which the conscious mind unfolds. The work of our imagination, no matter how free it may seem, is unconsciously guided by general-human principles and patterns. If this were not so, no reader would ever be able to re-experience the contents and structure of a work of art. Imagination does not originate in conscious volition or whim, it occurs—which is why, in the realm of poetry, it is called inspiration. Jung's research into the working of the human imagination thus also implies the question of the origins of poetic creativity. Here is where the sciences of literature and psychology meet.

II

Throughout Jung's work, we find numerous interpretations of literary themes. But there are three essays which deal directly with literature.[30a] The following is an attempt to summarize his most important ideas.

Jung endeavored to find a clearcut dividing line between the psychological and the aesthetic consideration of literature.

> Only that aspect of art which consists in the process of artistic creation can be a subject for psychological study, but not that which constitutes its essential nature. The question of what art is in itself can never be answered by the psychologist but must be approached from the side of aesthetics. A similar distinction must be made in the realm of religion. A psychological approach is permissible only in regard to the emotions and symbols which constitute the phenomenology of religion, but which do not touch upon its essential nature. If the essence of religion and art could be explained, then both of them would become mere subdivisions of psychology.[31]

This was Jung's first formulation in his essay, published in 1922, "On the Relations between Analytical Psychology and Literature." In "Psychology and Literature," published in 1930, the psychological part has been expanded. "The investigation of the psyche should therefore be able on the one hand to explain the psychological structure of a work of art, and on the other to reveal the factors that made a person artistically creative."[32] Here, Jung assumes that the work of art itself has psychological structures which do not necessarily derive from the psychological conditions of its creator. This is a new view, as against Freudian psychoanalysis which always explains the work of art through the personal complexities of its author. Jung's view is based on the hypothesis of the creative collective unconscious. Jung regards not only the individual psyche but also the collective psyche as a self-regulating system. Experience shows that contents and value systems which constitute the "spirit" of a period and philosophy are by necessity incomplete and one-sided. There is no philosophical system so all embracing, so generally valid, that it cannot be attacked and contested; there is no article of faith so firm that human doubt did not have to reject or, at least, reinterpret it in the course of time. Currents of thought succeed each other; what was valuable for one period often becomes valueless for the next. Seen in psychological terms this would mean that changing archetypal ideas attain validity and develop into the cultural canon of an era. Out of all the possible modes of human existence those which best lend themselves to coping with existing conditions are unconsciously selected. Views which help us come to terms with the greatest variety of encountered conditions and which, at the same time, produce meaningful relations, constitute the valid prototypes of the collective consciousness.

To repeat: one of the most important results of Jung's researches is the insight that the human soul strives toward totality; that is, towards the realization of all its innate possibilities. This is a goal we can never quite reach. This may well be the reason why conscious collective ideas and their unconscious prototypes with their necessary one-sidedness are continually being undermined from within. The result is "Civilization and its Discontents," a condition that calls for relief. New ideas emerge which try to compensate, to complete, or to replace the old philosophy. These ideas usually occur to individual, creatively gifted people, such as the poet who can receive them, give them shape, and so make them accessible to the general public. While Freud believes that the poet refashions his own unconscious wish into a work of art, Jung sees him as the instrument of a collective creative power. "Whenever the creative force predominates, life is ruled and shaped by the unconscious rather than by the conscious will, and the ego is swept along on an underground current, becoming nothing more than a helpless observer of events."[33]

Friedrich Hölderlin, the German poet, saw himself as "an arrow of the god Apollo. The god shall make use of the poet to let his divine rhythm leap forth from the bow."[34] The poet becomes an instrument destined to give expression and form to those yet unformed ideas that lie dormant in our souls. They take possession of him, transcending his personal life-sphere with their wealth of memories; otherwise they could not become generally meaningful. Artistic sensibility and talent are usually characterized by the vividness of fantasies rising from the unconscious and striving to take on form; and also by the ability to *give* them form. According to Jung's psychology, the unconscious mind stands in a compensatory relation to its own conscious contents and drives, so that works of art illuminate and compensate for the one-sidedness of the spirit of the time. Jung says: "Thus, just as the one-sidedness of the individual's conscious attitude is corrected by reactions from the unconscious, so art represents a process of self-regulation in the life of nations and epochs."[35] We find a similar trend of thought in Goethe:

> All supreme productivity, every important observation, every invention, every great idea that bears fruit and has lasting effect, stands not in anyone's power and is above all earthly force. Man must regard these things as gifts from on high, as pure children of God, and he must receive and venerate them with joyful gratitude. It is related to the daemonic which can overpower him and do with him as it pleases and to which he gives himself up unconsciously, while believing himself to be active under his own power. In such cases man can often be regarded as the tool of a higher world government, as a vessel that has been found worthy to receive a divine influence. I say this while I think how often a single idea has given new form to an entire century, and how certain individuals have put their stamp on whole epochs and have remained a recognizable and salutory influence for generations.[36]

The fact that totalitarian dictatorships expend so much effort on controlling and censoring art shows an instinctive knowledge of the compensatory aspects of works of art. Wherever the live mental processes are to be hamstrung in favor of a rigid collective system, creative-artistic freedom must first be curtailed. The artist must be allowed only to glorify existing conditions; his work is to have an educational effect in accordance with the ruling ideas, the ideology.

Given this knowledge, Jung finds it wrong to try to explain the creative act and the literary work through the personal history and problems of the writer alone—although depth psychology at first

tended to do so. It is true that the biographies of writers often are
treasure troves of psychopathological phenomena. Neuroses, psychoses, addictions, sexual perversions quickly reveal themselves to
the psychiatrist's trained eye. But all attempts at interpretation which
try to dissect works of literature on the basis of their author's personal difficulties reduce the work to a demonstration of symptoms.
"The personal psychology of the artist may explain many aspects of
his work, but not the work itself. And if ever it did explain his work
successfully, the artist's creativity would be revealed as a mere
symptom. This would be detrimental both to the work of art and to
its repute."[37] Jung offers the following example: "A knowledge of
Goethe's particular relation to his mother throws some light on
Faust's exclamation: 'The mothers, the mothers, how eerily it sounds'!
But it does not enable us to see how the attachment to his mother
could produce the *Faust* drama itself, however deeply we sense the
importance of this relationship for Goethe the man from the many
telltale traces it has left behind in his work."[38]

Jung tries to explain the writer's personal problematic through the
fact that the writer has to subordinate his humanity to his need to
create. His conflict consists in the fact that "two forces are at war
within him: on the one hand the justified longing of the ordinary man
for happiness, satisfaction and security, and on the other a ruthless
passion for creation which may go so far as to override every personal desire."[39] Rilke alludes to this basic conflict in his requiem for
Paula Becker-Moderssohn: "For, there is somewhere an ancient hostility between life and the great work."[40] A deeply moving document
testifying to the extent and power of this "hostility" is to be found in
the correspondence between Kafka and Felice Bauer.[41] "How can
we doubt," says Jung, "that it is his art that explains the artist, and
not the insufficiencies and conflicts of his personal life? These are
nothing but the regrettable results of his being an artist, a man upon
whom a heavier burden is laid than upon ordinary mortals."[42] He
usually must "pay dearly for the divine gifts of creative fire."[43] Thus,
if we are to regard the author's human-personal problems from the
viewpoint of the creative work, his suffering becomes psychologically
meaningful; it stems from the fact that he is as a rule not allowed to
travel "the broad highway of normal man"[44] or to identify completely
with the conscious trends of his epoch. He feels lonely and "thrown
back upon himself," as Heidegger says. This condition again has
meaning in regard to the work, but "the artist's relative lack of adap-

tation turns out to his advantage; it enables him to follow his own yearnings far from the beaten path, and to discover what it is that would meet the unconscious needs of his age."[45] Jung is quite generally of the opinion that the artist's suffering—for himself, his world, and the general spirit of his age—is the very thing that opens his consciousness to those compensatory images and ideas that arise from the unconscious. Jung arrived at this knowledge through countless experiences with mental patients undergoing psychotherapy. This is why he sees neurosis not merely as a negative, senseless pattern, but in some cases even as a signal or a call to deeper self-awareness, self-knowledge, and self-realization. No doubt this is why he never delved into the personal diagnoses or neuroses of literary personalities for a key to the understanding of their work; to him "every great work of art is objective and impersonal, and yet profoundly moving. And that is also why the personal life of the artist is at most a help or a hindrance, but is never essential to his creative work. He may go the way of the Philistine, a good citizen, a fool, or a criminal. His personal career may be interesting and inevitable, but it does not explain his art."[46] I consider this formulation of Jung's a little exaggerated; but it is as legitimate a position as are the psychoanalytical interpretations of the Freudian school which merely dissect the author's instinctual conflicts. How far the artist's personal sphere has influenced his work—the relationship between private biography and the contents of literary creations—is a matter that must be examined in each individual case and that will, of course, show very different results with different artist personalities.

Thus Jung's main interest is the work itself and its archetypal background. In considering the work of art from the psychologist's viewpoint, Jung first of all makes a basic distinction between categories of artistic creation which can be clearly recognized. The first category contains "works, prose as well as poetry, that spring wholly from the author's intention to produce a particular result. . . . He exercises the keenest judgement and chooses his words with complete freedom."[47] In this type of work the conscious artistic knowledge seems to have been responsible for everything, including the idea. Certainly, it has arranged the idea, related it to the whole, and determined its form. The poet "is wholly at one with the creative process, no matter whether he has deliberately made himself its spearhead, as it were, or whether it has made him its instrument so completely that he has lost all consciousness of this fact."[48] At any rate, the material from which he fashions his works seems not to be foreign to his conscious mind; it consists of

> materials drawn from man's conscious life—with crucial experiences, powerful emotions, suffering, passion, the stuff of human fate in general. All this is assimilated by the psyche of the poet, raised from the commonplace to the level of poetic experience, and expressed with a power of conviction that gives us a greater depth of human insight by making us aware of those everyday happenings which we tend to evade or to overlook because we perceive them only dully or with a feeling of discomfort. The raw material of this kind of cre-ation is derived from the contents of man's consciousness, from his eternally repeated joys and sorrows, but clarified and transfigured by the poet.

For the sake of clarity, Jung calls this kind of work *psychological*, because "the poet has done the psychologist's work in them . . . no obscurity surrounds them, for they fully explain themselves in their own terms."[50] The psychologist in turn can, at best, annotate or criticize such works; they remain throughout within the boundaries of what is psychologically comprehensible. "Countless literary prod-ucts belong to this class: all the novels dealing with love, the family milieu, crime and society, together with didactic poetry, the greater number of lyrics, and drama both tragic and comic."[51] They "have been known from the beginning of time—passion and its fated out-come, human destiny and its sufferings, eternal nature with its beauty and horror."[52]

But there is a different class of literary works, which comes,

> as it were, fully arrayed into the world, as Pallas Athene sprang from the head of Zeus. These works positively force themselves upon the author; his hand is seized, his pen writes things that his mind con-templates with amazement. The work brings with it its own form; anything he wants to add is rejected, and what he himself would like to reject is thrust back at him. While his conscious mind stands amazed and empty before this phenomenon, he is overwhelmed by a flood of thoughts and images which he never intended to create and which his own will could never have brought into being. Yet in spite of himself he is forced to admit that it is his own self speaking, his own inner nature revealing itself and uttering things which he would never have entrusted to his tongue. He can only obey the apparently alien impulse within him and follow where it leads, sensing that his work is greater than himself, and wields a power which is not his and which he cannot command. Here the artist is not identical with the process of creation. He is aware that he is

subordinate to his work or stands outside it as though he were a second person; or as though a person other than himself had fallen within the magic circle of an alien will.[53]

Jung calls this type a *visionary* work of art. It often comes over the poet as a kind of primal vision and it can "rend from top to bottom the curtain upon which is painted the picture of an ordered world, and allow a glimpse into the unfathomable abyss of the unborn and of things yet to be. Is it a vision of other worlds, or of the darkness of the spirit, or of the primal beginnings of the human psyche? We cannot say that it is any or none of these."[54] Such works in which we encounter the primal vision are, according to Jung: Dante's *Divina Commedia*, Goethe's *Faust*, Part II, William Blake's drawings and poems, the grand and sometimes scurrilous images in E. T. A. Hoffmann's novel *The Golden Pot*; James Joyce's *Ulysses*, which "is a work of the greatest significance in spite of or perhaps because of its nihilistic tendencies."[55]

"In more restricted and succinct form"[56] according to Jung, such works as *She* by H. Rider Haggard, *L'Atlantide* by Benoit, *The Other Side* by Kubin, or *The Green Face* by Gustav Meyrink are also based on a primal vision. Contrary to the "psychological" works in which well-known and familiar things are described and expressed, in *visionary* literature "we are reminded of nothing in everyday life, but rather of dreams, night-time fears, and the dark, uncanny recesses of the human mind."[57] This is why such works are not accessible to the spontaneous understanding of the general reader; they call for interpretations and commentary.

We can see why Jung, the explorer of the unconscious ground of the soul, was powerfully attracted to works of visionary literature. They gave him profound insights into the secret workings of man's collective-psychological life. These same forces, conjured up by the artist, can also, in a negative sense, erupt in individual psychoses or in religious and pseudoreligious mass hysteria, flooding the conscious mind. What matters most is whether such experiences can be accepted, sufficiently understood, and integrated into the conscious mind and thus enrich it profoundly, or whether they completely overwhelm it, and carry away its powers of discrimination from where they are anchored in everyday life—into unknown and no longer controllable regions. This is why we almost always find, in cases of insanity, that archetypal images have taken over the sufferer's consciousness and have produced a state of "possession." But the primal images can also release those helpful forces "that ever and anon have enabled humanity to find a refuge from every peril and to out-live the longest night."[58] This is why Jung, the physician and psy-chotherapist, was mainly interested in the relations between the ego, its radius of consciousness, and the basic archetypal data, the contents of the collective unconscious. When the ego is made aware of its own boundaries and allows them to open out towards the uncon-scious life in an understanding, orderly, and even value-judging manner, the result may well be a relation to the ground of one's own soul, the end of self-estrangement, and a maturing of the entire per-sonality. Jung's extensive research into symbols also serves to facili-tate a proper understanding of the unconscious contents of our mind and the way they function, so that they cannot produce dangerous obsessions by taking our consciousness unawares. Instead, these un-conscious contents should enlarge and deepen our consciousness and enrich the entire personality. For this reason, Jung rated the *visionary* type of literature with its deep-probing symbolism so highly, for, "he who speaks in primal images, speaks as a man with a thousand voices; he grasps and overpowers us and at the same time he raises that which he describes from the particular and transitory sphere into the eternal; he elevates individual destiny to the destiny of man."[59]

This brings us back to the actual problem of literary evaluation. Jung's valuation, which was psychological in viewpoint, cannot pos-sibly be identical with aesthetic-artistic values. It would be utterly absurd to ascribe greater artistic value to a book like Haggard's *She* than to, say, Goethe's *Wahlverwandschaften* (Elective Affinities) or to *Faust*, Part I, which Jung cites as examples of "psychological" liter-ature. Jung was fully aware of this discrepancy. He wrote: "There is a fundamental difference of attitude between the psychologist's ap-proach to a literary work and that of a literary critic. What is of decisive importance and value for the latter may be quite irrelevant for the former. Indeed, literary products of highly dubious merit are often of the greatest interest to the psychologist."[60] Literary critics have reproached the depth psychologists for their interest in literary works of extremely doubtful value.[60a] But Jung explains quite clearly that his interest in literature stems from quite another side. For him as a scientist literary products are primarily documents of a mental activity he wishes to illuminate in depth. He asks: what is the human psyche like; what laws can be inferred from its functioning; and how is human consciousness to cope with unconscious problems of the psyche for its own good? The words of the visionary poets, being "products of the unconscious," provided him with the most valuable insights for these researches. I would here like to call attention to the work of Jung's student, Aniela Jaffé about *The Golden Pot* by E. T. A. Hoffmann, a beautiful example of psychological interpretation and illumination of archetypal contexts in a literary work.

III

Jung did not actually make any direct contribution to the problem of *literary* evaluation, the subject of this paper. As a psychologist he did not feel qualified to do so. But the possibilities of a psychological contribution to this question of literary criticism are worth pondering anew.

We must first of all study the question of values in analytical psychology. Jung had an empiric view of his method of investigation: he considered himself a scientist who, because of the nature of the psyche with its images and fantasies, had to enter into many questions in the field of liberal arts as well. In its empiric investigation of psychic phenomena, Jung's psychology, like most natural sciences, makes no value judgments. It merely tries to illuminate, to discover laws and relationships. But, while pursuing this activity, psychology very soon comes to the realization that value and valuation play an enormously important part in the human soul. The "highest good," "the hard-to-reach treasure," seems to be an archetype we find expressed in countless symbols. Many myths and fairy tales feature the treasure which lies at the bottom of a deep lake, or is guarded by a dragon; the golden fleece; the water of life; the king's fairest daughter; the devil's three golden hairs, the golden ball. In alchemy, we hear about the philosopher's stone, or the mysterious hermaphrodite Rebis; in the history of religion it is the kingdom of God, Nirvana, or the gnostic Nous, meaning the spark of the Spirit that has leaped upon matter and brought it to life. We notice that these value symbols are often connected with a goal. They are each a goal to be reached and they mobilize psychic energies. Only the victorious dragon fighter can reach the treasure; the king's lovely daughter must be freed, the devil's three golden hairs must be plucked from his head. The philosopher's stone shall be purified *deo concedente*, that is, with the help of God; the gnostic tries to free the spiritual spark from the embrace of matter.

This archetype, then, contains an intense dynamism: its character is one of fascination and appeal; but it can be misunderstood in the everyday life of the conscious mind. For instance, the treasure, or gold, can be pursued in a purely material sense. This would mean that the dynamic primal idea of the highest good has been projected onto concrete possessions. The psychologist often sees the accumulation of capital experienced as a heightening of personal worth. Figures of speech such as: how much is he worth? (meaning: how much money does he have?) speak volumes about this correlation. The epidemic of suicides during the stock market crash of the nineteen-thirties can be interpreted to mean that the loss of money can come to mean the total loss of one's self, which means that life and the person have lost all value and meaning. But even some of the early alchemists said clearly: *Aurum nostrum non est aurum vulgi*—our gold is not the common gold. They wanted to say that what they sought was the "philosophic gold" of higher knowledge. Medieval icons and Madonnas are almost always painted on a gold ground which may be taken as a symbol for the fact that they were meant to represent contents of highest imperishable value. The New Testament doctrine about how immensely difficult it is for a rich man to attain the Kingdom of God can be psychologically interpreted to mean that the highest good must be freed from the projection onto external possessions before its supratemporal meaning can be understood.

It is similar with the treasure in the form of the virginal princess. Here we can see the high value placed on sexuality, its one-sided overestimation as a means of self-assertion. There is a more or less conscious sense of: I am a whole man only when I have conquered the most beautiful woman of all, and am envied by all. The woman becomes a value object which lends value to the person of the man. But the primal image of the virginal princess points to deeper and more all-embracing values. In contrast to the active-male principle which wishes to grasp the world and itself by means of rational categories, the princess symbolizes the values of the soul, of empathy, of relating to all that lives and to the mysterious skimmer of life itself. In Goethe's *Faust*, for instance, it is the image of Marguerite that awakens Faust's vital spirits.

Only through extreme effort is the highest good to become accessible to the hero who—for the psychologist—symbolizes human consciousness. The attainment of the treasure therefore stands for enrichment and expansion of consciousness, for the exploration and full savoring of being, for creation itself, as it is reflected in the human mind which ascribes meaning to it. The highest good is, therefore, that which we sense, experience, and interpret as the meaning of life.

This question about the meaning of existence, perhaps one of the most urgent questions man can ask, has been answered variously to satisfy the inner needs of certain epochs and certain individuals; it has been answered through the centuries, by religions and philosophies. But the question keeps reappearing as an archetypal urge towards the expansion of consciousness; today, when traditional world hierarchies are becoming ever more questionable, the answer must be sought by each person individually.[60b]

We have seen that value is an archetype which powerfully attracts and affects human consciousness. It fascinates, it demands action, and religious people have at all times experienced it as commandments from God which must be fulfilled. In practical life, we are powerfully attracted, stirred, and even moved to certain activities by certain ideas, events, or persons which touch upon this unconscious idea of value. Many valuable cultural achievements can result from it. But there is an extremely dangerous side to it, too; archetypes can seduce as well as guide us. Ideas which embody the highest value for us can take possession of us, can turn us into fanatics, and therefore, as is sometimes the case, they can work as negative values. The persecutions of heretics and the inquisition were conducted in good faith "in the name of Christ." Millions of men are slaughtered in senseless wars for "God, Emperor, and Fatherland." All demagoguery makes its appeal to certain emotional value ideas in us.

Based on these insights the analytical psychologist now endeavors —in his own special field which is the psychotherapy of persons in conflict with themselves—to accept and support the value drives he finds existing in the patient's psyche and, above all, to raise them as completely as possible into the patient's conscious mind.[61] To become aware of his unconscious values and their consequences and possible dangers is of decisive importance for a person who does not wish to fall victim to them. Experience has shown that increased awareness can both help people towards maturity and heal them in the psychotherapeutic sense. This makes the enrichment of consciousness extremely valuable for the analytical psychologist. The full self-realization of the personality, the process of individuation, is the psychologist's own highest good, his most important task, the answer to the question of fate and the meaning of life.[62] In the process of self-discovery and the search for meaning, the psychologist's task consists in illuminating and interpreting the various stages, in helping to overcome error, and in never losing sight of that ultimate value, the potential unity and wholeness of the personality.

Increased awareness brings with it the ability to distinguish between real values and false ones, and to place the various individual values within an entire value hierarchy. Consciously or unconsciously, we are always bestowing certain values on things, events, our fellow men and ourselves; we make value judgments. To judge is principally an act of our conscious mind, and value judgments especially are made, according to Jung, through the conscious function of feeling, not of thinking.[63] For example: our "conscience" judges good or evil through a *feeling* of guilt, and our *sense* of justice tells us what is just and what is unjust.

We evaluate by measuring the new object against existing inner value ideas. Evaluation can never be objective in the strict sense, since those factors which constitute our sense of value are based on subjective, psychic assumptions. That is why value judgments about events, persons, or even works of art always tell us as much about the judge as they do about the object being evaluated. To become aware of one's psychic value hierarchy and to question and test its standards again and again becomes an important, predominantly moral task for anyone who wishes to be as just as possible towards his fellow men and even towards himself. These inner value categories must be questioned and examined repeatedly; they change, expand, and deepen as our awareness grows. The greater the range of my consciousness, the greater the breadth of experience I have encountered, the larger and more differentiated will my value judgments be. Then I will face any new thing I must evaluate without narrow prejudice, but with understanding for its singularity; I will test and judge everything in a larger context.

We have shown that the highest good as an archetypal idea can be grasped only by means of symbols, for example, as the "hard-to-obtain treasure." A true symbol, it cannot be translated into a perceptible object of definite size and shape, but it points beyond itself into the realms of the abstract; realms that are constantly being reinterpreted by the religions or metaphysics of the day. But, as we have seen, the dynamic of the primal idea of the highest good is effective on various existence levels in our daily life and can do enormous damage when misunderstood in a one-sided, narrow way; when, in short, we do not become fully conscious of its actual place in the hierarchy of values.

Because the value archetype is so inexhaustible and ambiguous; because it can actualize itself in such an infinite variety of ways at various times and in various individuals, the evaluation of literature creates a problem for the psychologist. There is not only a history of literature; there is also a history of literary criticism, as René Wellek has proved in his massive work.[64] Such a history shows how value categories can change, how the collective values of various epochs create, among other things, ever new and different criteria. Goethe, in his day, described two basically different approaches to literary criticism which he judged to be destructive and productive respectively.

> The former is very easy: for one need only set up an imaginary standard, some model or other, however foolish it may be, and then boldly assert that the work of art under consideration does not measure up to that standard and therefore is of no value. That settles the matter and one can without further ado declare that the poet has not come up to one's requirements. In this way the critic frees himself of all obligations of gratitude toward the artist. Productive criticism is much harder. It asks: what did the author set out to do? Was his plan reasonable and sensible, and how far did he succeed in carrying it out? If these questions are answered with discernment and sympathy we may be of real assistance to the author in his later works.[65]

It is obvious that if we evaluate literature according to preconceived "models" we are bound to fail to do justice to a large number of works. There is, on the other hand, the danger of progressive relativism if we abolish actual valuation and judge a work only by its "inner harmony." This is why literary criticism must work out a standard which, while it does not postulate narrow, preconceived axioms, still has "validity beyond the changing times and other relative factors."[66]

For this purpose, the critic and literary historian, Siegfried Melchinger, seeks to establish two general criteria by which a work which claims to be art can be judged and placed on the "art" value scale. His first criterion is "necessity of origin," his second "the dimension of completeness." By "necessity" he means "that a work had to become a work of art and could become nothing else; a demand which also contains within itself the decision in favor of a specific form of art (such as verse rather than colors or musical notation); a criterium of specification which makes a work distinct and different from all others by the very fact that it cannot possibly be anything else or in any way different from what and how it is."[67] The decision for art "which at the same time includes the decision for one specific art-medium"[68] is, according to Melchinger, "irrational in character. It cannot be explained by science, nor can it be replaced by technological manipulation, nor can it be controlled or directed by ideological commands. It is determined solely by something that has been given to an individual, something he cannot change or determine, namely his talent."[69] Thus the road of criticism leads via the category of necessity to one of the central tasks of critical judgment: "to determine whether the work under consideration is marked by talent or not."[70]

The criterion of "completeness" is, for Melchinger, a dimension by which the work of art potentially counteracts all that is "incomplete, transitory, decayed, inadequate in human existence."[71] Therefore, the more completeness "a work can attain within and for itself, the greater will be its duration."[72] "We can tell whether there is talent in an artist and whether a work ranks as a work of art (or whether, perhaps, an author merely claims to be an artist, and a work merely assumes the attitude of a work of art) by the deep struggle for completeness that has produced it; by the dimension which the talent (self-evident in this case) has set out to reach in order to give the work a certain degree of durability beyond the purely contemporary market value."[73]

Wilhelm Emrich, in his interesting essay "Wertung und Rangordnung literarischer Werke," gives the following basic definition:

> What constitutes the specifically artistic quality of a work of literature is the fact that the various contents and forms which the author utilizes or produces out of his imagination are combined into a fabric of interrelations. This fabric, made from structure and language, liberates the various contents and forms from their specific historical context and opens up an inexhaustible wealth of meanings which, in turn, can develop representative or symbolic meanings that are equally applicable to other periods, other forms of life, other ideas. What constitutes a non-artistic work is the fact that the reflection it contains does not represent an endless continuum, but breaks off very soon, or reaches its end because its contents and forms do not point beyond themselves, do not contain a multiplicity of meanings,

but remain within an unequivocal realm which is quickly exhausted. There is no need for any further contemplation or exploration and, therefore, none takes place.[74]

According to Emrich a work of art can be graded by the wealth and inexhaustibility of the "fabric of relations" it presents to the reflective mind. This fabric of relations which, in the best cases, makes "infinite reflexion" possible, is not to be confused with "complicated" or "profound" problems, for, while such problems *can* be contained in a work of art, we can also encounter them in a cheap commercial novel, where the problem-laden profundities turn out to be simply emotional trivia and intellectual banalities that do not call for independent reflection and so do not open up any vistas or depths. It is often the very "understatement" of problems, their "indirect" presentation through the relations between seemingly quite "superficial" events that signal the highest art. The simple, "apparently superficial" folk tales and ancient myths which seem to consist of mere "sequences of events" are actually infinitely reflexible. We can see the proof of this in the fact that all these "simple" myths have been re-created again and again through the centuries, and are still being re-created in ever new forms by poets, playwrights, and novelists."[75]

Walter Muschg sees three main arteries that have run through the works of great literature since times immemorial: magical enchantment, mystical inspiration, and the naïve joy in living and in the earth's beauty.[76] Three primal images representing the poet are based on these: the magician, the seer, and the singer. For Muschg the work "genius" refers to someone or something deeply in accord with the most ancient types. "We say 'great' and we mean the return of something ancient. The secret of a poet's greatness is his connection with the archaic forms of the spirit of poetry. It can be traced only in the very greatest; it is this connection which makes them the exceptions among the lesser lights."[77]

The three authorities on literary criticism quoted above will have to suffice us. As a psychologist I will not presume to judge the competence of their statements; I am not even sure whether my selection of these authorities would be considered truly representative by literary critics today. However, the criteria cited above seem to bear witness to the fact, which every layman knows, that there are great works of poetry, some of them very ancient, whose "fabric of relations" to this very day gives rise to inexhaustible questions, and opens ever new dimensions of experience which in turn demand ever new interpretation and appear fraught with ever new meaning.

A psychologist cannot evaluate works of literature in the aesthetic-artistic sense or create criteria for them in that sense. But evaluation and the search for general value standards is an activity of the psyche which can be studied from the psychological point of view. And here it becomes apparent that the literary value categories cited above correspond with general value ideas that have been discovered in the human soul. We have said that the archetype of the highest good with its unconscious call to action motivates us to strive for value and to recognize value; in other words: to become aware of our own unconscious values. The further we progress in increasing awareness and recognizing the relative importance of certain values we had unquestioningly accepted from our families or peer groups, the more we shall discover the contents of a "fabric of relations" that is both inexhaustible and timeless. We thus gain a far larger sense of values and may experience an encounter with the "ultimate values" of our existence.

We find such images, symbols of the supratemporal, everywhere in the great literature of all times. They are fraught with meaning and are experienced as values by us. The criteria of literary evaluation cited earlier are based on this same spontaneous, archetypally determined value experience. As value categories, they appeal to our emotions and assume a living relationship between the work and the value-conscious reader. The question is, whether the "inexhaustibly reflective fabric of relations" of which Emrich speaks is intrinsic to the work, or whether the work merely acts as a catalyst, stimulating within the reader his own fabric of relations which, in turn, is projected back onto the work and so conveys a sense of value through it. There is no unequivocal answer to this question, since the experience of value becomes possible only in fruitful mutual relation; the poet touches something in me which seems to me of high value and, reciprocally, makes me receptive to the work's larger message. The value categories described above seem to be the result of such mutual relations between the work of art and the discriminating, emotional reaction of the reader or critic. In their emphasis on the supratemporal, in their infinite reflexibility, in their relation to the primal image, they point to an infinitely meaningful highest value which we can only vaguely sense as the deepest meaning of our life, and which our conscious mind can grasp only in a fragmentary way. Thus they leave enough room for appreciation of the irrepeatable uniqueness of the work on the one hand, and for its translucency for eternally human questions of existence on the other.

We now must ask ourselves how far we can do justice to contemporary literature with such criteria. Do they not create the impression that everything great has already been written, once and for all, by authors we consider classical in the widest sense? The psychologist's answer to this basically literary question might be that, as Jung has pointed out, the primal images have—at all times—the effect of extremely potent life forces. We cannot say that they have been revealed once and for all in the Bible, in the Upanishads, in Dante, Shakespeare, or, if you wish, in Goethe's *Faust*; that they have been given their final validity only in those works. The classics are historic documents we must, first of all, understand in the context of their period. But, in addition to this, their "infinite reflexibility" as Emrich calls it, provokes a search for new approaches in *every* period. There are libraries full of interpretations of all the works named above. But the primal images or archetypes are not historic entities. As Muschg says, the relation to archaic contents is not to be understood as an historical activity but rather as something that takes place within the psyche. The archetype itself is abstract, but it can take on the guise of thousands of possible symbols in which it manifests itself to the human consciousness. And so, ever new symbols arise, conveying a connection between the modern consciousness and the eternally human in a vaguely sensed way and, at the same time, opening up new possibilities of consciousness.

In literature, too, new types of word construction and word combinations can continually arise behind which there sounds the "primal word" as Gerhard Hauptmann has said. Whether anything of the kind is happening in our period, how far certain authors working in the style of surrealism, or the *nouveau roman*, or the theatre of the absurd, are opening up such new dimensions and creating space for the inexhaustible "fabric of relations," is a question which, as we well know, contemporary criticism cannot really answer, because lack of distance means lack of perspective. But there is room, and need, for detailed discussion and evaluation.

All in all, the psychologist can state that the literary value criteria mentioned above correspond to general human archetypal value ideas: that they bring those ideas to mind and are therefore of sufficient depth and breadth to allow us to approach true literature without being hampered by prejudgments or narrow, preconceived notions.

The criterium of "infinite reflexibility" of a "poetic fabric of relations" corresponds, in the realm of psychology, to the archetype
which is inexhaustible for the conscious mind. A conscious valuation,
no matter how broad, can never grasp more than the fragments of
the creative unconscious which manifests itself in a work of literature. This is why literary evaluation as such becomes a problem; this
is why a work of art must be studied and considered anew in every
period. As W. B. Yeats said:

> Man can embody truth
> But he cannot know it.

[*Translated from the German by Maria Pelikan*]

Notes

1. S. Freud, *Collected Works* (Standard Ed.) Vol. 8, p. 235.
2. *Ibid.*, p. 234.
3. G. Bally, *Einführung in der Psychoanalyse* Freuds (Hamburg, 1961), pp. 113–14.
4. Freud, *Collected Works*, Vol. 20, pp. 64–5.
5. Bally, *Einführung*, Vol. 16, p. 115.
6. Freud, *Collected Works*, Vol. 21, p. 133.
7. *Ibid.*, Vol. 12, p. 224.
8. *Ibid.*, Vol. 9, p. 151.
9. *Ibid.*, Vol. 21, p. 177.
10. *Ibid.*, Vol. 9, p. 153.
11. C. G. Jung, *Memories, Dreams, Reflections* (New York, 1963), pp. 154–55.
12. *Ibid.*, p. 150.
13. *Ibid.*, p. 151.
14. *Ibid.*, p. 363.
15. E. Jones, *The Life and Work of Sigmund Freud* (New York, 1955), Vol. 2, p. 140.
16. C. G. Jung, *Collected Works* (Princeton, 1960), Vol. 8, pp. 202–03.
17. *Ibid.*, p. 204.
18. *Ibid.*, Vol. 6, p. 618.
19. *Ibid.*, Vol. 9, p. 5, n. 9.
20. *Ibid.*, Vol. 6, p. 601.
21. J. W. v. Goethe, "Maximen & Reflexionen," in *Schriften der Goethegesell-schaft*, Vol. 21 (1907), p. 314.
22. Quoted by Jung, *Collected Works* (Princeton, 1966), Vol. 15, p. 80.
23. F. Strich, *Der Dichter und die Zeit* (Berne, 1947), p. 23.

24. Jung, *Collected Works*, Vol. 6, p. 603.
25. *Ibid.*, p. 605.
26. *Ibid.*, Vol. 11, pp. 330–31.
27. *Ibid.*, Vol. 7.
28. W. Dement, *The Physiology of Dreaming* (New York, 1958).
29. Jung, *Collected Works*, Vol. 8, p. 253.
30. Jacobi, *Die Psychologie von C. G. Jung* (Zurich, 1959), p. 127.
30 (*a*). Jung. (1) "On the Relations between Analytical Psychology and Literature." (2) "Psychology and Literature." (3) "Ulysses." In *Collected Works*, Vol. 15.
31. Jung, *Collected Works*, Vol. 15, p. 65.
32. *Ibid.*, p. 86.
33. *Ibid.*, p. 103.
34. Quoted by W. F. Otts, *Theophania* (Hamburg, 1959), p. 107.
35. Jung, *Collected Works*, Vol. 15, p. 83.
36. Goethe, *Conversations with Eckermann* (New York, 1960).
37. Jung, *Collected Works*, Vol. 15, p. 86.
38. *Ibid.*, p. 86.
39. *Ibid.*, p. 102.
40. R. M. Rilke, *Sämtliche Werke* (Wiesbaden, 1955), Vol. 1, p. 655.
41. Frankfurt a.M., 1967.
42. Jung, *Collected Works*, Vol. 15, pp. 102–03.
43. *Ibid.*, p. 102.
44. *Ibid.*, Vol. 15, p. 83.
45. *Ibid.*, p. 83.
46. *Ibid.*, p. 105.
47. *Ibid.*, p. 72.
48. *Ibid.*, p. 72.
49. *Ibid.*, p. 89.
50. *Ibid.*, p. 89.
51. *Ibid.*, p. 89.
52. *Ibid.*, p. 90.
53. *Ibid.*, p. 73.
54. *Ibid.*, pp. 90–1.
55. *Ibid.*, p. 91, n. 7.
56. *Ibid.*, p. 91.
57. *Ibid.*, p. 91.
58. *Ibid.*, p. 82.
59. *Ibid.*, p. 82.
60. *Ibid.*, pp. 87–8.
60 (*a*). For instance, B. A. Muschg, "Psychoanalyse und Literature-Wissenschaft." In *Pamphlet und Bekenntnis* (Olten, 1968).
60 (*b*). See A. Jaffe, *Der Mythus vom Sinn* (Zurich, 1967).
61. Jung, *Gestaltungen der Unbewussten* (Zurich, 1960).
62. Jaffe, *Mythus.*
63. Jung, *Collected Works*, Vol. 6.
64. R. Wellek, *A History of Modern Criticism* (London, 1958).
65. *Ibid.*, Vol. 1, pp. 223–24.
66. S. Melchinger, "Keine Mässtabe," in *Schriften zur Zeit*, Vol. 22 (1959), p. 18.
67. *Ibid.*, p. 28.
68. *Ibid.*, p. 29.
69. *Ibid.*, p. 29.
70. *Ibid.*, p. 29.

71. *Ibid.*, p. 31.
72. *Ibid.*, p. 31.
73. *Ibid.*, p. 31.
74. W. Emrich in *Sprache im technischen Zeitalter*, Vols. 11–12 (1964), p. 983.
75. *Ibid.*, pp. 990–91.
76. W. Muschg, *Tragische Literaturgeschichte* (Berne, 1953), p. 169.
77. *Ibid.*, p. 262.

Leonard F. Manheim

THE PROBLEM OF
THE NORMATIVE FALLACY

YET ANOTHER "FALLACY" IN LITERARY CRITICISM! MANY A CRITIC HAS
been belabored with the club of the "intentional fallacy" (basing critical judgments allegedly on the announced intention of the author
rather than on examination of the work itself) and its cousin-german
the "genetic fallacy" (considering the work from the viewpoint of
its sources in the life-history of the author). Ten years ago Maurice
Beebe listed some others:[1] the "exhaustive fallacy" (William York
Tindall's comment on the impossibility of analyzing any work in all
of its aspects or seeing it "from every possible angle of vision simultaneously"); the "progressive fallacy" (an attempt "to make progress
a criterion of artistic greatness and to judge a writer in terms of a
scale of improvement"); the "selective fallacy" (known in the old
system of propaganda analysis as "card-stacking," that is, drawing
"unwarranted conclusions from selected, partial evidence"); and
the "argumentative fallacy" (in which "a critic quarrels with an
artist's view of life"). And there are still others.

It all started with Ruskin, of course, when he denounced the "pa-
thetic fallacy," in which the emotions of a human being, usually the
author, are ascribed to non-human beings or even to inanimate objects. In its crude form it is indeed rather silly ("Poor rock! Everybody sits on him."), but a little more profound consideration will
reveal how ubiquitous the phenomenon is, how indispensable it is
to the communication of almost any emotional state from the author
to the reader. For, in truth, the phenomenon is a well-recognized
psychodynamic mechanism, formally isolated and named in early

psychoanalytic theory. It is a special form of *displacement of affect,* well known by now under its more common name, *projection.*

Leaving aside, however, the validity of the various modes of denunciation implied in these several classifications, consider for a moment the noun which is common to all of these pejorative terms. The technical meaning "fallacy" in logic is "any reasoning failing to satisfy the conditions of logical proof or violating the laws of valid argument." Ruskin may have originally had in mind the less technical meaning implying any deceptive or false idea, but the strict logical reference in the term has undoubtedly played the largest role in its adoption, as indicated above, for all sorts of critical procedures which fail to satisfy those who set themselves up as critics of criticism. How much more effective it is to say, "You are guilty of a fallacy." than to say, "I don't think I quite agree with you." For being guilty of a fallacy implies that one has been guilty of *violating a rigorous system of proof,* proceeding for the most part deductively from one recognized truth to another which follows from it. And the ultimate source of the "recognized truth" is a basic major premise which is either assumed or revealed, depending on whether you are a mathematician or a theologian. The reader is probably far ahead of the writer, remembering that when you do not accuse the other fellow of committing a *fallacy,* you are likely to proclaim that he has fallen into a *heresy,* the violation of another kind of dogma.

This introduction, therefore, has been an avowal of the inaccuracy of the title of this paper. For I am really not referring to the "normative fallacy" but to a "normative obsession" or a "normative compulsion." What reader of a critique of criticism would have read this far, however, if I had started off with a title which gave evidence that I was approaching criticism through psychopathology? For that is precisely what I intend to do. My contention, quite simply, is that absolute evaluation, the measuring of a work of art against some universally accepted norm, is not a valid function of criticism but is, rather, a product of the critic's being "hot for certainties in this our life." Let me develop my point—and give my literary reader a chance to cool off—by examining a parallel in another discipline, the law.

The late Jerome Frank was a remarkable combination of practical lawyer, active jurist, and legal theoretician. Holding undergraduate and law degrees, as well as an honorary LL.D., from the University of Chicago, he went from a research post at Yale Law School into the active political arena as counsel to several New Deal agencies back in the nineteen-thirties and then was a member of the Securities and Exchange Commission until 1941, when he was appointed to the bench of the United States Circuit Court of Appeals. It is from his major theoretical work, *The Law and the Modern Mind*, that I wish to quote at some length:

> This, then, is our partial explanation of the basic legal myth: The filial relation is clearly indicated as one important unconscious determinant of the ways of man in dealing with all his problems, including the problem of his attitude toward law. The several components of this explanation may be summarized thus:
>
> (1) The infant strives to retain something like pre-birth serenity. Conversely, the fear of the unknown, dread of chance and change, are vital factors in the life of the child.
>
> (2) These factors manifest themselves in a childish appetite for complete peace, comfort, protection from the dangers of the unknown. The child, "unrealistically," craves a steadfast world which will be steady and controllable.
>
> (3) The child satisfies that craving, in large measure, through his confidence in and reliance on his incomparable, omnipotent, infallible father.
>
> (4) Despite advancing years, most men are at times the victims of the childish desire for complete serenity and the childish fear of irreducible chance. They then will to believe that they live in a world in which chance is only an appearance and not a reality, in which they can be free of the indefinite, the arbitrary, the capricious. When they find life distracting, unsettling, fatiguing, they long to rise above the struggle for existence; to be rid of all upsetting shifts and changes and novelties; to discover an uninterrupted connection between apparently disjunctive events; to rest in an environment that is fundamentally stable. They revert, that is, to childish longings, which they attempt to satisfy through "the rediscovery of the father," through father-substitutes. Even when the fear factor is absent, the desire for father-substitutes may persist; father-dependence, originally a means of adaptation, has become an end-in-itself.
>
> (5) The Law can easily be made to play an important part in the attempted rediscovery of the father. For, functionally, the Law apparently resembles the Father-as-Judge. [At this point (p. 19) Judge Frank has a footnote which reads in part as follows: "Law and Religion are, of course, not the only activities affected by the search for fatherly authority. Science, too, suffers when it is made to bear the burden of being a complete guarantor of cosmic certainty." He refers here to Appendix III in his book entitled *Science and Certainty: An Unscientific Conception of Science*, pp. 285–88.]
>
> (6) The child's Father-as-Judge was infallible. His judgements and commands appeared to bring out of the chaos of conflicting views rules concerning right conduct. His law seemed absolutely certain and predictable. Grown men, when they strive to recapture the

emotional satisfaction of the child's world, without being consciously aware of their motivation, seek in their legal systems the authoritativeness, certainty and predictability which the child believed he had found in the law laid down by the father.

(7) Hence the basic legal myth that law is, or can be made, unwavering, fixed and settled.[2]

Let us return, then, to the possibly still fulminating man of letters, smarting under the insinuation that positive evaluation is not a critical function so much as it is a neurotic compulsion. Even for those who have always been more or less dimly aware of the futility of evaluative certainty, there have been moments of unwary relapse. David Hume, it will be remembered—certainly one of the most mature relativists who ever lived—strove to exorcise the demon of judicial criticism, only to fall into a vague reliance on some kind of all-pervasive standard of "taste."[3] The twentieth-century formalist, himself often the object of denunciation for his avoidance of the evaluative aspect of criticism, has "projected" the accusation onto the psychoanalytic critic. In 1958 Professor Paul Obler, by his own avowal a formalist, presented to the first official meeting of Discussion Group Ten of the Modern Language Association a rather comprehensive account of the historical development of psychoanalytic criticism, ending that account with a "Formalist Critique" in which he raised some fundamental questions, citing as his authority the leading theologically oriented critic of our century: "Does the psychoanalytic critic . . . evade the primary responsibility of criticism to analyze and/or evaluate the work? Has such a critic permitted himself, in the words of C. S. Lewis, 'to be diverted from the genuinely critical question, 'Why, and how, should we read this?' . . . 'why' meaning not 'with what intention?' but 'impelled by what causes?' "[4] In other words, the old cry is raised that the psychoanalytic critic does not "evaluate" the work, does not fulfill his obligation as a critic to be a giver or interpreter of the law, that he neglects his "normative" function. Yet avoidance of judicial evaluation is what every psychoanalytic critic must assume as a matter of course, and what every other emotionally mature critic ought to strive for.

The critic's dilemma in this respect is exactly that of the self-respecting, mature jurist or legal theorist. The conservative (read, infantile-minded) student jurisprudence, like the conservative theologian, wants to be assured of the existence of an arcane *Lex* and *Aequitas*, lacking the comfort he might once have received from an authoritarian *Yahweh* or *Elohim*. It is very hard to be a pragmatist in a world which still wants a philosophical absolute. But the full-grown scholar-critic must stick to his guns: he must be content to add a new word of interpretation, a new document that bears on the work, a bit of relevant biographical information, and, best of all, a new *explication de texte* in depth, in order that he may truly render the greatest service to the society which still dins into his ears, "WHY should I read this and not that? What makes literature 'good' or 'bad?' "

Perhaps I should let the matter rest there, having hopefully disposed of the irrational grasping for absolutes in evaluative criticism (not that such a rational extirpation will ever wholly scotch the serpent of irrational obsession). Yet it would be well to add a few words about *relative* standards. Even if we cannot hope to determine what literature is 'good' *per se*, what are the chances of finding out what is valuable in the work of art in terms of extraliterary standards? (We certainly owe ourselves the duty of trying to do that, for we must admit that in applying a psychodynamic basis to literary analysis we may well be using an extraliterary discipline. But of that more later.)

One extraliterary standard we may term *theological,* using the term in the broadest possible sense. Here we need not go beyond Plato. It is a commonplace to repeat that Plato did not have a high opinion of art as a means of direct contact with the ideal world of eternal things, hence his insistence that the "imitation of an imitation" must be kept out of the education of the neophyte philosopher-king. But that, of course, is not all that criticism owes Plato. There is always the nagging question of why the great philosopher-poet had such a low opinion of poetry. If we consider the aspect of Platonic doctrine set forth in the "Ion" or the "Phaedrus" (although it is always difficult to tell whether Socrates is developing a doctrine of his own or merely exposing the weakness of some other doctrine), we find the apparent conviction that the poet is indeed divinely controlled, but that his inspiration makes itself known through irrational, "enthusiastic" behavior. The poet may be to a great extent divine, but he is by that very token a madman.

Possibly there may be an explanation of this paradox, other than the current ones, that we do not always know what Plato-Socrates really thinks and that he may have changed his mind from one dialogue to another. I suggest that Plato, even without the aid of psychoanalysis, had discovered that one of the main features of artistic creation is that it makes use of unacceptable material, "id-material," the product of unconscious, irrational drives. But Plato had not progressed as far as the ego psychologists who suggest how the creative mind can make use of such material without being over-whelmed by it. Highly suspicious of the sources of art in the irra-tional, unphilosophic depths of the human mind, he repudiated art altogether as a means of communication with the divine and sub-stituted therefor, a combination of rational dialectic and personal mysticism as the way out of the cave into the sunlight of things eternal.

Many of Plato's followers took no account of his reservations. To Shelley, of course, it was the poet rather than the philosopher who had direct access to eternal verities and ideas, and was thus the unacknowledged lawgiver to mankind. When Shelley sings his "Hymn to Intellectual Beauty" we may feel *for* him and even *with* him, but, unless we experience the same mystical communion, we are not intellectually "convinced." The "theological" standard of critical judgment is, perforce, extremely vague. Not only will the individual's mystic communion with the divine be incommunicable and therefore uncertain, but, when a system of religious dogma may be involved, the standard will vary with the dogmatic basis as well as with the individual experience. Once again we are left with some-thing far short of an absolute basis for critical evaluation.

Where the extraliterary criterion is other than supernal, the old problem arises again, for will not absolutes in ethics, in politics, in economics, in any other discipline be as much colored by the norma-tive obsession as the direct literary touchstone? The tortuous ways in which critics as diverse as Matthew Arnold, John Ruskin, the neohumanists, the Marxians, the general social meliorists, and others too numerous to mention have attempted to avoid this dilemma have been manifold. To me they often seem to be engaged in a beautiful game of chasing will-o'-the-wisps. This is not to deny the *practical* aspects of their criticism nor the depth and ingenuity of their in-sights; I am dubious only of their search for the absolute through the evaluation of literature by means of some other, nonliterary discipline.

I said above that the psychoanalytic critic is likewise engaged in applying a nonliterary discipline to literary art. That is true, but I believe that our approach is fundamentally different. We are not concerned with standards but with prognostication. No appeal to psychodynamics will ever furnish us with an objective criterion for direct evaluation, but we may be able to hazard an educated guess as to what the response of readers will be, so long as that response is dictated by drives and impulses which are common to mankind, or, to limit ourselves perhaps to what we know best, to mankind as influenced by the patterns of western civilization. Perhaps we may be able to discover what works (even among those which have not yet stood the test of time) will "please many and please long."

There is no time and space here for me to develop this concept adequately, but I can at least suggest some collateral readings. Most of them will be recent, for only in the last few years has the psychoanalytic critic directed his attention less to the source of literature (the dynamics of the author) and to the content of the work itself (particularly its characters, when we are dealing with fiction or drama), and more to analysis of the reader's response, the probable reasons for that response, and the probabilities of future response to existing and not-yet-existing writings.

Here I must throw modesty to the winds and refer to the group of critics who have been associated with the Discussion Group (General Topics 10, MLA) and the journal (*Literature and Psychology*) with which I have been associated for the past eighteen years. I should mention first Simon Lesser's *Fiction and the Unconscious*,[5] which devotes many of its pages to reader response. Louis Fraiberg's first important work, *Psychoanalysis and American Literary Criticism*,[6] was more or less historically oriented, but it is most admirably supplemented by his "New Views of Art and the Creative Process in Psychoanalytic Ego Psychology,"[7] in which stress is laid on the creative process, with some attention to the reader's necessary response to that process. I might mention some portions of my own "Toward a Psychoanalytic Theory of Literature,"[8] and the introduction and some of the essays in *Hidden Patterns: Studies in Psychoanalytic Literary Criticism*.[9]

But by far the most important study of evaluation in terms of reader response is Norman N. Holland's *The Dynamics of Literary Response*.[10] That book contains a chapter on "Evaluation" (Chapter 7, pp. 193–224) which in its original form[11] furnished the springboard from which my present study takes off. I cannot quote as much as I would like, but the following will, perhaps, suffice:

> It would seem there is no sensible way of getting from the text to an evaluation. But surely this cannot be so—and it isn't. "Nothing,"

wrote Henry James, "will ever take the place of the good old fashion of 'liking' a work of art or not liking it: the most improved criticism will not abolish that primitive, that ultimate test." James is right, and his dictum provides a toehold for a psychoanalytic approach to the problem of evaluation. The route from text to evaluation proceeds through someone's mind, someone who likes or dislikes what he has read. The classics, the masterpieces, are those that have pleased the best readers[12] for a long time. We come, inevitably, to the "test of time."

Like any other theory of evaluation, it has its weaknesses. One trouble with the test of time is that it takes so long, usually a century or two. How can it help the critic confronted with today's book or tomorrow's movie, which he must pronounce on the spot good, bad, or indifferent? What does it mean when a critic says such-and-such a book or poem of today is "good" when it has not had time to take the test of time? We can solve that problem by saying that the critic is making a *prediction* that the work will pass the test of time. He is saying, in Dr. Johnson's phrase, that this is a work that "can please many and please long."

. . . .

What in the text leads someone to make the prediction it "can please many and please long"? Behind that question is another: What does it mean to say something will please people in an aesthetic way? How does the aesthetic pleasure of a poem differ from the simple sensuous pleasure of a well-mixed martini?

From the point of view of our model [a back-reference to the first section of the book, entitled "The Model Developed"] literature is a species of play. That is, to play is "to hallucinate ego mastery." Both play and literature can be understood in this sense as first, letting a disturbing influence happen to us, then, second, mastering that disturbance. . . . When literature "pleases," it . . . lets us experience a disturbance, then master it, but the disturbance is a fantasy rather than an event or activity. This pattern of disturbance and mastery distinguishes our pleasure in play and literature from simple sensuous pleasures.

Saying a literary work is "good" then, from the point of view of our model, is predicting that it will pass the test of time; that it "can please many and please long"; that it is a widely satisfying form of play; or, more formally, that it *embodies a fantasy with a power to disturb many readers over a long period of time and, built in, a defensive maneuver that will enable those readers to master the poem's disturbance.*[13] [Stress is mine.]

Even with my omissions and stresses, that is a rather substantial chunk of highly concentrated conclusions, but it embodies most succinctly the gist of the psychoanalytic theory of critical evaluation. If it proves to be too concentrated, I can only suggest: Read the book.

A few more words, then, on strategy. I suppose that, like me, most of my readers for the most part are engaged in day-to-day teaching of literature and not usually in expounding theories of criticism. It should not be thought that I suggest that the teacher of literature should answer the question, "Why is this work good?" by replying, "I am sorry, but my analyst prohibits my answering that question." The student will often be content with an objective answer that does not undertake to expound eternal verities and absolute standards, but which lets the instructor use his special information to tell the student how the work has impressed members of the "in-group" of which the instructor is a member and which some of the students, at least, hope to join. The psychoanalytic reasons for not offering an authoritative judgment and the psychoanalytic method of accounting for past, present, and future judgments may be tacitly passed over. The student, with some exceptions as hereafter noted, may be objectively content with such a historically oriented reply.

He may not be, however. At this point let me recall an old joke with which the reader may not be familiar.

> A distinguished foreign lecturer opened his talk at University A with a cheery "Good morning, ladies and gentlemen." The students replied, "Good morning, professor." At University B he uttered the same greeting and in each and every student's notebook there appeared an entry: "Good morning, ladies and gentlemen." At University C he had no sooner uttered his greeting when a student in the back row said, "I disagree with that."[14]

Now if you teach at University A you will not find out easily what effect your critical judgment has had on your students, if indeed it had any effect. At University B you will be encouraged to go beyond an historical account of critical evaluation and pronounce one evaluative judgment after another based on nothing but your own predilections. (You probably will do that in any event.) You will be in the fine company of the allegedly defunct impressionist critics and teachers. They are far from defunct. You still say, "This is a fine book. This will afford you a lot of amusement. Here you will find a wealth of wit and wisdom"—and all without citing any authority or using any method except your own personal influence. You are saying in effect: "I love you, dear students, and I am sure that you love me. I would never mislead you; you must know that. (I think) this work is good (or bad), and I want you to agree with me. (*Understood*: No real father could be more solicitous for your happiness and your freedom from uncertainty.)"

And the student, who will often be feminine, possibly even female, may respond in kind: "How true! How valuable! What a good teacher! That is the man (woman) who ought to rate high on our student-evaluation-of-faculty list. How glad I am that I came to the Multiversity of Siwash! What a wonderful thing education is!"

But not always (*vide* the response at University *C*). The attitude toward the father and the father-figure is loaded with ambivalence. Judge Frank stressed the aspect which views the Father-as-Judge as infallible, whose "judgments and commands appeared to bring out of the chaos of conflicting views rules concerning right conduct," whose "law seemed absolutely certain and predictable." But in the negative phase of affective bipolarity all of this is reversed. Certainties are rejected; chaos seems preferable to authority; individual judgments, no matter what their basis or lack of basis, are superior to all pronouncements of teachers and rulings by administrators.

In its most restrained form this manifestation is to be found at the annual meeting of the in-group (such as MLA meetings) where younger scholars, usually avid for recognition, will hold forth in papers which seem designed always to demonstrate that "Whatever was—ain't!" And in its least restrained form there will be student revolts in which students storm university buildings, lock faculty and administrators out, lock themselves in, and seem to desire nothing less than to break open the minds and bodies of their teachers and lodge themselves within those authoritarian bodies and minds—until their own bodies and heads are beaten and broken by the recognized agents of violent authority, the police.

And then the Students for a Democratic Society "leaders" step in with their seductive extrascholastic absolutes: "Free the oppressed! Only violence will lead to universal peace! Down with the monsters who have mismanaged the civilization they must now quickly hand over to us!" And then the fat will be in the fire. As it is. And all, I suggest, because the normative fallacy has led faculties and administrators into gross mismanagement of the student's bipolarity in relation to his fatherly Alma Mater.

Notes

1. M. Beebe, "Modern Fiction Newsletter," in *Modern Fiction Studies*, IV, 2 (1958), pp. 179–83. The quoted language in the descriptions which follow are excerpts from Professor Beebe's comments.
2. Originally published in 1930. The quotation is from the sixth edition (New York, 1949), pp. 18–21. It is interesting to note that Judge Frank does not rely on Freud as his major authority, indicating at one point that he fears the tendency of those who would arrogate to Freud the position of Father, a position which Freud would be the first to disclaim.
3. The Hume essay is in M. Schorer, et al, *Criticism* (New York, 1958), pp. 439–449.
4. P. D. Obler, Literature and Psychology, Vol. II, No. 4, pp. 50–59, at p. 59.
5. S. Lesser, *Fiction and the Unconscious* (Boston, 1957).
6. L. Fraiberg, *Psychoanalysis and American Literary Criticism* (Detroit, 1960).
7. In *Literature and Psychology*, Vol. XI, No. 2 (1961), pp. 45–55.
8. In *Shenandoah*, Vol. XVII, No. 3 (1966), pp. 61–68. Originally delivered as a paper at the meeting of MLA Discussion Group General Topics One (Poetics and Literary Theory) in December 1965.
9. Edited by Leonard and Eleanor Manheim (New York, 1966).
10. New York, 1968.
11. In *Literature and Psychology*, Vol. XIV, No. 2 (1964), pp. 43–55.
12. In referring to the "best" readers, it seems to me that Professor Holland may be begging the question by assuming an absolute standard for judging who the "best readers" are.
13. Holland, *Dynamics*, pp. 201–03.
14. The joke originally named three New York City institutions: Columbia, NYU downtown, and City College. But, apart from the fact that such local references may be lost on readers unfamiliar with New York stereotypes, it is also apparent that the Columbia stereotype (or image) has undergone some marked changes of late.

Stephen C. Pepper

THE JUSTIFICATION
OF AESTHETIC JUDGMENTS

ARTISTS AS A GROUP TEND TO BE AMBIVALENT ABOUT CRITICS AND
aesthetic standards. This mixed attitude makes a good point of departure for a study of aesthetic standards for in a certain sense the
artists are the experts in this region. Their judgment need not be
final but it would be unwise wholly to neglect it. It would be unwise,
for instance, to take a dogmatic stand on either pole of their ambivalence—either on the side of total skepticism and denial of any justifiable aesthetic standards, or on the side that certain aesthetic
standards are objectively justifiable beyond question.

Recently, due largely to the influence in English-speaking coun-
tries of the emotive judgment theory of value supported by the linguistic analytical school of philosophy, a skeptical view of standards
has been in the ascendency. It stemmed originally from G. E. Moore's
presentation of the "naturalistic fallacy" in ethics which applied to
values generally including the aesthetic. Briefly it stated that "good"
could not be identified with "pleasure" or any other "natural" character, for the reason that it always made sense to ask after any such
identification whether pleasure was "good." Consequently, Moore
argued that "good" could not mean just pleasure or any other sub-
stituted character. He argued further that "good" must mean an
abstract (sort of Platonic) entity known by an "intellectual intuition."

A. J. Ayer, coming after Moore, rejected this last conclusion. He
questioned the existence of any such Platonic abstract entity or of
any peculiar intellectual faculty to intuit it. But he was still impressed with Moore's linguistic argument for the "naturalistic fallacy"
and suggested that the reason "good" could not be identified with

any natural character was that it did not refer to anything knowable at all. It was simply a term referring to emotional attitudes of approval. And "bad" was reciprocally a term for expressing disapproval. It followed that sentences including "good" and "bad" and their equivalents as grammatical predicates—such as "charity is good" (virtuous, noble, estimable)—are not declarative statements of fact which must be true or false or probable, but are expressions of emotive attitudes which are neither true nor false nor probable. Such sentences are really exclamations, or optatives, or imperatives. From this approach it follows that there can be no cognitively justifiable moral or aesthetic standards, since moral and aesthetic "judgments" are not declarative statements that can be justified as true or false or probable. Notice that like Moore's argument, Ayer's also is purely linguistic.

This is the most skeptical theory of value ever propounded. For the gist of the argument is that, basically, values are not open to cognitive control in terms of evidence for the truth or falsity of statements expressing them. Here, we can say, is the extremity of the skeptical pole of the artists' ambivalence about standards. And perhaps there is no better ground for questioning its soundness than the artists' ambivalence on the subject. On the one hand, the artists are eager to protect the spontaneity of their creative expressions. But on the other hand, they are also eager for their works to be judged excellent and worthy and firmly established so in truth.

The latter pole of the artists' ambivalence will be my focus of interest in this article. I am going to assume that there is something in the artists' deep sense of a kind of objectivity of aesthetic values which justifies their ambitions for "greatness" and for "fame" that is something more than notoriety.

My procedure in this article will be to work from certain linguistic formulations of aesthetic criteria towards the evidences supporting these formulations and thence on to progressive complications of the evidence as we get deeper and deeper into the practice of aesthetic criticism.

We do not have to go far in the study of aesthetic criteria before we discover the power of definitions in critical judgments. Especially in appraising the works of new movements in art, we find critics resorting to definitions. We find remarks like these: "Free verse, whatever else it is, cannot be regarded as poetry." "*The Death of a Salesman* fails of being a tragedy." "Doggerel is not poetry." "*Kim* is neither a novel nor a short story." "Detective stories are entertainment, not literature." Or, in general, "X has no aesthetic value because it is not a work of art." Judgments of this sort are the most damaging ones a critic can make of an artist's work, for they mean that in the critic's judgment the artist has completely missed his target. To appraise a poem as a poor one is much less damaging, for it allows that the poet hit the target even though far from the bull's eye.

I am now going to make the statement that underlying all aesthetic judgments (or value judgments generally) can be found a definition of the field of value concerned, and that this is the ultimate criterion of value in *discourse*. I specify in discourse, for definitions are linguistic structures for use in communication. We shall presently be led to consider value criteria outside of discourse but in view of the complexities of the subject it is best to begin with these specific criteria. Even this statement that the definition of a field of value is the ultimate criterion of value in *discourse* will sound to many as a rather drastic one. But if it is accepted, it will lead to a great clarification of the subject.

Before going any further, let me illustrate. Suppose a number of men are appointed to judge a competition of English poems in the form of the Petrarchan sonnet. We shall obviously need a definition of the latter. However this definition is derived, it is going to be something stated in communicable symbols, that is, in discourse and probably in words. For if we do not have some communication with one another as judges about the criterion we are using for distinguishing a Petrarchan sonnet when we meet one, there will be no significant judgment made in the competition.

Now a definition of a term such as the "Petrarchan sonnet" specifies the characters required of that form or those found common to the class of objects under discussion. This set of defining characters demarcates the field. In short, they constitute the criterion the judges will use for including a poem in the competition. It must have fourteen lines in iambic pentameter, the lines must be divided into an octet and a sestet, there must be a certain distinction of thought between the octet and the sestet, a certain rhyme scheme, and possibly a few other characteristics. A poem of sixteen lines, or one divided in the manner of the Shakespearean sonnet will not be admitted to the competition.

The definition therefore does function as an effective aesthetic criterion in this competition for this type of poem. In fact, its effectiveness goes further than determining what poems are acceptable, it also determines the quantitative standards for the best and the worst within the field. If any of the defining characters can be quantified, or if they entail other characters that can be quantified, these constitute the relevant standards for determining the degrees of excellence of the poems included. Several of the defining characters listed above do entail quantitative elements. The requirement of fourteen lines is, of course, fixed and incapable of quantification. But the requirement of iambic pentameter is open to a wide range of degrees of excellence. It is the most richly developed of all the verse structures in the English language. The judges will keenly watch how this is handled. And this is not a matter of rhythm only, but of the sounds embedded in it and the relation of sound to sense.

The character of thought in the definition of the Petrarchan sonnet is also open to degrees of excellence. There is not only the management of the thought of the sestet in relation to that of the octet but the question of its depth, subtlety, and novelty. Moreover, the thought and the iambic verse demand each other for the fullness of the excellence of each. There are degrees of a poet's skill in bringing this about. And so it goes. And all this comes out by simply noting the functions of the definition in discourse in giving the basic criterion for what is or is not relevant in a field of art and the quantitative standards growing out of it.

But, of course, this is only the beginning. For at once one asks what justifies the authority of the definition. In the illustration above, we imagined a poetry competition with a prize offered. But the acceptance of the illustration would depend on two other factors not mentioned. The first is that Petrarchan sonnets are to be found in our aesthetic environment, so that the definition is not fanciful and arbitrary, but conforms to verifiable descriptions of such objects. The second is that in selecting the Petrarchan sonnet we are already somehow assured implicitly that the form is one capable of great beauty. This latter assurance does not lie in the definition we found for the sonnet itself but from some further outside source that gave its appraisal to that definition.

These two factors will lead us beyond aesthetic evaluation by definitions in *discourse* to aesthetic facts outside of discourse, and to evidences of natural norms in human nature and social structures which are the justifications for the effectiveness of the aesthetic definitions as basic criteria in *discourse*.

Take first the descriptive factor involved in any aesthetic definition functioning as a basic criterion in discourse. It is essential (if men are to respect them) that value criteria, whether in ethics or aesthetics, be not fanciful or arbitrary but responsible to the subject matter evaluated. This can be achieved for definitions in discourse only if they can be shown to be truly descriptive of processes going on that actually do function evaluatively outside of mere words. In short, the definitions that behave as basic criteria in discourse must be *descriptive*. These are the sort of definitions used in the sciences to distinguish types of natural processes and objects whether in physics, chemistry, biology, or the social sciences. Whether it is a chemical substance, a species of bird, a primitive social structure, or a religious ritual, it is defined by the description of it. And so too are the forms and techniques of the arts described by their definitions, including the form of the Petrarchan sonnet.

This is important to notice (particularly in view of some skeptical trends in contemporary criticism) because it shows that when descriptive definitions function as aesthetic criteria they are subject to verification. Such criteria are true or false. And obviously they are trustworthy only so far as they are true. If a poem is highly rated as a Petrarchan sonnet, this value judgment must be based on the observation that the structure of the poem conforms to the true description of the structure of this form of poetry and to a high level of excellence specifiable by the descriptive definition of the form. This is the sort of judgment art juries are regularly asked to make for the distribution of honors and prizes among artists, and for the acceptance of works for exhibition or for publication. There is nothing extraordinary or unaesthetic about it. Quite the contrary. Every human society that includes art as part of its culture arranges for such judgments.

The only relevant question when such judgments have been made is whether they were true or not. And this is the question that frustrated artists regularly raise, and often quite legitimately. The reason can be brought out in a moment.

But first we must take up the second of the two grounds of justification mentioned earlier. The first was that the definitions used as aesthetic criteria should be supported by facts. This is provided for by insisting that the definitions be descriptive definitions and that the descriptions be true to the subject matter described. The second was to justify the selection of a descriptive definition as an aesthetic criterion at all. Why should we take the descriptive definition of a Petrarchan sonnet as an aesthetic criterion anyway, any more than a descriptive definition of granite or lava or of the chemical composition of water?

Here we encounter the really difficult philosophical problem, which is how to recognize an aesthetic fact (or more generally a value fact) when you meet one. A supposedly easy solution is that there are not any value facts. This is the position of the value judgment school heralded by A. J. Ayer, and still widely held. It is, in my opinion, a hasty solution that impatiently just gives up the problem. It is, moreover, a purely linguistic solution produced by defining value judgments as those expressed by optatives, imperatives, and the like as sentences that are neither true nor false as opposed to propositions or declarative sentences which alone may be true or false. Had Ayer and his followers come at the problem from our direction—that is, by first observing the facts as to how evaluative judgments come to be made among groups of people and even by individuals—he would never have taken the supposedly easy way out of defining value judgments as verbal forms not open to verification.

In the light of our preceding analysis this is simply a descriptive definition on Ayer's part. For he obviously offers it as the true disposition of all value items. This definition, tested by only what little factual material we have brought out by evaluating a group of Petrarchan sonnets, is almost certainly false. And if he wishes to escape such facts of evaluative procedures by holding that his definition is, like the optatives and imperatives, not a propositional form and so neither true nor false, then clearly we need not take his view seriously at all, since it does not purport to be true.

I believe that—in a variety of subtler ways following the subtleties of the later linguistic analysts—this sort of refutation would apply to them all. It would apply to any writer who finally succumbed to identifying a value judgment, no matter how belatedly, after allowing all sorts of intermediate legitimate reasoning about values. It would apply to any writer who finally succumbed to identifying the ultimate value judgment with an imperative or some other form of language not open to a test of truth or falsity.

So, I will not take this way out. I propose to face head on the problem of how to recognize value facts in our experience. What we need is evidence for a descriptive definition of the whole field of values as distinct from non-value facts. Or if perchance all facts have a value ingredient, then we need at least a series of descriptive definitions which will distinguish the various kinds of values from one another. Particularly in this paper I should like to have a descriptive definition of aesthetic value, as distinguished from other values.

What we need here is the most extensive evidential backing possible. One way of getting this is to consult the most adequate world hypotheses for their considered ways of describing values and distinctions among values. For the aim of world hypotheses is to organize all evidence, without restriction, in the most adequate way possible. By this means, whatever status is given to values in these systematic organizations of the world's evidence has all this evidence behind the conferred status. I undertook to do this in my book *The Basis of Criticism in the Arts*.[1] I then followed up with a general examination of these systems of unrestricted evidence in my book *World Hypotheses*.[2] In my study of the history of human thought four relatively adequate world hypotheses stood out above all others. Four somewhat divergent descriptive definitions of the aesthetic values appeared. The divergencies arose more from the emphases given than from exclusions. Each philosophy recognized the pertinence of what the others stressed as aesthetic standards but put those standards in subordinate positions. The philosophy of naturalism stressed pleasure; that of the Platonic and Aristotelian formists stressed cosmic ideals in artisanship, forms of life, and the normality of man; that of the Hegelian organicists stressed the organic whole; and the Deweyan contextualists stressed the vividness of the qualities of immediate experience. In using these basic criteria on specific works of art, I found that those which, on the whole, the consensus of criticism held up as the "greatest" stood high in all of these criteria, while those about which opinions differed stood high in some and low in others. I ventured the overall judgment that we had a high degree of objective justification for the supreme aesthetic worth of the works which excelled by all these criteria. For the others the judgment could be taken to be just about what the divergent evaluations brought out. If works of art stood low by all criteria, this was the best of evidence available to us that their aesthetic value was not significant.

These criteria were all, by our analysis, represented linguistically by descriptive definitions. But something further comes out by the fact that the subject matter described is, by the evidence of the world hypotheses, independent of the linguistic definitions that describe it. In short, now we have discovered objective criteria from which the descriptive definitions are derived, not vice versa. That is, according to the total evidence of the world hypotheses, the values lie by this evidence where they are placed. For naturalism, the pleasurable satisfactions themselves in the experiences producing them establish the aesthetic values of the experiences—whether any man descriptively defined them so or not. And the ideal forms of Aristotle, including that of the fully normal man, establish these as values whether a critic ever evaluated them with his descriptive definitions or not.

Moreover, all four of these norms are recognized, even if they are not given priority, by each of the four relatively adequate hypotheses in their organizations of the world's evidence. For instance, though naturalism gives priority to pleasure and satisfaction, it recognizes that the fulfillment of ideals is a great source of satisfaction, and that in the organization of aesthetic experience there is an increased spread of satisfaction, and that through the vividness of any experience satisfaction is enhanced. And though contextualism stresses the vividness of immediacy, it recognizes that intensely painful experiences tend to be avoided and pleasant experiences extended, and that a skillful organization of vivid experience increases its duration, and that vivid experience is increased in depth if it is expressive of powerful social ideals and the basic emotions of the fully vital man. So the evidence of all the relatively adequate hypotheses supports the objectivity of all four of these evaluative criteria in the sense that they operate in human experience independently of the judgments of critics and aestheticians and the linguistic formulations given them. In other words we have discovered the evidence for the existence of aesthetic norms independent of their descriptions. Thus, the descriptions are justified if they truly describe the action of these norms.

So now we arrived at the basis of the justification of our descriptive definitions functioning as aesthetic criteria. A critic is justified in his evaluations if his descriptive definitions truly describe actual aesthetic experiences and their objects.

How do we know through our world hypotheses that the descriptive definitions which the critic uses are describing the aesthetic field of experience? The answer is simple. It is because they are all describing the same common-sense objects and experiences—that is, pictures, poems, novels, dramas, pieces of music and the experiences of them; and because each world hypothesis acknowledges aesthetic criteria of the others, although each differs in its determinations of priority.

We are now in a position to go back to the question raised by the frustrated artist whose work is not recognized. Under what conditions will the artist's complaint be justified? Take first the competition for the best Petrarchan sonnet. A frustrated poet has handed in an eighteen-line poem following the regular Petrarchan form except that he has lengthened the sestet. He felt the thought justified the change. Let it be admitted by the critics that the eighteen-line poem—as a poem—was superior to the poem awarded the prize. I nevertheless think that we should have to agree with the action of critics. The frustrated poet is asking for a change of standard from that specified for the competition. Both standards, that for the total aesthetic field and that for the limited Petrarchan sonnet, would be descriptive definitions of objects within the aesthetic field. The frustrated poet may say, as he frequently does, that no good modern poet would want to write a Petrarchan sonnet anyway. It is an old, outworn form completely alien to the whole trend of modern writing. He compromised, as far as he felt he could, just by adding two extra lines. The competition on the terms specified is pedantic and hypocritical and obstructive to contemporary creative writing. Any conscientious group of critics should give the award to the best poem, the devil with the constricting rules.

We may sympathize with the frustrated poet and agree with his comments about creative writing. Yet the critics would be violating the aesthetic standards set up and well understood if they had awarded the prize to this poet. The trouble, if it is a trouble, in this case is with the conditions laid down for the competition. There could only be one legitimate complaint: that there was some unstated implication that the Petrarchan sonnet is the most perfect, or perhaps the only true form of poetical expression. The juries chosen for foundation awards are sometimes justifiably suspected of this sort of suppressed judgment. If so, the standards they use are literally false. They do not descriptively define the area of their judgment accurately. Their judgment is then likely to be biased and in error.

Now, however, let us set aside the arbitrary limitation of the rules of a competition and substitute the character of a style of poetry, and here we meet the more realistic situation. A new style is always in the making, and a traditional style is always in ascendancy. Perhaps the reason is partly that the new style has not quite found itself yet. To even the most advanced critic, there may be a question as to whether the new style does fall within the aesthetic field or—if it does—whether it has much capacity for high aesthetic achievement. I purposely do not say "poetic." That may be arbitrarily demarcated. It need not concern an artist much. If a novel must have an articulated plot, most modern stories are not novels although some are great literature.

To handle this situation there is a common recourse today by many philosophers to the "open texture concept," or the "family resemblance concept" which owes its prominence largely to the influence of Wittgenstein. His famous example is the concept of "game." There is a great variety of games from bridge and solitaire to polo and skiing. Wittgenstein finds no common characteristics to define clearly all these activities within one class. They simply have a family resemblance which can be traced from any familiar instance to the other instances. The instance chosen to anchor the concept is known as the paradigm case.

Some aestheticians today are suggesting that concepts like "poetry," "painting," "architecture," and the overall concept "work of art" are of this type. In ordinary language probably most aesthetic concepts are. On this assumption a new style of poetry or painting could easily be added to the "family" with no strain on the concept. The only requirement is that the "ordinary man" pick it up obligingly for the ordinary language he speaks. I doubt if the "fur lined cup" or the "caged sugar lumps" of the Dada school have been accepted yet as works of art by the ordinary man, or ever will be. The art historian, of course, accepts them in his way, and they are well housed in an art museum.

The great trouble with the "open texture" or "family resemblance concept" as an aesthetic criterion is that it lays aesthetic evaluation open to the whims of "ordinary language," which incidentally for many concepts varies from language to language. To the aesthetic skeptics this is no drawback. But we have been calling attention to evidences of much objectivity in aesthetic judgment. So, at least for the concept of the aesthetic field and the work of art as an object definable in terms of the aesthetic field, we should want to hold to a concept which in principle seeks rather well-defined boundaries. This does not require that the descriptive definitions now used in *discourse* should have firm boundaries. Those derived from the world hypotheses listed earlier evidently do not. But they do aim for such boundaries, assuming that in actuality the objects and experiences being described do sufficiently separate themselves from other objects and experiences in the nature of things.

This leads me to allude to my most recent study of aesthetic values, developed in the last chapter of *Concept and Quality*[3] just published. The key concept here is what I call a "selective system." An easily-grasped example of a selective system is a goal-seeking purposive structure. Here is a system of dynamically controlled acts, all directed towards a final goal by a drive or a need which sets the organism towards that goal. Subordinate acts with their instrumental objects are selected as means towards reaching the goal. Some of these prove to be in error and are eliminated. Other acts are corrected and incorporated into the purposive structure until the final goal is reached which reduces the drive and satisfies the need. Such a structure is an actual performance that goes on, whether described by a psychologist or not. And the structure is normative in its dynamic operation. It is a natural norm. It selects and thereby evaluates certain acts and objects by the criterion of whether they do or do not further the aim of the structure towards the achievement of its goal.

Now there are a number of these dynamic structures or "selective systems" active in human individual and social behavior, and several of them are natural norms of aesthetic values indicating the very criteria disclosed by the world hypotheses above. Take the criterion of pleasure stressed by naturalism. This is found in the terminal act of typical goal-seeking purposes. For instance, in the ordinary thirst drive the final act is the drinking of water which can be extremely pleasant after moderate thirst. We tend to draw out the pleasure of that consummatory activity as long as we can.

We have behavior dispositions for many such consummatory delights. The selective system for these is to seek the optimum condition for the greatest enjoyment for the longest time. We can obtain these delights not only in drinking and eating but also in seeing and hearing. The visual arts and music cater to these pleasures. And the dynamics of this consummatory selective system can be seen in the way people choose their position before pictures for the optimum view, or choose seats in the theater for the optimum seeing and hearing. The prices of the seats reflect the action of this selective system. And, of course, the artists have already chosen and organized their materials for the potentially optimum and longest-lasting effect. So we will sit for two hours listening to music or watching a play. Put all these selective consummatory activities together in an organized study, and you have the typical hedonistic aesthetics of the philosophy of naturalism.

I just mentioned the importance of organization in the way pleasurable materials are composed by artists for maximum delight. But there is another human area where organization works quite independently. This is the selective system of the integration of the personality and the nervous system. This consists in the dynamic selection of dispositions for the greatest harmony of human action.

It develops the organic whole characteristic of the Hegelian organistic philosophy. Frustrating dispositions are thrown out by the action of this selective system which aims for a harmonious, well-integrated person. The achievement of such a person is the ideal normal man of the Aristotelian formistic philosophy.

Cultural patterns with their social institutions constitute another dynamic selective system which has important bearings on aesthetic values. Social institutions demand the fulfillment of social ideals. Going still further into detail in the matter, ideals stressed by formism are clearly expressed in much religious art, and in nearly all art of excellent representation. And there is a dynamic urge for integration in cultural patterns whenever these develop a cultural lag.

Lastly, in an indirect but effective way the selective system of biological natural selection leads to a demand for vividness of awareness towards an intelligent and swift adjustment to changing situations for the survival of the individual and his society. For one of the functions of art is to enhance such vivid perceptions in preparation for the problematic situations man is bound to encounter.[4]

There are still other aesthetic consequences which follow from the interrelationships among these selective systems. But the larger point I am anxious to make by these last references to the dynamic action of selective systems is to emphasize the evaluative action of natural norms. I wish it to be seen that aesthetic evaluations by descriptive definitions in *discourse,* or by any other purely linguistic means, have no authority in their own being but derive their justification from the evidence which supports them and, ultimately, from natural norms and natural valuations. It is the latter which justify the descriptive definitions as far as they truly describe the evaluations that go on in nature—that is, the evaluations that go on in the natural dynamic selective activity of a man's person and his society and in his adjustment to his environment. And these evaluations by natural norms do go on and are observable and verifiably describable.

I return finally to the frustrated artist who claims he is not receiving the recognition he deserves. His claim is justified if there is a natural norm of aesthetic value that supports his claim. Suppose he is breaking out a new style of art, as did Wordsworth and the free-verse poets, a style that gathers up many aesthetic values into a fresh configuration. Then his claim may well be justified, whatever his contemporary critics may say. For an aesthetic style is in the nature of a social institution, an integration of the social aesthetic needs of a period with all the dynamic sanctions such social institutions gather into themselves as natural norms. Or he may, like Blake, reverberate to the deep emotions of the human personality, independent of any social institution, but with its own powerful sanctions. But if the artist's claim does not receive the sanction of any natural aesthetic norm, if his work is imitative and merely dragging on the habits of an outworn style, or merely exhibiting the superficial eccentricities of his own thin inhibited personality, then his claim has no aesthetic justification.

Notes

1. S. C. Pepper, *The Basis of Criticism in the Arts* (Cambridge, 1945).
2. Pepper, *World Hypotheses* (Berkeley, 1942; paper bound edition, 1961).
3. Pepper, *Concept and Quality* (Open Court, Indiana, 1967).
4. For the expansion of this insight see I. Jenkins's *Art and the Human Enterprise* (Cambridge, 1958).

Wladimir Weidlé

THE APPRECIATION AND
UNDERSTANDING OF
A WORK OF ART

THE RELATIONSHIP BETWEEN THE APPRECIATION AND UNDERSTANDING
of a work of literature (as of any other work of art) varies considerably, and even the meanings of these two terms contract or expand
in accordance with the concept we may have of an art in particular
or of art in general. If a work of art is in our opinion first and fore-
most a work of language—a language which, to be sure, does not
necessarily have recourse to words or, even if it has, employs them
very differently than does the language of science or the language of
everyday life—then our first effort must be to understand it: to understand what it says, or what it tells us since, being a work of language,
it says something.[1] On the other hand, if we identify it fully with the
aesthetic object which we have extracted from it and which we substitute for it after having approved it aesthetically, then any other
effort or attitude becomes superfluous, nothing else really being required than our decision to approve it.[2] There is nothing in this approval that compels it to become deeper or to be transformed into
a more intimate and fertile attachment unless understanding and
appreciation have from the beginning taken a common path and
mutually sustained each other, instead of being reduced to an act in
which the role of understanding has become purely contingent: to
the mere granting of a certificate of aesthetic validity.

We are all prone today, no matter what our opinions regarding art
may be, to award such certificates, even if only tacitly, implicitly—or
to refuse them—to all works of art at first encounter without even

asking ourselves whether the work in question requires a closer examination, an effort to understand it completely. It is true that we have to begin, as we always have done in such cases in the past, with an examination of the surface; we need only decide whether it suffices to remain at this level of contact or to recognize that this examination, while legitimate as a beginning, remains by its very nature obviously superficial. This question, harmless at first glance, arises, along with the choice that it implies, in a particularly pressing, even alarming, manner as soon as the criterion according to which the certificate has been awarded is based only on the requirement of a rather short excitement, as is increasingly the case, or, even more frequently, on mere astonishment. In the past, and even when we had learned to consider the element of "art" within the work of art separately from the rest of it, we granted awards of merit to those works of art which conformed with a particular aesthetic—that of a grand, durable style which continued to persist or that of a tradition with developments which are manifold but accepted in its essentials by everyone including those who presented their versions for examination: the most nonconformist geniuses and the most docile artisans alike. Such an aesthetic could only have been normative, but since it did not have a complete consciousness of itself (a style, a tradition, as long as they are active, possess only partial self-awareness), the rules that it established (apart from such techniques as meter, the grammar of music or architecture) remained imprecise and fluid and caused no great harm to the work it sought to regulate. It was moveover "impure." In other words, although within the framework of this aesthetic a certain kind of langauge was called for, attention was nonetheless given to what was being voiced by this language, and there was no propensity to question the conviction universally accepted (and precisely for that reason rarely formulated) that art *speaks*, that the work of art has something to say. In the great majority of cases furthermore, the recognition of artistic validity was granted spontaneously and without the least doubt in any of the arts, the only question being the degree of excellence of the work and the rank it deserved relative to other works of the same art which it more or less resembled. The result was to render appreciation inseparable from understanding.

We are now almost two centuries removed from this situation, very far away from it since the last half century, still further away in the last twenty years. First came the end of all specific and normative aesthetics (the one cannot do without the other), confirmed by the birth since 1750 of what we call aesthetics. The correlative of this aesthetics is no longer a definite kind of painting, of poetry, of music, but painting, poetry, music and thereupon, by a kind of speculative short circuit, art in general. Aesthetics was not born of an attentive consideration of what the diverse artistic activities of man have in common; its point of departure, as its very name indicates, is the effect on the perceiver of the object he perceives. The consequences have been multiple. I will limit myself to the essential ones.

1. The word "art," thanks to aesthetics, has become a term of praise or (if preceded by a negative) of blame.[3] We all employ the word in this way. Little has come of the rare attempts (to which in my opinion it would be well to return) to give it a descriptive meaning, that is, to conceive of art—anthropologically, not aesthetically—as a kind of language and the several arts as so many of its variations. In the presence of a work of art which we do not approve of aesthetically we all proclaim: this is not art.

2. Aesthetics has led us to confuse a work of art, a work of artistic language, aesthetically approved by us, with any natural or artificial product or other which we are inclined to approve in the same fashion, and it is by no means certain that there exists anything which could not under certain conditions (under the influence of mescaline, for example) be approved of aesthetically.

3. Aesthetics has taught us to be satisfied with that kind of approval which can very well do without any kind of understanding, and to substitute it for a comprehensive appreciation which would be capable of determining the rank and quality of a given work and its human value—matters with which precisely aesthetics, if it remains true to its principles, is not concerned and could never be concerned, for they evade its judgment.

A curious levelling takes place—not only of appreciation but of the works themselves which have been or are to be appreciated. For during the course of our century little by little art itself has succumbed to what we may call the aesthetic fallacy. Since it has been less and less considered as a language, it has managed in several ways no longer to be one. Since it has been judged only by the effects it has produced, it has ended up producing only effects. And since approval, that is a small aesthetical "yes," has been deemed sufficient to promote a work (or, for that matter, anything) to the dignity of a work of art, the poet as well as the painter, the architect as well as the musician increasingly take the attitude of courting only that approval. This is an approval which casts aside understanding and for which an object of minimal aesthetic value—that is, an object aesthetically acceptable, if only barely so—becomes, by this very fact, a work of art. Furthermore, since few criteria for approval continue to exist in our time other than the novelty of effect capable of producing surprise, the situation is clear. It is not the triumph of art for art's sake but the triumph of art as the aesthetician conceives it, particularly the aesthetician who is satisfied with his minimal approval: the triumph of art for the sake of aesthetics.

There is nothing which requires understanding in strictly nonobjective painting or sculpture. The image speaks as long as it is not a mechanical copy of the visual; the painting without an image is silent. This does not, of course, prevent me from possibly finding it "good," "less good," "astonishing," "suggestive," or even "beautiful." Nor is there anything that calls for understanding in functional architecture which remains mute about the human meaning of its function, in atonal music which can just as well be played in reverse as not, in so-called concrete poetry which may intrigue or amuse me but is completely incapable of telling me anything at all. This poetry (since it claims this title) has been aestheticized to the point where it willingly gives up the producing of poems which aspire to more than a minimal aesthetic value, but in relation to the rest of literary art it clearly occupies a marginal position, and this art as a whole is, by common consent, the most difficult to aestheticize radically. This may indeed be so, and we surely hope it is, but those who believe it all too frequently do so for the wrong reason. In this domain the expressions "language," "understanding," and even "communication" become markedly ambiguous and should only be employed with a great deal of circumspection. One of the most firmly held principles of current criticism, for example, is the denial of the notion that poetry is a form of communication.[4] In one sense, it is not; it is not the communication of a "message" which could be transmitted in some other way; but if we are right (as I believe) to think that it communicates *another kind* of message or content (in the sense of the German word *Gehalt* but not *Inhalt*), then we cannot say that it communicates nothing at all. Poetry is language and consequently requires understanding; but it is a different language and needs to be understood differently. Those who know that my mother tongue is German or French are thereby in no way enlightened on the question of whether I understand, in this other sense of the word, a given poem by Hölderlin or Baudelaire. I can approve of the poem aesthetically; even more, I can love it without having understood it

totally. Does a total understanding indeed exist? Understanding in
this sense is like a slow impregnation, a perhaps endless progressing,
but the further I go, the deeper I penetrate, the more convinced I
become that the poem or the poet is saying, is "communicating"
something to me.

Moreover this poetic language (P) which is not the language of
words (L), although they are present (but fused with semantemes
to whose meaning their everyday significance contributes no more
than do their sound and their rhythm), is by no means the only
"other" language at the disposal of literary art. Often combined with
it is the essentially different language of "fiction," of imaginary figures
and events, that of the novel, the short story, and the drama. We
understand this language of fiction (F) with the aid of another—P
or L or most frequently a combination of the two—but language F
may well make use of the language of film as indeed of the animated
cartoon or of the pantomime. Whatever the case, it remains language
in spite of any literary theory which insists upon regarding it as the
material, the subjective matter, the "contents" of a narrative or dramatic work. This unnecessarily clouds the issue and obscures the
notion of art as language, the only notion which can be set up in contrast to the "aesthetic" notion of art which reduces it to the production of objects requiring merely that kind of approval which we
have already analysed.

These two languages (P and F) of literary art,[5] these two arts—for
we must finally conclude that there are two of them and not only
one—are both tied to language in the ordinary sense of the word, but
this connection is not the same in the two cases as we instantly realize
when confronted with the problem of translating a lyric poem, a
closely written essay, or a novel. Poetic language (P) is linked with
ordinary language (L) through that concrete aspect of manifestation of L which in French is called a *langue*. It is a very close even
inextricable link; one must understand Italian with a comprehension
appropriate to L if one wishes to understand Dante or Leopardi
with a comprehension appropriate to P—which does not prevent the
comprehension of P from being very different from that of L, nor
does it prevent, because of this very difference, a close relationship
between the comprehension of P and the understanding of F. The
latter becomes accessible to us in literature, in reading, by the inter-
mediary of L, or by a combination of P and L, but it retains its inde-
pendence from L or PL in a way that P could never be independent
of L. The imagined figures and events which constitute F remain to

a certain extent behind L or PL, while P always remains anchored, built into L, or, more precisely, L_1, a concrete *langue* which in each particular case "represents" the language. There are those who understand L (that is, actually L_1 or even L_1, L_2, L_3, . . .), but who do not understand P (or rather the element P of a P_1, for, no matter what the advocates of "pure poetry" may think, P is never present in its pure state). They do not even notice the presence of P, while those who do not understand F simply believe that there is nothing there which requires comprehension: they take a language which transmits, which *communicates* a meaning for a self-sufficient concentration of facts or events.

The two languages-arts, indiscriminately encapsuled within what we call literature, each require, as do the speaking arts in general, an adequate understanding which is by no means the same in the two cases, but which, however, contrasts in the same manner with the understanding of ordinary language. Most of the errors of literary criticism, even such criticism which has not been misled by an excessively aestheticizing literary theory, are the result of a refusal or inability to distinguish P from L, F from P, and the three kinds of comprehension which are appropriate to these three languages. Many an appreciation has been the worse for it, which gives us evidence of the degree to which appreciation is dependent on understanding (and on the interpretation which results from it), if we take care not to confuse it with its poor relative, minimal approval.

Notes

1. It is an utterance (*"énoncé"*) or a group of utterances. The German *"eine Aussage"* expresses it well, whereas one could hardly call it in English "a statement." This word has a connotation which limits its use to discursive language. That is why, when we attempt to find "statements" in poetry, we only discover "pseudo-statements." (The term is I. A. Richards' and corresponds, I fear, only to a pseudo-concept.)
2. On the danger of confusing a work of art with an aesthetic object, see my communication of the same title to the meeting in Athens (*Actes du IV. Congrès International d'Esthétique,* Athens, 1960), and my lecture delivered in Munich in the same year, "Das Kunstwerk: Sprache und Gestalt," reprinted in *Sprache und Wirklichkeit* (Munich, 1967).

3. "An appraisive term," as W. B. Gallie has so aptly called it in a study, "Essentially Contested Concepts," published in 1956 and reprinted in the anthology *The Importance of Language*, Max Black, ed. (Englewood Cliffs, 1962); see especially p. 133 et seq. Gallie nevertheless appears not to have grasped that there is an alternative to this excessively aestheticizing conception of art which condemns it to be nothing but an object, and that there can be an aesthetic appraisal which takes degrees and nuances into account and is not limited to a mere yes or no, approval or disapproval.

4. It is well to recall, for example, the famous and in many respects excellent essay by Cleanth Brooks, "What does Poetry Communicate?" which forms a portion of his book *The Well Wrought Urn* (New York, 1965). In reference to an analysis, excellent in itself, of a poem by Robert Herrick, he notes: "To say that Herrick 'communicates' certain matters to the reader tends to falsify the real situation," which is true if we assume that he is communicating facts or the material of verbalization. But the "real situation" is nevertheless that of a communication which is fused with the verse (melody, rhythm, or significant words)—a communication dependent upon the verse and transmitted by it yet remaining distinct from it. Thus criticism errs in abandoning all idea of language with the declaration: "The old description of the poet was better and less dangerous: the poet is a maker, not a communicator." The Greeks, however, did not forget that he was also a speaker who naturally, to be sure, "made" his poems, but at the same time *spoke* through that which he made. It has become rather dangerous to stress this idea of "making" since we have been taught to transfer it to the creation of aesthetic objects.

5. See my study, "Die zwei Sprachen der Sprachkunst," in the *Jahrbuch für Asthetik und allgemeine Kunstwissenschaft*, Vol. 12, 2 (Festschrift Gantner, Teil 2).

TENTATIVE CONCLUSIONS

David Daiches

LITERARY EVALUATION

ALTHOUGH LITERARY CRITICISM HAS ACQUIRED MANY FUNCTIONS IN THE course of its long history, the function most often demanded of it by the lay reader—as well as that implicit in the Greek etymology of the word "critic"—is judgment, discrimination, the placing of a given literary work in a scale of values. But the simple question "How good is this work?" is not really a simple question at all. A definition of literary value comprehensive enough to be applicable to all varieties of literature yet straightforward enough to yield a definite placing in the scale of merit when applied to specific works is the end and not the beginning of a long inquiry. "How good *as what?*" is the counter-question to be expected of any sophisticated critic when asked the direct question about how good a work is. Literature serves and has served a great variety of functions, has assumed a great variety of forms. The obvious temptation to any critic faced with this variety is to take refuge in relativism: this was good of its kind, was good in its day, it achieved the end set himself by the writer and expected by the contemporary reader. This position is by no means confined to modern critics.

> A perfect Judge will read each Work of Wit
> With the same Spirit that its Author writ,

wrote Pope, and again:

> In ev'ry Work regard the Writer's End,
> Since none can compass more than they Intend.

But even this is easier said than done. How do we discover the "Spirit" in which "its Author writ"? By delving into his biography, by making a historical study of literary taste and fashion in his day, by inferring it from what he has actually written (and here there may well be a strong element of subjectivity on the critic's part), or by something of all three? Again, suppose one has clearly determined the author's intention and the "Writer's End"—must we not discriminate between ends? Something may be good of its kind, but how good is the kind? Is a perfect limerick good literature in the same way as a great tragedy is? If not, are we to have two different standards, one for each genre with no communication between them, or could we subsume both standards in a more comprehensive one in which, say, the limitation of scope and simplicity of form of the limerick would represent a disqualification so far as "greatness"—the highest award—was concerned but would not prevent the award of a prize for "goodness"? But can we really compare a limerick and a tragedy in any significant critical way? (I take these two forms as two extremes, but the question applies across the whole range of literary forms and genres.) If we can, what is the relation *critically* between an imperfect tragedy and a perfect limerick, between a dull and pretentious epic and a sparkling two-line epigram, between (say) Cowley's *Davideis* and Hilaire Belloc's *Bad Child's Book of Beasts?*

If, with many modern critics, we refuse to make comparisons of this sort and content ourselves with giving an analytic description of the individual work, we are to some degree renouncing the critic's function. For if criticism implies discrimination, discrimination involves comparison. Critical comparison need not mean placing in a rigid order of merit, with *King Lear* scoring five points more than *Phèdre*, or *War and Peace* out-pointing *Emma*, though this is more because once a certain degree of high excellence has been recognized in a work of art it becomes increasingly difficult to pinpoint merits beyond this degree than because such scoring *sub specie aeternitatis* is inherently absurd. We can agree with Saintsbury that "in the house of poetry are many mansions" and inhabit each with pleasure at different times and in different moods while at the same time refusing to be a mere relativist in matters of value and to content ourselves with describing works of radically different sorts as being good of their kind and incommensurable.

Can we, then, make a beginning by discriminating between ends and placing them in a hierarchy of value? This was done by neoclassic critics, who had a clearly formulated doctrine of literary "kinds" arranged in an order of merit. But one of the characteristics of literature is that it tends to transcend its overt aims. A poem designed to probe the ultimate depths of experience may be dull and pretentious, while an apparently light-hearted squib, a whimsical lyric written for amusement, or an "occasional" poem designed for an ephemeral occasion, may indirectly probe those depths more effectively. Art is never confined by the ostensible aims of the artist: as D. H. Lawrence said, "Never trust the artist, trust the tale." Robert Burns wrote "The Cotter's Saturday Night" as a poem of high and profound seriousness, and his "To a Louse, on Seeing One on a Lady's Bonnet in Church" as an amusing little squib. But there is no doubt that the latter is the better poem—not merely better of its kind, but better as an illumination of the human situation, for its meanings reverberate away as they do not in the former poem.

The writer's intention cannot, then, be taken as a guide to the value of his work, but on the other hand it may very well help in our *understanding* of the work. If we are reading a literary work that was produced in a different civilization from ours or in an earlier and very different period of our own civilization, we must first know what it is we are reading. We must know the language, the conventions within which it is written, the range of reference and allusion which give significance to the imagery, and so on. Knowledge of the writer's intention may help us here. If, for example, we know that a poem was intended to be declaimed at a public celebration, we know how to approach its language, at what distance to stand when reading it, as it were. Such knowledge is not always conveyed in the title of a work. In reading a Greek drama, we must know something of the Greek myths it draws on and refers to and also something of the conventions governing the Greek theatre and of the religious and ritual elements. (We must, of course, know Greek too if we are to have any confidence in our critical judgment; but the question of literature in translation raises a host of other problems that do not properly belong here.) What a work of literature *is* is thus not altogether an ontological question. If we came across *Oedipus Rex* in an anthology of modern drama, with no previous knowledge of it or of Greek tragedy, we might well read it as a black comedy about sex instead of a tragedy about fate. And, of course, language itself is historically determined, so that a work written in the past, even in our own language, contains meanings which one can only see if one knows the relevant history of the language. Again, knowledge of the conventions within which a writer is operating enables us to approach the work properly. Tolstoy had great fun, in *What is Art*, in mocking Wagnerian opera by describing it as though it were meant to be nineteenth-century realistic drawing-room drama. We must know how to pose ourselves before a work, and if it is a work of the past such knowledge must come in some degree from history.

The first law of criticism, then, is the priority of understanding. We must understand what a work is before we can read it and so before we can judge it. The question of liberty of interpretation is crucial in any discussion of evaluation. If by ingenuity of subjective interpretation we can find virtually any meanings in any work, then evaluation—certainly the comparative evaluation of different works— becomes impossible. If one is free to interpret anything as anything, then evaluation becomes a wholly subjective matter and normative criticism becomes simply a personal game. Any structure of words can be used as the taking-off point for unlimited personal fantasies, and if the only question asked by the critic is "What can I make this work mean to *me*?" then the answer can have little or no objective value. I recall once in a seminar on poetry that a student interpreted an Elizabethan sonnet in a way that involved understanding certain words in senses that they could not conceivably have borne for an Elizabethan, and when I remonstrated he replied calmly: "But I'm explaining what the work means to *me*; isn't that what criticism is all about?" I could not get him to see that it is what the *work* means to him that matters and that he was not reading the work at all. One could build personal fantasies out of a column in the telephone directory by ingenious interpretation of words, but that would not make the directory a work of literature.

This suggests that there are dangers in regarding analysis as the primary critical technique. The practitioners of such a technique all too readily fall into the belief that what is analyzable is good—and of course with sufficient ingenuity anything is analyzable. If you are faced with, say, a poem and are invited to exert your analytic ingenuity on it, you take it as a challenge to find the maximum number of subtle meanings. And if a criterion such as paradox or complexity is the one being applied as the test of literary quality, the critic can just soldier on until he has demonstrated the necessary elements of paradox or complexity. It is clear to anyone who has observed students—and I mean intelligent graduate students—engaged in practical criticism that the decision whether a work demands and repays subtle analysis is generally made *before* the task is undertaken, which means that the value judgment precedes the analysis. "Demonstrate the complexities in this work" is generally the task assumed by these critics, rather than the profounder task of inquiring into what if any complexities exist in the work and in what way do they contribute to its merits as literature. It is interesting that an age which has repudiated what Professor Wimsatt was the first to call the "intentional fallacy"—the bringing into critical judgment of the author's intention—on the grounds that it confuses biography with criticism, has been much less ready to repudiate what might be called the fallacy of personal ingenuity, in which the critic's biography (surely much less relevant than the author's) is directly involved. For it is a mistake to suppose that analysis is necessarily objective and is on this ground to be opposed to the subjective impressionist criticism which consists of a report on how the work affects the critic (the "affective fallacy"). Unanchored ingenuity in searching for conceivable meanings in making an analysis of a work can in fact involve the critic's autobiography much more drastically than an attempt to justify a work in terms of its effect on the reader.

The first requirement of the evaluative critic is to know what a work *is*, to understand its language, to be at home in its area of reference. This is partly a matter of historical knowledge. Even on the simplest level of lexical meaning critics can make the most dreadful howlers by assuming, for example, that a word meant the same thing to Shakespeare or Pope as it means in educated English or American speech today. Language, it cannot be too often stressed, exists in history, and a structure of meanings built up in a past work of literature can only be recognized for what it is by a reader who is aware both of the previous history which defines the possible meanings of a word at any given time, and of the area of reference or suggestion which is available to particular writers in particular times and places. The acquisition of such knowledge is a precritical activity: it is not criticism, but a prerequisite for criticism. Another critical prerequisite is that the reader should be sure that what he is reading and discussing is truly the work that the author wrote, not a botched, misprinted copy: he need not be a bibliographer or textual critic himself, but he must know how to use the work of bibliographers and textual critics. A work which is partly what its author wrote and partly what incompetent copyists or printers made it out to be, can of course be evaluated for what it is, and in the case of a long work such as a Shakespearean play, occasional misprints or dubious readings will not prevent a just estimate of the work as a whole, although it may affect one's judgment of a few individual passages; but a short lyric in which (to take an example which actually occurred in an important edition of Yeats) some of the lines are transposed and one line omitted altogether, cannot be justly evaluated at all.

Assuming, then, that the critic has the historical knowledge to enable him to read the work (and that it is a work of the past) accurately, to stand at the proper distance from it, to appreciate to what area of literary activity it belongs, and to what areas of culture and experience it reaches out, how should he proceed? In spite of the dangers of analysis, to which I have drawn attention, it is clear that some kind of descriptive account of the work is necessary for the critic. The question that divides two significantly different critical approaches is whether the descriptive account should precede or succeed the formulation of precise criteria of value. Should we say, "A great poem should have the qualities a, b, c, etc.," and then proceed to look at the poem to see in what degree it possesses those qualities so that it could be precisely graded on a scale? Is the critic's procedure a syllogism: "A great work should possess the qualities x; this work demonstrably possesses the qualities x; therefore this is a great work"? Evaluative criticism of this kind is what one might call the classical extreme: there are "rules" which define a good work of literature, and the critic proceeds by applying them. The opposite, the romantic extreme, is the purely subjective, impressionist judgment: this moves me though I cannot tell exactly why, it does something to me (A. E. Housman on the physical effect on him of true poetry). No serious critic today would accept either extreme. Yet, though I myself would unhesitatingly reject the schematic syllogistic kind of procedure implied in the classical extreme, I would agree with the underlying classical assumption that in order to be able to make a responsible value judgment about a work of literature the critic must know what it is that literature is and does, must have some general conceptions of its nature and function. He must know, for example, that the value of a poem does not lie in its acrostic cunning or in the degree of ingenuity expended on its verbal patterning, nor on the other hand does its value lie in the degree to which the writing of it afforded relief to the poet. He must have clear ideas about the *ends* of literature and about the different *means* which can achieve those ends—and he must be able to distinguish between ends and means. Pattern, for example, is clearly an important means in literature, but the existence of pattern (however complex, however subtle, however ingeniously analyzable) is in itself no necessary guarantee of the literary quality of the work. I said earlier that literature tends to transcend its overt ends. But I am not now discussing overt ends or intentions, nor am I referring to the differing ends which distinguish different genres: I am referring to those implied ends which represent the ultimate justification of imaginative literature. And it does not take any lengthy process of philosophical investigation and argument to define those ends which represent the ultimate justification of poetry, fiction, and drama. All the critic—as distinct from the aesthetician or the philosopher—needs is an awareness of the illuminative function of literature. The function of literature is to illuminate human experience—that is why we still read and enjoy Homer, Dante, Shakespeare, and Tolstoy. The devices of craftsmanship which the critic can identify in particular works must, if they are to be seen as relevant to an evaluation, be seen to be means to some kind of human illumination. Of course, one is at liberty to believe that works of literature are interesting and valuable simply for the qualities of verbal texture and design that they exhibit. We are dealing here with a basic question of first principles. Verbal designs can be amusing or intriguing or pleasing in any of a variety of ways, but they do not seem to me to be among the most valuable products of civilization. The reason why literature is valuable, why we esteem the literary artist among the highest of our culture heroes and consider a life devoted to the production of literature well spent, is that literature illuminates life—illuminates it uniquely and at the same time more powerfully and movingly and directly than can be done by discursive discourse *about* life.

This may seem a sentimental commonplace, but no discussion of evaluative criticism can proceed far without some indication of where the discussion starts from. The above statement about the ultimate (if implicit) value of literature is inferred inductively by introspection about the kinds of pleasure and insight that literature has actually afforded one. It is an empirical conclusion, like Dr. Johnson's "Nothing can please many, and please long, but just representations of general nature" or "by the common sense of readers uncorrupted with literary prejudices, after all the refinements of subtilty and the dogmatism of learning, must be finally decided all claim to poetical honours." Such generalizations cannot themselves be of any help in practical criticism, but they represent certain principles—the end and not the beginning of a long exposure to many varieties of literature—which determine the starting point of criticism and the direction in which it moves. (Incidentally, Johnson's generalizations may seem crude and indeed plain wrong to us, but if we understand his language and the context within which he wrote we will be more inclined to agree with them: the phrase "common reader," for example, means something very different in an age of mass literacy from what it meant in an age with a relatively small and uniformly educated reading public.)

If, then, the classical extreme represents a truth—that we must have some notion of what literature is all about before we can set about judging particular works—the romantic extreme also has its element of truth. While literature cannot be judged on the grounds that it "sends" any given reader, it is nevertheless true that literature does affect people and that in the last analysis it is in the way that it affects sensitive and experienced readers that its value lies. This "romantic" position may seem to some modern critics an awful surrender to autobiography, but in fact it represents simple common sense. Literature, like all the arts, is produced by people for people ("The poet," said Wordsworth, "is a man speaking to men"), and people respond to it because they get something out of it. If we cannot test the quality of literature by the crude process of counting heads, this is because a proper responsiveness to it can only be achieved by long and careful exposure to a great variety of its forms, rather than because it is inherently absurd that what is most widely esteemed is best.

If the reminder that literature is created by man to fulfill a human need sounds both vague and naïve, that is because the practicing "new critic" of modern times has been so busy trying on the one hand to liberate criticism from loose impressionist chat, insisting on precise, technical language applied to the individual work only, and on the other hand to demonstrating the difference between literary and other modes of discourse by eschewing any appeal to general human values which could be relevant also to those other modes, that he has avoided discussion of ends. Yet the recognition that ultimately some sort of affective theory is implicit in all evaluative criticism does not imply that what literature does for people is the same as or even in any way resembles what anything else does for them. Literature is indeed unique, in that it gives special kinds of pleasure and a special kind of insight that nothing else affords. But the pleasure and the insight remain its ultimate end, however much we may distinguish different subcategories of pleasure and insight applying to different kinds of literature, and however much the practical critic is concerned with examining and demonstrating the means by which those ends are achieved. Indeed, the practical critic will usually take those ends for granted, concentrating on a study of the means: that is why it is important every now and again to remind ourselves what the ultimate object of all literature and all criticism really is.

If literature serves a human need, then the best literature is that which can be seen to have served it for most people over the longest period of time. This would seem at least to be one criterion on which to judge the literature of the past. "The reverence due to writings that have long subsisted"—to quote Dr. Johnson again—"arises therefore not from any credulous confidence in the superior wisdom of past ages, or gloomy persuasion of the degeneracy of mankind, but is the consequence of acknowledged and indubitable positions, that what has been longest known has been most considered, and what is most considered is best understood." The test of time, however, is not as simple a matter as Johnson would have us believe. In the first place, there still remains (as Johnson very well knew) the critical test of finding out exactly why any given work stood the test of time: in virtue of what qualities was it admired by so many people over such a long period? In the second place, once a work or an author has become regarded as a "classic" it becomes part of an established culture which is handed on by the educational machinery of a civilization without any necessary spontaneous feeling on the part of each new generation that the estimate is critically justified. Homer was read in fifth-century Athens as a great educator, the schoolboy's guide to the moral life, which cannot have been the view of those who produced it and certainly was not the view of those who venerated the *Iliad* and the *Odyssey* in the eighteenth and nineteenth centuries. True, the fact that different generations have admired Homer for different reasons is a tribute to the richness of these two epics, and the same can be said about Shakespeare, who was admired in the eighteenth century for his "knowledge of the human heart," in the nineteenth century for his ability to create character, and in the twentieth century for a number of reasons including his dramaturgy, his command of language, his mastery of dramatic structure, and his ethical subtlety. But there are also classics that seem to have remained classics over centuries through a kind of cultural inertia, works that few people read, that are only rarely valued and even then by specialist scholars, yet which remain in the canon of classics. In England *The Faerie Queen* is such a work: whatever one's view of Spencer's incomplete heroic poem (and personally I would rate it fairly high), it would be ridiculous to maintain that it maintains its place as a classic because generations of readers have known and loved it.

We must, then, distinguish between live classics and dead classics. Works can become classics for a variety of reasons and some maintain their place in an established culture without any exposure to the test of popularity even among the more sophisticated and highly literate minority. Shakespeare is the supreme example of the true classic: his reputation built itself up steadily, from the seventeenth century when he was esteemed but generally rated lower than Ben Jonson to the eighteenth century when he was regarded as the great natural genius who could get away with anything, to the nineteenth century, by which time he was the undisputed top figure in English, and in the view of many, in world literature. At every stage in the development of this reputation Shakespeare was read, acted, and discussed. Here is a clear case when we can say that Shakespeare's appeal to different sorts of people judging by different standards at different times is proof of the richness of his work and the multiple values contained in it.

Thus the capacity of a literary work to be different things to different generations may be a sign of its greatness. The test of time reveals this multiplicity and releases this potential. It is true to say that we can be surer of the worth of a work of the past than of something only recently produced. Yet there is a paradox here. I have already discussed the difficulty of knowing just what a work of the past really is, the dangers of radical misunderstanding through lack of awareness of the way language has changed since it was written or of the conventions which determined its form. This should mean that only works by our own contemporaries can be certain of receiving a full and just appraisal from us. But this is not so. Our own contemporary literature is notoriously difficult to judge, for reasons diametrically opposite to those that cause difficulties in our evaluation of older literature. When we read recent works we are liable to carry too much of the world common to writer and reader—that is, to the writer and ourselves—with us in our interpretation and evaluation, so that we do not read the work but look through it at the world we and the writer know. It is difficult to distinguish the point at which the work stands on its own, containing its meanings within itself. When we read older works we may err through lack of knowledge of the area of reference that gives resonance to the writer's language; with new works we may err through knowing that area of reference all too well and thus by assuming that the writer has effectively used it in the work whereas in fact he might simply have made a perfunctory gesture towards it. In short, a new work is difficult to distinguish from its environment. There are, of course, other reasons militating against a just evaluation of the work of our contemporaries, especially at this moment in cultural history when the speed of change in artistic taste and fashion is faster than it has ever been. We may be fooled by fashion in two quite different ways: we may admire something because it is written in a mode we have justly learned to admire, or we may admire something because it avoids all fashionable norms in an attempt to strike out in a radically new direction and, feeling committed to support the avant garde in the interests of the health and vitality of the arts, delude ourselves into believing that the new is good simply because of its newness.

Provided that at each stage the readers have acquired enough historical knowledge to understand the language and the conventions of a literary work, it is true to say that if it has been valued by many generations of sensitive and experienced readers it is likely to be of high merit. But we can go further and say that the vitality and expressiveness and human interestingness of some works are so overpowering that they can communicate a great deal of their power and meaning even to readers who have not acquired this historical knowledge. Again, Shakespeare is a case in point. The English language has not changed so much since Shakespeare's day that a reasonably intelligent reader or spectator of his plays, even if without special knowledge, will not receive a complex and moving experience. The greater the gap in language and culture between one's own age and the date of the literary work under discussion, the more difficult it is to depend on the simple time test. A Greekless modern reader who reads the *Odyssey* in translation is at the mercy of the translator and can have little certainty about the way language is used in the original. And the way language is used in a work of literature is a central question in any discussion of literary value, since it is this which builds up a reverberating world of ever-deepening meanings in the light of which the illumination of human experience (the ultimate end) is achieved. Of course, the greater the work, the more multiple the means employed for achieving this end. The fact that Lady Macbeth talks of her "*little* hand" (the affectionate diminutive of a lover) after she had in an earlier scene renounced her femininity illuminates in an instance of tense pathos, which is yet in terms of the dramatic action not pathos at all, a whole area of meaning relative to the self-delusiveness of ambition. An awareness of this device, and of the innumerable such details of structure and language and their interrelations, can survive translation up to a point, and if it can survive translation it can surely survive being read by someone who knows only twentieth-century English and has no background in Elizabethan language or habits of thought. The greater the work, the more likely it is to contain within it some proportion of devices which can survive a lack of special knowledge in the reader. It is also true that the shorter the work, the less the possibility of such survival. In my own experience of university teaching I have found again and again that a sonnet of Shakespeare's or Sidney's or a short poem of Donne's can be *radically* misinterpreted (so that the student is not reading the poem in front of him at all) in a way that, say, *Julius Caesar* or *Middlemarch* cannot be. (Because much modern criticism infers its basic methods from the analysis of short poems, this is disturbing.)

Any discussion of the test of time as a proof of greatness brings us back to the "affective" question. Apart from the special case of dead classics preserved by an educational tradition unconnected with human response, literary works survive because different people have kept on responding to them. It is true that there is today a very large subarea of orthodox academic evaluation deriving from this response, and in that subarea values are given and not discovered, but if we investigate, for example, the great surge of interest in the metaphysical poets during the first half of this century we can see that there was a genuine poetic rediscovery, a genuine human response and a sense of a human need being met, involved here, and the academic consequences were secondary. Yet even the academic consequences have meant for several generations of students real excitement and discovery, academically guided and stimulated though they might have been. The rediscovery of previously neglected works, incidentally, is an interesting variation of the time test. An age can suddenly recognize itself, or imagine that it recognizes itself, in an earlier age by the discovery that the art of that earlier age responds with peculiar urgency to the imaginative and emotional needs of the later age. Such rediscovery does not necessarily mean that the works thus rediscovered are lower down in the scale of value than works which have never lost their popularity and high esteem, though this may be so in particular cases. The temporary eclipse of a writer may be due to changes in literary fashion which prevent that writer from being properly read. The whole question of changing taste in the arts is highly complex and involves many factors both cultural and social. All I shall say here is that the resurfacing of a writer or a work after a period of obscurity may be due to an over-estimate resulting from the special needs of the rediscovering genera-tion, but it is just as likely—indeed, I think history shows it to be more likely—to be testimony to the inherent quality of the work or writer, which cannot be indefinitely kept down by fashion, ignorance, or prejudice.

But none of these generalizations is of much direct help to the individual critic endeavoring to establish the degree of literary merit in a given work. They may be of indirect help, by reminding him that a work which has survived many generations must possess special qualities, which he had better look for. And the questions of means and ends to which I referred earlier may help him by en-couraging him to couch his description in terms which suggest his evaluation. And this indeed seems to me the nub of the whole prob-lem. Structure, texture, imagery, the use of metaphor, the presence of mythic elements, complexity, paradox, rhythm and sound, ethical or psychological suggestions and implications—whatever elements in a work we point to must be in order to show how the work as it progresses builds up a totality of meaning which moves and illumi-nates. Of course there are many kinds of moving and illumination, and no one would seek the same effects from *King Lear* and *The Rape of the Lock*. But the human relevance is paramount. One need not classify different "kinds" of literature, each with its appropriate area of human significance, as the neoclassic critics did, or reduce all literature to the embodiment of archetypal varieties of myth, as Northrop Frye does; but we must be aware of differences in mood and tone which determine the area of human experience that the work illuminates and, more significantly, the nature and quality of the illumination. To demonstrate this does not require a syllogistic argument of the kind described above, if only because the most con-vincing kind of criticism is less a logical demonstration than a per-suasive reading, a sort of acting out of the work in the presence of the reader so that the reader, as he follows the discussion, can see how the language works, how the structure operates, and so on, and watch the work flower open (or, if the judgment is adverse, wither away) as the criticism develops. The best kind of evaluative criti-cism is *loaded description*. The effective evaluative critic cannot simply speak in his capacity as expert, assuring his less expert readers that this really is the genuine article, as an expert in antique furniture or in the history of art will guarantee the authenticity of a Chippendale chair or a Rembrandt painting. The expertise of the critic must communicate itself to the reader by the way in which it is expressed. We do not accept his evaluation because of his credentials, but because of the persuasiveness and the particularity of his description of the work in question. Thus, good evaluative criticism is self-justifying. It is not a question of asking whether the reader agrees with the critic but rather of asking whether the criticism, read back into the work, is immediately seen as providing a convincing and illuminating way of reading the work. Evaluative criticism which cannot be seen in this way, however ingenious or learned it may be, is not really evaluative criticism.

But evaluation, even if it does not mean awarding specific grades to every work, does involve comparison. How can we distinguish *relative* merit by the method of loaded description that I have been advocating? In the first place, I believe that comparison can and should play a considerable part in actual critical description. This is particularly apt when works are of roughly the same period and deal with roughly the same theme. Thus, in discussing Marvell's "To His Coy Mistress" the functioning of the imagery as well as the special tone of the poem can be made clearer by comparing the language and the tone with that of Herrick's "To the Virgins, to Make much of Time," with its more open-worked and indeed repetitive imagery ("The glorious lamp of heaven, the sun"—as though Herrick had not confidence in his own metaphor and had to go on to explain it). A third poem on the same theme, Waller's "Go, Lovely Rose!," could also be introduced into the discussion. This poem, with its logical progression of imperatives ("Go . . . Tell . . . Bid . . . Then die . . ."), stands in its intellectual texture midway between Marvell and Herrick, and in literary quality—that is, in the way language is used, in the range of thought and feeling compressed into the poem, in the originality and haunting nature of the tone, and so on—it is possible to rank the three poems in order of merit, with Marvell's first, Waller's second, and Herrick's third.

This suggests that evaluative description should also be conducted in a context wider than the individual work under consideration. If I were talking to students about the Marvell poem I would insist that they read beforehand all the three poems I have mentioned so that I could feel free to make comparisons and contrasts at any point in the discussion. No evaluative criticism can be properly carried out by an unstocked mind or before an audience with unstocked minds. One must know the range of possibilities of an art before one can judge the success of any given example. The greatest potential literary genius in the world, if deprived throughout his life of all literature beyond the level of Edgar Guest, would be impoverished to an intolerable degree and both his judgment and his own creative work would suffer. If, as I remarked earlier, the first law of criticism is priority of understanding, the second law is the necessity of experience. Or one might say that full understanding of a given work is impossible without experience of a range of works. Only wide reading gives one an awareness of the possibilities of the medium and enables one to develop *taste*, which is simply the sum of discriminations made available by attentive reading in a large variety of literary modes. One might well think *The Duchess of Malfi* the absolute summit of English poetic tragedy if one was ignorant of Shakespeare, and, conversely, no one who has not read a great deal of other couplet poetry of the century can fully appreciate Pope's unique genius in handling the heroic couplet.

The intensive critical description of an individual work should, I believe, always take place in a context of shared knowledge (shared between writer and reader or between speaker and audience) so that allusion, comparison, illustration, contrast, parallel, or whatever it may be, can be brought in naturally to fill out the argument, thus at the same time making clearer a point about the work under discussion and setting going normative implications that apply also to other works. I cannot in fact imagine a critic really getting going on a piece of practical criticism, with the intellectual excitement and quickening of sensibility which this involves or should involve, without feeling impelled at some stage to illustrate or expand his point by reference to other works. Gradually a world of values is built up, with reference both to the work under discussion and to other works, by a combination of specificness of description and range of allusion.

With great and complex works, critics may agree about the value but disagree about the reasons that account for it. This is inevitable, as I have remarked, with an overpowering genius like Shakespeare whose plays can be fruitfully read in so many ways and at so many levels. With this sort of work, no critic can tell "the truth" about the reasons for its being great: he can only provide his contribution to a perpetual discussion. But again we must insist that the critic reads the work, and not his own fantasy, and that he does so within a wide range of reading. (There are cases where a critic can perform a useful service by reading his own fantasy derived from the work and not the work itself, for the power of the work to generate such a fantasy may itself be relevant to its value. But total liberty of interpretation is a denial of the importance and indeed of the reality of the actual literary work.) With works of less universal appeal there are more likely to be legitimate differences of opinion about their value. Exactly how good, for example, are the works of Gay, James Thomson, Southey, Trollope? Many works look better to us if we can use our own historical imagination to enable us to supply areas of reference and even habits of mind which the original authors took for granted in their audience, so that our judgment of such works will depend in some degree on our knowledge. Debate arises when the question of whether a given work is *worth* our acquiring the relevant knowledge to enable us to read it better. The late E.M.W. Tillyard once remarked that he regretted that he had not time and energy to enable him to cultivate the taste for eighteenth-century Miltonizing verse, and for this he was savagely attacked by F.R. Leavis who regarded as a typical academic heresy the view that one should by scholarly effort make an attempt to appreciate everything, of whatever merit or lack of merit, that was written in the past. Leavis had a point: to work oneself into a state of mind which would enable one to enjoy inferior work of the past that was highly acclaimed in its own day is no more critically respectable than to try and put oneself into the state of mind of those who prefer comic books to Shakespeare in order that one should appreciate comic books. Whether a work of the past justifies the acquiring of the knowledge and understanding that will enable one to read it "properly" depends on how good it intrinsically is, yet how good it intrinsically is may not be discoverable until we have acquired that knowledge and understanding and read it in the full certainty that we have read what is really there. The way out of this circular argument is simply to ask whether the work on first reading invites the search for fuller understanding. There is no way out of a dependence on a first reading. However puzzling, obscure, alien, impenetrable a work may be, if it has real literary quality enough will get through to the experienced reader at first reading to invite him to further reading. I remember when, as a student, I first read Yeats's "Byzantium." I knew little of Yeats then except some of the early poems, and I had not the vaguest idea what Yeats was talking about in "Byzantium." But the poem haunted me and worked on me; I could not get its images and rhythms out of my head; and eventually I was driven to a study of Yeats which enabled me to read his later poems with full understanding and appreciation.

Works of the past may be considered minor when only a proportion of informed and sensitive readers feel themselves invited by them to acquire the further knowledge necessary for their full appreciation. And legitimate differences of opinion must be allowed to exist here. But if someone says that he fails to see why Shakespeare is a greater dramatist than Dekker, then we cannot simply invoke the *de gustibus* argument and shrug this off as a minority opinion. The person who believes Dekker a greater dramatist than Shakespeare is demonstrably wrong, and any critic who finds himself so outrageously at variance with what Johnson called "the common sense of readers"—in this case informed and experienced readers extending over a long period of time and many changes of literary fashion—should simply admit that he has a blind spot and leave it at that. No one has any obligation to admire what is conventionally regarded as admirable in art, but if absolutely the whole world is out of step with you it is the part of modesty to consider whether it is not you yourself who are out of step.

If it is true that the ultimate *raison d'être* of literature is its appeal to readers and thus its "affective" potential, it must follow that there is an element of subjectivity in all literary appraisal. But this does not mean that the critic can be content to point and shout his praise (as that distinguished critic F.R. Leavis does in his book on Lawrence, where the method largely boils down to quoting a passage and saying, "There now, isn't that absolutely splendid?"). Evaluative criticism is description presented in such a way that the reader is carried into the work with new insight and appreciation (or condemnation, for this applies to damnatory as well as to appreciative criticism). If the subjective element in the original appraisal is too strong—if, that is, the critic is bringing to the work emotions and attitudes deriving from something outside the work and not seeing the work itself with sufficient clarity, which personal circumstances can lead even the best critic to do at times, particularly with contemporary literature—his description will be likely to sound too highly pitched and so be unpersuasive. Again, the use of comparisons will enable a critic to guard against taking too naïvely an unearned emotional quality in a work. This seems moving and memorable, but put it beside *that* and you will see that it is merely sentimental. In critical debate, when one may be trying to prove that another critic has mistaken sentimentality for emotional profundity, for example, the nicely chosen comparison can be an extremely effective weapon.

From what has been said it will be clear that the balance between the subjective and the objective in literary criticism is a very tricky business. Up to a point a critic is one who has trained himself to see the work, in Arnold's phrase, "in itself as it really is" and who refrains from bringing into his criticism irrelevant personal emotions. But on the other hand, great literature appeals to one's innermost self in a profound and moving way, and all one's experience, all one's knowledge of life, all one's involvement in human relations and in the general "complex fate" of being human, is relevant to one's response to it. Shakespeare's tragedies appeal desperately to one's deepest knowledge and feelings in a way that, say, the novels of Peacock do not. Is this a difference between the great and the good? And is this bound up with the difference between art and craft, the former using craftsmanship in the interests of the most profound imaginative exploration of experience and the latter using it in a more relaxed and self-sufficient way? And is it with respect to the latter category only that differences of opinion about value are inevitable and desirable? I am inclined to believe that this is so, that art includes craft as the great subsumes the good but that craft (or the good) is not necessarily art (or the great). Of course I am using these terms arbitrarily, but the distinction I am trying to make must have occurred in one way or another to most readers.

Some works invite what can be called committed reading, with the result that the critic runs the risk of becoming too deeply and personally involved in his own commitment to be able to argue persuasively with those who do not share that commitment (again, we might cite Leavis on Lawrence). The invitation to commitment is itself a quality, and provides a criterion by which to judge certain kinds of writers (Blake, for example, or Whitman, as well as Lawrence). But the very highest kind of literature transcends that kind of invitation: we are not "committed" in this way by Shakespeare or Tolstoy. The invitation to commitment is divisive, and not always on literary grounds: there are sensitive and experienced critics who cannot get through to Lawrence as a writer because the commitment he seems to be inviting them to make is both nonliterary and unacceptable. The state of profound, almost trance-like contemplation in which the greatest literature leaves us (and this indeed is one criterion of great literature) is not "kinetic" though it is revelatory.

In the lower ranges of literature are all sorts of mixed kinds, partly documentary, partly sociological, partly historical, and one of the problems in defining the task of the literary critic is precisely that literature is so wide-ranging, often so "impure," with the spectrum

ranging from the almost wholly documentary to the wholly imaginative. One must find a technique of description that enables one to do
justice to these mixed kinds, to demonstrate the effectiveness of the
literary devices which make the documentary element so much more
vivid and persuasive. The novel in particular tends to be a mixed
form. In calling these mixed forms "lower" I am not so much implying
a value judgment as suggesting a scale between the high visionary
and the low documentary, with every possible kind of combination in between. The relation of this scale to a scale of quality is not
easy to determine: it can be argued that the purely visionary is not
by any means the greatest and that a grip on contemporary social
fact, however indirectly or obliquely demonstrated, is the mark of
the greatest writers.

It will be seen by now that I have no absolute "right" critical
method to prescribe. If I might state an article of faith—which I have
developed over more than thirty years of reading and discussing
literature—it is that literary criticism is an art, not a science, and
justifies itself by its practice, not by its theory. The kind of loaded
description that I recommended earlier brings all the critic's faculties into play as he tries to recreate the work in all its vitality and
reality by letting his own words play over the words of the original
in order to light them up and display them in all their vitality, their
order, their resonance. This is at least true of the kind of criticism
which tries to demonstrate by description the qualities of a work
which make it a true work of literary art. Criticism of this sort is a
kind of creation—not the irresponsible taking off from the work into
something quite new and different which Oscar Wilde recommended,
but taking inspiration from the work in order to demonstrate it in all
its glory. Great art prompts great criticism: both in the end are
justified by the degree to which they provide illumination. And really
effective critical description strikes sparks off the work under discussion in order, as it were, to provide illumination of experience in
its own right. The ultimate test of effective critical description is that
the reader does not have to go on afterwards and define his criteria
or formulate a scale of values. Awareness of the criteria is implicit
in the understanding.

Howard Lee Nostrand

THEME ANALYSIS IN THE
STUDY OF LITERATURE

PAST DISCUSSIONS OF DIFFERING APPROACHES TO THE ARTS SUGGEST THAT
the hazards of such discussion spring partly from unspoken premises.
The participants talk past one another because their underlying assumptions, insufficiently examined and often unconsciously held, are
wrongly imagined to agree or to conflict. Today, when critics from
radically different cultures are merging their discussions of the arts,
it becomes more important than ever to attempt a systematic account
of the premises underlying each position that is argued.

What premises are required for a "themal" study of literature?
The approach proposed in the present paper seeks to describe, in the
form of interrelated "themes," what a given reader or audience finds
in a literary work of art. This approach might be called "thematic";
but that term has been used for various procedures, some of whose
faults we can avoid. Let us try borrowing the hybrid adjective
"themal" from Morris Opler of Cornell University, the anthropologist
who has done the most to illuminate entire cultures by abstracting
their unique patterns of themes.[1] It seems conducive to clarity to
adopt Professor Opler's neologism, because his approach to the
themes of a whole culture follows the same inductive procedure that
is proposed here for approaching works of literature. Indeed, the
"themal" study of a people's literature and of its social behavior
should produce comparable conclusions, and thus shed light on the
relationship between the literature and the surrounding culture.

We shall come back to this use of the themal approach after we
consider the reasons for analyzing literature. First we shall look at

the premises which it seems necessary to postulate concerning the nature of literature itself; then the reasons for analyzing it; and then the nature of the analysis in terms of themes. The assumptions that prove necessary in this last section may be avoidable in other forms of literary analysis; but the premises that will be posited in the first three sections, concerning literature and the justification for analyzing it, seem inescapable in any study of a literary work, and in fact, *mutatis mutandis*, in the study of the other arts as well.

The present essay will nevertheless be limited to literature, defined broadly as composition in words which elicits a contemplative response. This definition includes, for those who find the distinction tenable, both imaginative literature (positing a fictitious alternative to reality) and literal discourse (referring directly to the world believed by the author and his fellow culture-carriers to be real). That distinction is not assumed here, because no assumption concerning the point at issue is required for analyzing literature. (My own view is that literary works distribute themselves along a continuum which extends from the predominantly literal to the completely non-literal use of language.)

PREMISES CONCERNING THE NATURE OF LITERATURE

The physical presence of a literary artwork is composed of symbols, organized in a structure which itself contributes toward the embodiment of that which is symbolized. To apprehend a work of art requires not only the perceiving of the symbolic structure, but beyond that, an inferring of what is symbolized. Let us call that which is inferred by the reader the "import" of the work: this term avoids the implication, sometimes false, that every work of literary art has a literal "meaning" or "message." And let us define "the reader" to mean either one person, or a group of readers homogeneous in some selected respects, or the audience to which a work is presented orally within a delimited culture area and period of time.

This premise will no doubt be unacceptable to radical behaviorists because of two presuppositions on which it rests: first, that verbal communication conveys more than the physically present stimulus to sense perception, and second, that the reader's response includes a striving to integrate and make sense of the literary experience, relating it, furthermore, to prior experience of art and life. The extreme behavioristic position, however, has been losing adherents to its reductive explanation of language and has in fact become increasingly hard to maintain, particularly since Chomsky's observations on B.F. Skinner's *Verbal Behavior*.[2]

The import of a work will necessarily vary according to the interests, attitudes, and concepts brought by the reader to his encounter with the work. While the physically-present symbol changes little, if at all, the import may vary widely even among readers belonging to a single culture and period; and the publicly accepted import of a work may change radically in the course of successive cultural movements, as has been shown, for example, for fables of La Fontaine.

Within the response of the reader which enters into the import of a work as he conceives it, one may distinguish components of emotion (affective charge), idea, and contemplation ("artistic remove"). The contemplative part of the response may be delayed if the work is perceived at first as an illusion of reality rather than as artistry. But it is postulated here that this third component of the response is essential to the import of the work. An essential difference between a literary tragedy and a highway accident, for example, lies in the contemplative attitude which every tragedian seeks to elicit. If the reader's response is entirely devoid of "artistic remove" he has not fully perceived the literary work, as "literature" is defined in the fourth paragraph of this essay.

It follows that any definition of a work's import for a category of responding persons must take into account somehow the element of reflection: for example, by valid sampling of all the contemplative responses within that category. The requisite degree of thoughtfulness, and the requisite evidence of it, are questions to be decided in view of the purposes to be served.

Literary works differ in the degree to which they are independent of their antecedent and surrounding context. The degree of self-dependence can be judged partly by the consistency of a work's import for culturally diverse readers, and partly by a comparison of its import for readers who know and who do not know the context in question.

Every work has some significant external relations, however, if only because its materials and structure bring elements of import to the literary composition: they do not, after all, acquire their entire significance from participating in the work. And some works take on a quite altered import, demonstrably closer to the author's presuppositions, when the reader considers external relations such as the antecedent tradition of literary form, imagery, or myth; the taste of the author's period; the esthetic, moral, religious, or social preconceptions and concerns of the author.

THE REASONS FOR ANALYZING LITERATURE

Analysis cannot substitute for direct experience of a work. It can, nevertheless, become a justifiable adjunct to the experience if it enriches one's understanding or enjoyment of the work—as can sometimes be done by clarifying its internal or external relationships. Even if one's own grasp of a work gains nothing from such analysis, the process or the findings of analysis may help to communicate one's appreciation to another person. Analysis is also justifiable if it contributes toward a surer basis for evaluating a work.

Beyond the purposes of grasping, teaching, and evaluating the individual work lie further purposes that are served by some forms of literary analysis. One of these, still largely within the province of literature, is to relate literary works to one another—comparing, grouping, tracing historical connections, aiming toward an articulated account of world literature.

Extending outside the literary domain is the purpose of knowing the relationships that literature may bear to the rest of a people's culture, including the other arts, and to the people's social system. Literature relates to society in three main ways: it reflects, innovates, and contributes toward stability and social control.[3] This purpose is of direct concern to literary scholars as far as the import of literary works can be enlightened by their external relationships.

A purpose which concerns us all, in our Socratic quest to know ourselves, is that of deepening our understanding of a people's way of life—our own or another—through understanding of its literature. This purpose is extraneous to a purely literary interest; yet literary scholars have reason to make sure that literature is analyzed, for this purpose as for others, by persons sensitive to a literary composition as an integral work of art.

One more purpose deserves to be listed among the major reasons for analyzing literature: that of comparing cultures, for the sake of self-knowledge and for the sake of the successful communication, between both cultures and subcultures, that is requisite for a cooperative national and international community. Parts of the comparative study of cultures lie in the domain of literary scholarship, notably comparative literature, comparative criticism, and the synthesis of literary history called world literature. These parts of the total enterprise are in some measure interdependent with the parts belonging to the rest of the humanities and to the behavioral and policy sciences.

PRAGMATIC CONSEQUENCES OF THE REASONS FOR ANALYZING

In order to serve any of the purposes just listed, the analysis of literature must elucidate the import of a work, including primarily the contributions thereto which are found in its symbolic structure and materials, but also including any important contributions found in the work's literary or its sociocultural context. Where the purposes to be served require descriptive knowledge of the synchronic variations and historical changes in what a work has meant for different groups of readers, the task of analysis includes defining and comparing the import perceived by the several readerships. This task is imposed independently by several more general purposes: to understand the mode of existence of works of art, to understand the relation between the arts and the rest of a people's life, and to understand a life style through its cultural and societal manifestations.

The literary context that may be relevant is likely to be extensive. In the case of works dating from past periods, the import for a reader at a subsequent moment may well involve not only antecedent traditions and movements, but those of intervening times. The literary context is the more extensive because the potentially relevant background includes not only written but oral composition, and the partially oral types such as *Aucassin et Nicolette* or the *commedia dell' arte*. Furthermore, while language is a symbolism separate from the symbolisms of the other arts and of social behavior, the history of literature overlaps with the histories of the visual arts and of music, by reason of shared import, mutual influences, and such composite art forms as Richard Wagner's *vereinigtes Kunstwerk*.

To trace the relationships between a literary work and its vast literary and artistic context requires some historically (or at least topically) organized conceptualization of world literature, a phenomenon that is *sui generis* yet not wholly self-dependent.

If the concept of historical movements is used in visualizing the history of literature, each movement must be defined inductively by enumerating the norms which a group of works are found to have in common. These norms regulate a work's structure, its subject matter, and style of language, and they influence the moods, sentiments, and attitudes it evokes. They are seldom explicitly stated in the work. Often they are unconscious values or presuppositions rather than rules consciously followed. But whether explicit or implicit in the work of art, the norms are a part of its import, which varies with the reader's perception.

A thorough definition of a literary movement, therefore, and of the historical continuity or contrast between movements, rests not only upon a thorough account of the symbols graphically or phonically present and verifiable in the individual artworks concerned, but also upon a thorough account of the import of each work, as perceived by the historian himself or by a readership he selects as valid for his purpose.

If instead of organizing literary history into movements one chooses the generation as the primary grouping,[4] or if one prefers to group literary works according to shared sets of themes,[5] the import of each work remains essential to these forms of generalization.

The other main context of the literary work, as important in its way as the context of world literature and art, is the sociocultural moment in which it has been gestated and produced. If the reader is of a different period, then the sociocultural context at both moments becomes relevant.

To place a work in a sociocultural context requires some structuring of this vast background, which otherwise is quite unmanageable. While no one of the alternative conceptual schemes need be postulated as an essential premise for literary analysis, it is suggested that the most serviceable at present, and the one with the most promise of future development, is the scheme proposed by the sociologist Talcott Parsons, which distinguishes a cultural subsystem (a people's values, assumptions, empirical knowledge, art forms, language, paralanguage, and kinesics) and a societal subsystem (the people's social institutions and other conventionalities governing interpersonal and intergroup relations).

As far as originality is valued, as it has been by Occidental critics since the Renaissance, the evaluation of a work requires distinguishing between the original, personal contributions of the author and the "interpersonal" elements shared by the work with antecedent creations. Originality must be assessed both in the symbolizing devices of the work and in its import, which may imitate import previously expressed either in literature or in another symbolism, notably a nonverbal art or some form of social behavior. The originality of a work cannot be fully assessed, therefore, without an account of its import expressed in terms that permit comparison with the import communicated through the other symbolisms.

The task of literary analysis consequently cannot be fulfilled by desultory insights into the work of art. While this may suffice for enjoying and teaching literature, an integral description of the work's import, in terms to permit comparison with nonliterary import as well as with other works of literature, proves necessary for evaluating originality and for the further purposes of analysis whose pragmatic implications we have explored.

The purpose of developing a national community of subcultures and an international community of cultural nationalisms calls for deliberate study of cultural themes and their evolving interrelations, as the themes are manifested in literature and otherwise. Richard McKeon summed up as follows the contructive possibility of mutual understanding and a cooperative advance of cultures:

> The invention and discovery of new hypotheses and principles, when they are not purely fortuitous, arise out of new variants of themes and new applications of techniques; and communication, when it is more than the elaboration of shared beliefs and postulates that unite communities, sects, and schools, depends on the discovery of the common themes to which particular doctrines give different concretion, the common values to which different communities give different expression, and the common techniques to which different methods give different principles, employments, and systems.[6]

THE METHOD OF THEMAL ANALYSIS

One method of elucidating the import of a literary work, and the method which best facilitates comparison with the import of symbolisms outside literature, is a certain approach designed to describe the work's essential import as a set of interrelated themes.

We shall first define the concept of a theme that best serves this purpose, then describe the method of inferring the themes of a work and, lastly, assess the limitations of this approach.

Since the purposes behind the themal analysis of literature are to elucidate the import of a work and to permit comparison with other import, the kind of theme to be sought is first of all a kind of import: it is not itself a symbol, even though it can never be expressed or referred to except in some symbolic form. The form does not have to be literary. The same import may be embodied in other symbolisms and, potentially, pervade a whole culture. Let us call the themes we seek "cultural" themes, in contradistinction to literary themes and to private themes. The analyst goes beyond the "literary theme" of Prometheus or Lucifer, which is part of a work's symbolism, to define the specific form of rebellion, of revolt, which belongs to the import symbolized.[7] At the same time, the analyst goes beyond such private preoccupations as those which Jean-Paul Weber has so well analyzed[8]—Gogol's obsession with noses, Mallarmé's with the pool he fell into as a child, Poe's recurrent symbol of the clock. These "themes," too, are symbols rather than referents, and their private import for the author acquires public, cultural importance only in the measure that it becomes significant for readers of literature.

We can restrict the kind of import that is to be called cultural theme. It centers around a value (that is, an imperative, a directive) as perceived by the author or reader or both. It is this element in a theme that makes it a concern more intensely felt than the dispassionate statement of a supposed fact or of a procedure that one could follow if one cared to. A theme carries the implication that its factual element ought to be acted upon; or if it involves the concept of a method, that this method ought to be followed.

A theme has a larger scope than a value, however. It includes whatever underlying assumptions of fact, pragmatic consequences, and relations to delimiting or supporting values, have a direct bearing on the value at the core of the theme to be defined.

A themal description of a work of art will thus bring to the foreground the focal concerns in the reader's perception of the author's intent: and it will also comprise, as a supporting middle ground, whatever bears directly on the defining of the focal themes. The same holds true for a themal description of a whole culture, so that any comparison built upon such descriptions will focus on the essential import of the entities compared.

The concept of a theme requires one more point to be clarified concerning its component materials: the relation of themes to the norms referred to previously: the norms used by René Wellek and Austin Warren, in the twelfth chapter of their *Theory of Literature*,[9] to illumine "The Mode of Existence of a Literary Work of Art," and used further by Professor Wellek as the basis for defining "Symbolism as an International Movement"[10] and other movements in the history of literature. The norms implicit in a work are essential to its import, and in fact are inseparable from the author's conscious or unconscious choice of structure, ideas, feelings, language, and relationship to the reader—the choice, for example, between the Romantic appeal to sympathetic emotion and the *Verfremdungseffekt* sought by Brecht, Camus, or Valle-Inclán. These norms are bound to be at least subordinate parts of themes (which we shall call subthemes), and they are occasionally prominent enough in a work to demand a place among its main themes.

The statement of a theme must take the form of a subject with predicate; and in many cases it should indicate a range of variation rather than an absolute. A theme has to be formulated as a subject and predicate because a topic alone is too indeterminate to satisfy the purposes that generate the need for literary analysis. It is to be expected that the predicate of each theme will be modified by other themes in the work.

In imaginative literature, some of the themes are not reducible to literal statement. Indeed, in the Western view which esteems originality, the arts are at their greatest when their "presentational symbolism" (as contrasted by Suzanne Langer with "literal discourse") expresses in the "mythical state" (Ernst Cassirer) an *aperçu*, a feeling, an orientation, at the growing edge of a civilization, which only later may be reduced by philosophy or science to the form of a literal proposition. When a theme of a work cannot be expressed literally, the analyst must respect the fact and refer to the theme in nonliteral terms, notably those of the work itself, or those of another presentational symbolism.

A theme or subtheme requires a "modal" statement—formulation as a range of variation along some continuum—when the predication about the subject is found to vary. This often happens. For the import of a complex work of art even as perceived by a single reader is often a summation of varying emphases that the reader has felt at different times.

A themal analysis of a literary work may best begin with two procedures carried forward together, the one independent and the other, derivative.

The independent procedure is to identify the theme expressions perceived by the reader in question. Let us suppose, in this exposition of the method, that the reader is the analyst himself, using this method to complete and synthesize his own perception of the work's import. In this case, at least, the analyst will be able to pick out the theme expressions in the light of his reading of the whole work. But in any case the perceived evidences of themes will include more than the verbal expressions in the text. The norms of structure and style will be more or less implicit. The form of a sonnet may be immediately self-evidencing to an observant reader who has never heard of

sonnets, while the form of a short story, with its economy of structure, may be less manifest, and the canons of the longer forms of
prose narrative may be hidden except to painstaking research. When
such formal canons are perceived by the reader, prompted or un-
prompted by knowledge extraneous to the text, they become a part
of the work's import for him. And this holds true for any other
esthetic or cognitive or moral implications inherent in the work as
he perceives it.

The derivative procedure is to indicate tentatively the one or more
subthemes—elements of potential themes—that each theme expression or other evidence is inferred to symbolize or to substantiate. A
convenient technique is to copy each theme expression on a library
card, with space at the top for pencil headings. One should note in
this first stage the relationships perceived between the subtheme one
is recording and any other subthemes, particularly in the immediate
context of the evidence recorded.

The second step is to group the theme expressions, putting like
with like according to the conjectured subthemes and not according
to the expressions. For if one groups like symbols together, as Archer
Taylor has done in his collection of riddles, and Stith Thompson in
his *Motif-Index of Folk Literature: A Classification of Narrative Elements*[11] one is headed in a wrong direction for our purpose, which is
to synthesize the import behind the symbols. This was demonstrated
by the unsuccessful effort of several distinguished Hispanists, writing in the *Bulletin of the Comediantes* between 1953 and 1959,[12] to
formulate the themes of certain Golden Age plays: the inquiry advanced toward the grouping of plots, subplots, and other symbolizing
devices, but among these it scattered the *disiecta membra* of the
themes symbolized.

Grouping together the expressions of like subthemes produces two
results that lead to the synthesis of main themes.

Some of the subthemes will be perceived as virtually identical. In
such a case the theme expressions confirm one another, and the number of reaffirmations constitutes one evidence of the relative importance to be ascribed to the subthemes. Mere counting of instances
does not alone indicate the relative importance; the analyst must be
sensitive to other evidence such as intensity of expressed feeling, and
the place of the instances, or the status of the characters speaking,
within the structure of the work.

The indispensability of an analyst sensitive to literature is evident
when a poem is studied whose import suggests no discursive mean-

ing. Other imaginative literature, however, may deceive a positivistic historian into thinking that he can excerpt passages and give them literal meaning independent of their context. If one snips out the raisonneur's speeches from Molière's *Le Misanthrope* (1666), one wrongly infers that the theme of *la mesure* in the play is a classical "neither-nor" kind of moderation; but the structure of the play contrasts this static position with an appreciative attitude toward Alceste, and thus gives a quite different predicate to the theme: the Romantic "both-and" sort of moderation, which was not reduced to literal statement until a later generation, perhaps first in Diderot's *Pensées philosophiques* (1746).[13]

The other result of grouping the like subthemes is that some of the groups, though distinctly differing in import, will be so closely related as to form a single theme. Other relationships—of antagonism or of near-irrelevance, unstable relationships, and ambiguous ones—indicate separate themes.

It is sometimes hard to decide whether a given perception of a work is more faithfully represented by treating a thematic component as a single theme or as two or more, particularly when the component embodies conflicting forces. The first criterion to apply is the evidence in the text itself: Is conflict the theme topic, that is, the value or disvalue, or is the emphasis rather on defining the forces that conflict?

If the text leaves the answer ambivalent, then it is the more useful solution to regard the conflicting forces as the themes and treat their interaction as a second level of descriptive statement. This choice facilitates comparison between the themes of the artwork and those of the culture as a whole. For on this larger scale, where the "universe" of theme expressions is infinite and the import is not simplified by artistic selection, the multilateral relations among the culture's values become so complex that they would become unmanageable unless the entities handled as themes were as homogeneous as possible. The conflicts, anomalies, and discontinuities in the culture can be best described as relations between themes. Charles Morris[14] showed the possibility of calculating the relative degrees of compatibility or conflict between the values in a value system. He constructed a billiard-ball model to express these relationships on a spatial analogy, as relative distances between the values.

In the themal study of a literary work the final stage of synthesis is to describe the relationships among the main themes of the work, if a plurality of themes has been found.

Some works of art may indeed have only one theme, but most can be better represented by a structure of themes, interacting, and in longer works of art, producing a series of configurations. The themes are relatively stable variables, even though some of them evolve; their interrelations are less stable variables.

Leo Spitzer's expectation that a work would be reducible to a single "spiritual etymon" was abundantly fruitful, one must recognize. So likewise was Ruth Benedict's expectation that a whole culture could be explained as Apollonian or as Dyonisiac.

But in anthropology Morris Opler has since achieved a higher fidelity by replacing these Nietzschean terms with a more complex description, discerning a dozen or so main themes whose precise substance and interaction are peculiar to the culture described. Similarly in literary analysis, Eugene Falk has achieved a higher fidelity by distinguishing a plurality of themes in a novel and tracing their successive encounters in the course of the work.

As a demonstration of sound inquiry into the relationships among the themes of a literary work, one could wish it were possible to quote the whole of Professor Falk's *Types of Thematic Structure: The Nature and Function of Motifs in Gide, Camus, and Sartre*[15]— including the substantial "Introduction" by Bernard Weinberg, who contrasts the "centrifugal" sort of thematism, leading away from the text to extraneous concerns, with the "centripetal" kind exemplified by this book, which leads toward the import of the work analyzed.

Professor Falk finds several distinct types of structure—distinct ways of juxtaposing theme expressions to make themes interact—which contribute to the unique import of the works he has chosen as examples of the structural types: *La Symphonie pastorale, L'Étranger, La Nausée* and likewise Michel Butor's "nouveau roman" *L'Emploi du temps*, analyzed in a later study not yet published. That study has been written for an eventual volume I am preparing which will compare diverse approaches to the themes of several French authors, including essays by the authors on the themes of their life work.

THEME STUDY IN PERSPECTIVE

The serious limitations of the themal approach to literature are those caused by the nature of literature itself and consequently shared by all forms of literary study.

The identifying of the evidence of subthemes and the synthesizing of themes are subjective processes; but unless one authoritative reader is postulated, no method whatever can establish the authorized version of a work's import. If on the other hand the problem for the analyst is to determine what import is in fact perceived by a given reader, then the factual conclusion he reaches can be checked by other analyses using this method or other methods, and a systematic method such as this one has the best chance of alerting the analyst to evidence he might be prone to overlook.

The framework of hunting for themes constitutes a reductive scheme; but so does the personal fancy of the most fancy-free interpreter of a poem. And for the purpose of completing the analyst's own perception of a work, the themal approach seeks such a wide range of evidence that it is free to exchange *aperçus* with any other method, from the most impressionistic to the reductive schemes that prescribe categories to be observed. An example of the latter is the fruitful scheme of seven continua developed by Will T. Jones.[16]

The themal method does not eliminate the human element of judgment; but the same is true of all other methods as far as they involve deciding what factual questions to ask, or what use to make of the answers obtained. In establishing the facts to be assessed, this method can draw upon verifiable results produced by more scientific methods: Robert Escarpit's revealing studies of the readership of literary works; Alphonse Juilland's inventory of theme expressions in the series he is editing, *Dictionnaire des idées dans l'oeuvre de . . .*, which is to include volumes on Simone de Beauvoir, André Malraux, Proust, and others; Roman Ingarden's phenomenological inventory form for classifying theme expressions observable in the sounds of a text, its units of meaning, and the objects represented.[17]

The limitations one would expect to find peculiar to theme analysis prove to be largely or entirely surmountable. It is not confined to peripheral features but can center upon a work's import. It does not have to impose an analyst's terminology and categories, but can let the work speak for itself with no distortion except the inevitable contribution of a given reader.

The unique advantage of this approach to literature is that it produces results admitting of close comparison with import expressed in the other arts and in social behavior, at the same time that it seeks a comprehensive description of both the arts and the culture as a whole, each in its own terms as far as that is possible.

There is no quarrel with those who object to hunting in literary texts for documentation on social reality—the position well argued by Michel Beaujour and Jacques Ehrmann.[18] For the comparing of independent bodies of import does not entail deducing the one from the other. Apart from this issue, something *can* be learned from literature about the surrounding society. A dissertation being written by Marie Pierre Koban, comparing the image of French youth in novels and in sociological inquiries of the latter 1950's and early 1960's, finds a theme of violent revolt in the novels, though the opinion polls asked no questions on the subject and therefore shed less light on the social behavior that was to break out in 1968.

The limitations of the themal approach to a whole society, somewhat different, are also surmountable. This topic is elaborated in an eventually forthcoming handbook on "Understanding Complex Cultures." In sum, the "subjectivity of the analysts" can be overcome through replication by other observers, particularly if the separate teams of analysts are drawn from different combinations of cultures, always including representatives of the culture studied. The "danger of circularity" can be avoided if a second team of observers takes a separate sampling of theme expressions. The "limitation that themal analysis is not quantitative" can be offset by building upon quantitative data wherever these are possible. The objection that "themal description takes no account of deviant behavior" can be obviated by modal generalizations: theme predicates expressing a range of variation. And the objection that "a thematic synthesis yields only logical relationships" (of compatibility or antagonism), and not structural-functional relations, can probably be met by centering each theme around a directive element, so that the themes constitute the value system of the culture. If the relationships in that system turn out on other evidence to be functional, or causal, we can utilize this knowledge without contradicting the essential insight of the themal approach: namely, the discovery of common referents that recur in diverse symbols and situations.

Applied to a life style as a whole, the method of themal analysis and synthesis is one among half a dozen approaches. The others include free, unsystematic intuition; the inventory of ready-made categories; the structural-functional model (some decades in the future); history (tracing cause and effect); and contrastive analysis. The synthesis of main themes can draw upon all these others. It is the one that holds the best promise of an integral understanding, in the culture's own terms, within the twentieth century—though there are rigorous-minded anthropologists who demand a more scientific description.

Applied to literature, this method will take its place somewhere among the large number of approaches, all potentially useful to one another: approaches to literary import, symbols, and ancillary phenomena; approaches from the humane disciplines and the social and behavioral sciences; approaches through free intuition and through methodical approaches that range from personal formulas to the several kinds of content analysis (contextual, qualitative, and quantitative).

Probably every study of literature, as far as it deals with the import of a work, seeks to identify what a given reader finds most important in the work and so is likely to make explicit one or more main themes. The method presented here is distinct in that it organizes the evidence for such themes and the method of inferring them.

So careful an approach to artistic import has rarely seemed worth the trouble until now. Literary history has pushed its development of precision more in the direction of symbols and external matters; criticism has typically sought the single interpretation or evaluation that seemed self-evident to the critic's intuition. At present, however, there emerges a pattern of reasons for exploiting the "centripetal" kind of theme study that seeks the essential import of a work of art.

Literary theory has shown convincingly, in the generation of René Wellek and Austin Warren, that the changing import of a work, involving changing norms perceived in it, is basic to its "mode of existence"; yet the question of precisely what this means, and how to handle the evolving referent of the symbols, is left for another generation. It is clear at least that henceforth the critical history of literature must deal somehow with the relativity of a work to its diverse and successive readerships. And the range of variation in the work's import becomes the more significant as social and cultural evolution accelerates, as authors strive to convey strange, new import, and as the critical traditions of East and West confront one another with their discrepant interpretations and evaluations.

Meanwhile, the "new criticism's" concentration on the literary work as a self-contained structure has led to a fresh interest in combining the gains of that movement with the realization that the work of art has significant external relations as well. As Walter Sutton of Syracuse University has put it, the concept of an organic whole carries with it that of an ecology: an interaction between the organic whole and an environment, from a prenatal stage to the entity's last discernible influence.

The relativity of a work's import to its readers during its life cycle, together with the dependence of literary history and the partial dependence of cultural history on the definition of that import, may be expected to occasion increased themal study of literature. Now is the time to examine the assumptions of such study and to inquire how it may be conducted so that its fruits will have the broadest use and the most lasting value.

Notes

1. See M. Opler, "The Themal Approach in Cultural Anthropology and its Application to North Indian Data," and appended bibliography *Southwestern Journal of Anthropology,* Vol. 24 (1968), pp. 215–27.
2. N. Chomsky, in *Language,* Vol. 35 (1959), pp. 26–58.
3. See M. C. Albrecht, "The Relationship of Literature and Society," *American Journal of Sociology,* Vol. 59 (1954), pp. 425–36. See also H. L. Nostrand, "Literature in the Describing of a Literate Culture," *French Review,* Vol. 37 (1963), pp. 145–57.
4. See J. A. Portuondo, *La Historia y las Generaciones* (Santiago de Cuba, 1958).
5. R. M. Albérès (pseud. of René Marill) suggestively divides the first half of the twentieth century into three periods, 1900–1914, 1914–1933, and 1933–1950, each with six or eight main themes. See for example his *L'Aventure intellectuelle du XXᵉ siècle, 1900–1950.* (Paris, 1950).
6. R. McKeon, *Thought, Action, and Passion* (Chicago, 1954), p. 12.
7. Diversity of nomenclatures adds to our difficulty of mutual understanding. Raymond Trousson recommends speaking of the *thème* of Prometheus and the *motif* of revolt, in his *Un Problème de littérature comparée: les études de thèmes; essai de méthodologie* (Paris, 1965), pp. 12–13.
8. J.-P. Weber, *Domaines thématiques* (Paris, 1963).
9. R. Wellek and A. Warren, *Theory of Literature* (New York, 1942), 3rd ed., 1956.
10. Belgrade meeting of the International Comparative Literature Association. 1967.
11. S. Thompson, *Motif-Index of Folk-Literature* (rev. ed.; Bloomington, 1955–1958).
12. Articles beginning with Vol. 5 (1, Spring 1953), pp. 17–23, and ending with Vol. 11 (1, Spring 1959), pp. 1–6.
13. This example has been developed in H. L. Nostrand, "On the Role of literary Historians in the History of Ideas," *History of Ideas Newsletter,* Vol. 2 (1956), pp. 54–58.
14. C. Morris, *Varieties of Human Value* (Chicago, 1956).
15. E. Falk, *Types of Thematic Structure* (Chicago, 1967).
16. W. T. Jones, *The Romantic Syndrome* (The Hague, 1961).
17. R. Ingarden, *Das literarische Kunstwerk* (Halle, 1931).
18. M. Beaujour and J. Ehrmann, *La France contemporaine: Choix de textes culturels* (New York, 1965).

Emil Staiger

THE QUESTIONABLE NATURE
OF VALUE PROBLEMS

EVERY GENUINE WRITER, AND EVERY READER ENDOWED WITH SOME sense of artistic quality, will react to the problem of literary evaluation with intense suspicion. The lover of literature in him will protest before he knows what he is protesting about. He considers it superfluous—indeed, humiliating—to have to justify his love, his admiration. Does love ever ask for reasons? Has any lover ever been dissuaded of the beauty of his beloved by scientific theories? What concern of his—in the encounter of his spirit with a great work of art, in that most tranquil, most concentrated, most intimate solitude of all—is a theoretical disquisition that is supposed to be acknowledged by all and binding upon all? The very idea is distasteful to him. He rebels against the artificial separation of the observed and the observer, against any attempt to remove what is beautiful—or, in more general terms, artistically perfect—into an objective, "disinterested" sphere, and such concepts as value and evaluation are a most disagreeable reminder of banks and stock markets. And he is not far wrong, either. For the purpose does seem to be a counting, accounting, and crediting to account, as well as an attempt to deal arbitrarily with artistic qualities, to manipulate them, and ultimately perhaps even to produce them mechanically.

Nevertheless, if we put the question broadly, if all we want to know is what we note when we read and interpret, what decides us to state with conviction: this is a thoroughly satisfying work, that is a doubtful, unsatisfying work—then the lover of literature within us (whom no literary historian or aesthetician can deny if he wishes to retain his vitality) will have no serious objection. The following remarks are an attempt to reply to a question framed thus broadly, a purely provisional reply that consists merely of general indications and is intended as no more than a sketch.

At first sight it would appear that *unison* forms the basis for the value of an artistic literary work. By this we mean all those things brought to the surface by an artistically adequate interpretation: that is, that everything we note in a text is governed throughout by *one* spirit, *one* rhythm, *one* spiritual gravitation.[1] In a novella of Kleist's, for example, the daring hypotaxis matches the pitiless, indeed, fatal, consistency of thought, the monstrous motifs with which life is put to a test it fails to pass, the abrupt yet uncommonly sharp visualizations of the things which testify to the author's most passionate involvement as well as to the recognition that man is not permitted a true confrontation with the fullness of existence. Again, in a poem by Brentano, the renouncing of clear contours, the delight in colors and shimmering lights, in the magic of intangible atmosphere, match the soft diction that luxuriates in sonorous vowels, the unhampered flow of the short, lucid sentences, the overriding power of the mood, the romantic self-forfeiture which is perceived as an inexorable destiny.

This harmonizing of the diverse aspects of an artistic literary work is what we call style, and we find ourselves confirmed in this by the numerous attempts, both early and recent, to grasp the nature of the beautiful. Let us take just a few examples. Plotinus declares: $\kappa \acute{a} \lambda \lambda o s$, $\H{o} \tau a \nu \ \dot{\eta} \ \tau o \hat{v} \ \dot{\epsilon} \nu \dot{o} s \ \tau \grave{a} \ \mu \acute{o} \rho \iota a \ \kappa a \tau \acute{a} \sigma \chi \eta \ \varphi \acute{v} \sigma \iota s$.[2] ("We speak of beauty when the nature of the One binds [governs or permeates] the parts.") And elsewhere: $\H{A} \mu \epsilon \rho \epsilon s \ \mathring{o} \nu \ \dot{\epsilon} \nu \ \pi o \lambda \lambda o \hat{\iota} s \ \varphi a \nu \tau a \zeta \acute{o} \mu \epsilon \nu o \nu$.[3] ("That which is indivisible made manifest in the Many.") Thomas Aquinas cites among various characteristics of beauty that of "*consonantia.*"[4] Crousaz, in his *Traité du beau*, written in 1715, defines beauty as a "*variété réduite à quelque unité.*"[5] Goethe speaks of "permanence within change,"[6] and sometimes of a "law that is made manifest,"[7] which in turn means that the One is revealed in the Many. Schiller's "freedom in manifestation"[8] and Hegel's "sensuous shining forth of the idea"[9] mean much the same thing.

Needless to say, all these interpretations are determined by *Weltanschauung*; that is, they must be detached from their context and integrated before we can make use of them. But they should signify no more to us than pointers to a very remarkable fact: namely, that under the most varied presuppositions beauty is continually con-

ceived as an interplay of the One and the Many, whether the "one"
be taken to mean God, idea, law, or whatever. And it is precisely
this interplay of the Many and the One which, as style, as unison,
appears to decide—or to be instrumental in deciding—the aesthetic
quality of an artistic literary work.

Yet is this really the case everywhere and categorically? We know
of very many masterpieces that satisfy this demand in every sense.
We need only think of Virgil's *Aeneid*, Dante's *Divine Comedy*,
Racine's tragedies, some of Ibsen's later plays, not forgetting the
great novels of Flaubert, or a work like Stifter's *Nachsomer* to recognize what it means to sustain one note for such prolonged periods.
Nor need we exclude Shakespeare's tragedies and comedies, with
their alternating verse and prose, high tones and low. Here the
greatest contrasts are reconciled and resolved in a unity, albeit an
enigmatic unity.

But what of Goethe's *Faust*? There is no denying that in the first
scenes the tone changes without the change being justified by the
subject. The monologue in *"Wald und Höhle"* bears the stamp of a
spirit that has scarcely anything to do with the Faust of the Gretchen
tragedy. We might, of course, say that everything ultimately resides
in the unique personality of Goethe. But this does not refute the
claim that some parts of *Faust* are stylistically as far apart as, say,
Torquato Tasso is from *Götz von Berlichingen* or from the Fastnacht
plays. The fault for this change in style, often deplored by Goethe
himself,[10] lies not with any artistic consideration but with the history
of the work's creation. It was more than sixty years before the work,
although still not complete, was at least concluded. During this time
the poet underwent constant change, and no effort of mind or will
enabled him to return to an earlier stage, even when now and again
he made the attempt and sometimes expressed his belief that he
had succeeded.[11]

But what is true of *Faust* applies more or less to all Goethe's major
works. *Wilhelm Meister* also lacks stylistic unison. Even in *Hermann
und Dorothea* we notice a transition from the first songs, still remi-
niscent of Voss, to the "noble simplicity and quiet grandeur" of the
second half. And it can sometimes happen that even a poem of a few
verses switches to a different tone, as, for instance, in the *"Mailied,"*
rightly considered one of the most glorious documents of the Sesen-
heim breakthrough, although at the end, with the "new songs and
dances," it lapses into Anacreonism.[12]

So we see that if unison alone is to substantiate the aesthetic stature of an artistic literary work, Goethe, the greatest of all German writers, makes a poor showing, and precisely because he is the most flexible, the most faithful to the spirit of life, the most mutable. One may content oneself—and quite properly—with the irresistible profound unison to be found in parts, both long and short, of his works, and even prefer these to the unswerving dreams of rigid consistency of other poets. Our first proposal for substantiating value appears inadequate.

But its inadequacy is demonstrated by yet another consideration. For we cannot dispute the fact that there is also a unison which, artistically speaking, is wholly irrelevant, the sustained convention, an impersonal style prescribed by public taste and perhaps even by books of rules. Wherever belief in a "critical literary art" is widespread, this danger is bound to exist. Many writers of the Enlightenment, for example, succumbed to it. Countless epigrams and ditties of the eighteenth century, numerous plays that followed the principles of Gottsched, are as alike in style as two peas, and according to the artistic concepts of our own day, devoid of artistic value. Even the cheapest popular novels may have stylistic unison yet evoke no aesthetic satisfaction in us. From this it follows that the only works which we acknowledge as works of art are apparently those which have an *individual character*, which testify to an unmistakable personality, and which are in some way unique.

It would be difficult, we must admit, to produce evidence for this thesis from earlier eras. Right up until modern times it has been true to say that it was taken for granted, theoretically at least, that a work of art must correspond to a norm and could only be judged in terms of the fulfillment of a norm. That this was not enough, however, was recognized by Madame de Longueville as long ago as 1656 when she remarked, after listening to a recitation of Chapelain's epic *La Pucelle: "Oui, cela est parfaitement beau, mais il me fait bâiller."*[13]

In Germany the youth of 1770 vociferously demanded originality, and in the 1790's Friedrich Schlegel used the concept "interesting" to substantiate the postulate that defines modern criticism: namely, that an artistic literary work can never be original enough, and that it is to be valued primarily as an expression of an individuality.[14]

A historical mind feels compelled to rebel against this and to remark that by this standard it would be impossible to do justice to the classics, the Middle Ages, and even early modern times. But such a mind would surely have to admit that it is the pulse of a towering individual that distinguishes, say, the core of the *Iliad* from the stereo-typed cyclic epic, that—to say nothing of the lyricists—even the Attic tragic poets stand out as individuals, and that we value the authors and poets of the German baroque (despite their earnest endeavors to do justice to a poetic canon and to compose in the style of Opitz) not least for their individuality. We need only compare, for instance, Opitz himself with Fleming or Dach.

But we have no intention of saying: The more individual the bet-ter! In the writing of artistic literary works as such there are limits to individual expression. The first is one of literary species. By "species" I do not in this case mean the "lyrical," "epic," or "dra-matic," as in my *Grundbegriffe der Poetik*;[15] neither do I mean lyrical poetry, epic poetry, or drama in the traditional sense. We would first have to engage in lengthy discussions as to what a drama, a lyric poem, a novel, an epic, actually is, and what reasonable demands may be made of each of these species. I am taking the concepts as simply, practically, and concretely as possible: hence by "lyric poetry" I mean short texts in verse, by "epic" a long text in verse, by "novel" a long text in prose, and by "drama" stage plays in any form they care to take.[16] Superficial and oversimplified though this may be, it is perfectly adequate for our purposes, sufficing as it does for the realization that not every species permits an individual to get every-thing off his chest. In lyric poetry, for example, I cannot embark on the sort of descriptions that come naturally to the epic. A poem is much too restricted in scope for them to be effective. Magical evoca-tion of mood or symbolic profundity are essential if the visible world is to acquire artistic significance in a few lines. Gottfried Keller often offended against this principle in his lyrics. In an epic, on the other hand, an underlying tone of drama or a constant emotional intensity is out of place. In the long run, the strain becomes too much for us—something that every reader, his admiration notwithstanding, has experienced with Klopstock's *Messias*. In plays, nothing is permis-sible that fails to project beyond the footlights—in other words, what-ever is too tender or too intimate, hidden allusions, and the kind of nuances detectable only by the most attentive reader. Where such things do find their way into an otherwise theatrically sound play, we accept them as homage to a few connoisseurs as, for example, those ineffably delicate intimations of spiritual depths which Hofmannsthal assigned to the simple, almost primitive comedy outline of *Der Rosenkavalier*. But when a drama consists entirely of such im-ponderables, love's labor is indeed lost. Its creator would have done better to write poems or novels.

We see, then, that a literary work must be *faithful to its species* if we are to accord it the highest rank. I say the highest, for now and again we find ourselves happy to make certain allowances when an author presents us with an abundance of beauty in an inappropriate vessel. Confronted by Goethe's *Torquato Tasso*, dramaturgical criticism falls silent. We would not care to be deprived of the lyrical effusions in Keats' *Endymion*. But however that may be: offenses against the scope of a species are always regrettable. For the time being, therefore, we will add this criterion to our list.

Yet we soon notice that it ought by rights to be conceived in still more general terms. Literary art is a linguistic art. It follows that it should also be *faithful linguistically*. It would not have occurred to anyone, even a few hundred years ago, to mention this specifically, but our modern linguistic skepticism forces the problem upon us in all its significance. Let me elaborate a little.

We see how during the last century the traditional dramatic form began to be questioned. Psychology was delving so deep that it became increasingly difficult to believe that a person could be represented by his visible and audible aspects. Yet theater depends on the visible and the audible. So playwrights saw themselves required to develop an art of the enigmatic, the unspoken, which still had to be intelligible to the audience. We have only to think of Ibsen, who became an almost unrivaled master of this method. O'Neill, in *Strange Interlude*, uses the device of a kind of ventriloquism intended to convey to the listener what the figures are concealing from others or even from themselves. We cannot help but admire the resources used by the modern playwright to convey the virtually inexpressible things he has in mind, but these resources do not gloss over the fact that the novel would be more suitable for such purposes. The novelist is not limited to a period of a few hours. He can extend himself as far as he likes; he can try to show off his subtle, almost endlessly ramified knowledge of human nature in psychological excursions or minutely depicted processes of consciousness. But even the novel appears to have already reached a borderline, a *ne plus ultra*, marked by such works as *Ulysses* or, still more, *Finnigans Wake*. The necessarily conceptual, that is general, nature of language must employ the most cunning artifices to meet the demands of the subjectivity it is intended to fathom. Is lyric poetry perhaps spared the stresses and pressures of our own time? Even most lyric poets no longer believe that the deepest personal thoughts and experiences can be communicated in a language that is used by and intelligible to many people. The very sentences that are formed by anyone are the ones least suited to express "my" existence, "my" unique inner self. But this implies that the moment I try to communicate "me"—taking the word in its strictest sense—I am no longer capable of any communication.

> Spricht *die Seele, so spricht, ach! schon die* Seele *nicht mehr.*
> ("When the soul *speaks*, oh then! the *soul* no longer speaks.")

Schiller did not act on this insight in his poetic practice, limiting himself instead to the communicable. Today the attempt is being made to meet this need with that hermetism which has brought to outright despair many a reader who is genuinely anxious to understand. In other words: the creator of literary works of art explores beyond the scope of language and expects it to accomplish what it never has accomplished and never can accomplish: the sheerly "individual word." The art of writing is canceling itself out—although from the loftiest motives. The result is the loneliness of the indecipherable and ultimately the blank sheet of paper which, because it never commits itself, leaves the floating, the unresolved, open. We have moved as far as we can from that Roman genre which Goethe called an "impaling"[17] and which he deplored as an ousting of life through the power of words.

What may we conclude from this observation? That there are ways of feeling and thinking, of viewing existence, which are perfectly suitable for linguistic works of art, and others to which the nature of language runs counter and which can find expression only via a labyrinthine detour or not at all. To say the same thing in familiar terms: not all periods, and within one period not all trends, all *Weltanschauungen*, are equally capable of artistic literary expression. So it would seem feasible to look at the problem of value from this standpoint also.

In German literature around 1800, Goethe is without doubt the writer most faithful to the nature of language. His organic thinking is just as favorable to the clear, graphic present, which he delineates with a single word, as it is to the functionality of the parts, the relationships, in which the word fits into the framework of a sentence. And at the same time the element of intimacy in which we find everything submerged provides appropriate scope for the musical delights of the language. By contrast, Kleist's "Nordic severity" leads to a hypertrophy of relative pronouns: in the frequent, logical, concessive, consecutive, final conjunctions, in the prolific punctuation. Obscured by all this, the subject itself threatens sometimes almost to disappear; the language remotely approaches the extreme of a mathematical formula. In Novalis there has been found to exist a "consumption," an evaporation, of nouns which would ultimately find its logical conclusion in whispering and breathing, whereas in Hölderlin's late poems the single word gradually becomes so heavily charged that the context of the sentence threatens to go astray.[18] Today, with our sharpened sense of the soul's unfathomability and our plague of overused words, we seem to be entering on an era in which a talent transgresses most against language when the expression of its individuality achieves its maximum truthfulness. How is the critic to react? All he can do is challenge the author to be faithful linguistically and ungenuine, or be genuine and cease to speak— unless he believes him able to endow his words with such incomparable luster as to make all skepticism vanish and empower the work once again to create a new sense of community.

Community! This brings us to a final criterion. For almost two hundred years we have been so in the habit of demanding the interesting, the individual, from our writers that little by little we have almost lost sight of literature's power to create a sense of community, or else we completely miss the point of this power, as if it were a matter of using literary means to win men for certain purposes. The very purpose, the very meaning, of existence is supplied by poets who, like Dante—transcending all political frontiers—found a nation; that is, unite a people to form a new reality. This is also inherent in Herodotus' claim, doubtless scarcely exaggerated, that the Greeks received their gods as a gift from Homer and Hesiod.[19] The range of understanding in the highest and lowest zones of existence, the accentuation of "reality," what is essential or unessential, significant or trivial, the perspectives from which a people is accustomed to look at things: this is what we should regard as the achievement of those few geniuses through whose works a new era in history begins—as with the founding of a religion or a law. It need scarcely be added that any literary work of art deemed capable of this power must embrace the widest possible circle with its subjects and concern as many people as possible with its thematic material; that is, that it must have the stuff of representative greatness. But are such things relevant to aesthetic evaluation? Only the snob would dispute this. We will gladly agree with him that a poem by Gerard Manley Hopkins may be as artistically perfect as the *Aeneid*. But if he then proceeds to place Hopkins on a par with Virgil we have ceased to discuss literature with him. It is the *weight* of a work of art in the balance of history that we would also like to see acknowledged, without reference to what happens to please us most today.

Where, then, have we arrived? Entirely empirically and with no claim whatever to completeness, we have assembled certain criteria according to which the attempt is made—generally speaking and without being clearly aware of it—to define the value of a literary work: unison, individuality, loyalty to species and language, the power to create a sense of community, weight. Are we now to apportion credit to these with a points system, awarding unison, say, three points, or individuality five? I shall not go on. Every fiber rebels against all such aesthetic bookkeeping. But it must be realized that no such method is practicable, for the maximal work that would score the highest possible number of points has never existed and indeed never can exist. What do we mean by this? Such a method is impracticable if only because of the difficulty of agreeing on the ranking of the various criteria, and because, even were agreement possible, we would still have no answer to the question of how to evaluate a slight impairment of unison—in Goethe's "*Mailied*," for instance—or of how to rate some spectacular individualistic infringement of the laws of species. No one can object to a reader of our twentieth century from finding the expression of individuality more important than the power to create a sense of community, and thus from preferring a writer such as Heinrich von Kleist to Schiller. And it was just as impossible to criticize Lessing for prizing above any other quality the power to create a sense of community.

Yet this concerns us less than the impossibility of a maximum. Everyone must admit that the individual and personal traits of an artistic literary work can only be intensified at the expense of their general significance, and vice versa. Schiller was already familiar with this problem in all its breadth. He, more than almost any other German, had the will to create great poetic works of universal human significance, and he was well aware of how this required the sacrifice of individual and personal interest, something which he too was convinced forms an irreplaceable element of true poetic art. He tried to unite the opposing forces in his concept of the "interesting perfected mind."[20] But how perfection, which he regarded as fulfillment of a norm, was to coalesce with the free play of the individual element, or to what extent the individual element could have universal validity, was a problem that not even a mind like his could solve satisfactorily. For it does in fact seem impossible, even wrong, to try to retain the atmospheric charm of the individual element in a series of songs, in the thousands of lines of an epic. The magic spell appears to wonderful advantage in the few verses of a poem by Anacreon, Mörike, or Verlaine, but when extended to any length it cannot but tire even the most gifted reader. We know that Croce has drawn a stern conclusion from this by conceding even in Dante only certain passages to be "poesia," assigning all the rest to other realms as "non-poesia."[21] Besides, we have already seen how difficult it often is to reconcile the demands of language as such with the faithful rendering of individuality.

But let us for a moment suppose that an author has approached the "maximum," that he has brought the opposing forces to a point of such happy equilibrium that nothing more is left to be desired, as if, aesthetically speaking, the circle had been squared. What would be gained by this? That we say: this is a perfect work, a work which supremely satisfies all our criteria? That we miss the presence neither of the individual element nor of universal validity, that we have neither to deplore an impairment of unison nor to regret that the work does less than justice to the nature of either language or species? The mere making of such a statement would be enough to jeopardize the rank accorded it. Our highly commended masterpiece would emerge as a mandatory model. And yet a model—as the term implies—is supposed to be imitated. But imitation is not compatible with individuality, that ineffable quality which eludes even the most gifted disciple. Consequently, when we look at something which is perfectly beautiful we observe the paradox that it is simultaneously inimitable and exemplary. Should it nevertheless be imitated—slavishly, not in a true continuation of tradition—the imitations would gradually strip the model of its merit. Concealed by the imitation, what is unique and original is ultimately almost unrecognizable as such. During the past century, for instance, the most knowledgeable readers were already finding it hard to appreciate Schiller's *Wilhelm Tell*, in its incomparable, hard-won, powerful simplicity, as one of the greatest theatrical works of all ages and all peoples. Their vision was obscured by the platitudes of Laube and Wildenbruch and the host of amateur playwrights, just as our judgment of Hellenic art was affected by the bad Roman copies, not to mention the plaster casts in our archaeological institutions. Besides, imitation cannot help but be a fake because it does not stem from the secret of individual personality, or—which amounts to much the same thing—because it does not do justice to the altered historical situation and sets itself the vain task of trying to halt the wheel of time. This is what prompted Friedrich Schlegel to exclaim, in half-jesting indignation: "Heaven preserve us from eternal works!"[22] We do not join in his plea. In our opinion, "classic" works—to use the word in an unadulterated sense —are admirable in all ages and are thus also desirable. But we do admit that this desire is often unattainable, that at times it must be very earnestly suppressed. For that classic equilibrium of which we will assume for the moment that, in terms of our criterion, it approaches the maximum, can only ever evolve—if it is to be genuinely alive—from a conquest of extremes and one-sided stylistic trends. So it is necessary that the ideal in art perish continually, that fashion and taste, even barbarism, thrust aside perfection in style. For only those things that have declined and perished can celebrate a resurrection.

This process—indispensable, demanded by the nature of history— would only be disrupted by an uncompromisingly binding and recognized value system. We would then hesitate to move on from what aesthetics has claimed and demonstrated to be supreme. Future generations would approach the artistic work of the hour with a guilty conscience and without the impetus of that vital quality of blind confidence. But this is something we need not fear. Throughout history we find no doctrine that has been permanently acknowledged by all those whom it concerned. When man encounters that which does not advance him or support his self-affirmation, he tends either not to understand it or, if he does understand it, to forget it in the shortest possible order. This kind of misunderstanding or forgetting is the normal relationship between the younger and older generations. The younger generation, of course, is continually asserting that it has overcome the older one, but often it can only say this because it is unaware of the older generation's achievements. And this is what seems to apply in our aesthetic issues. I cannot find that in substantiating taste judgments we have progressed much beyond that which the best minds in England and Germany brought to the surface around 1800 and during the ensuing decades. We have alienated ourselves from them. We take exception to transient externals and idealistic systematics whose assumptions we can no longer share. But in so doing we overlook the incalculable treasures of strictly phenomenological insight contained in, say, Schiller's or Hegel's aesthetic writings. To rediscover these and appropriate them in a new, no longer idealistic spirit would mark the most promising path toward well-founded aesthetics. It is hoped that the present essay will serve as a purely provisional fragment toward such a reawakening. It is not concerned with metaphysics, in whose service the idealists placed their research in aesthetics. It integrates concepts in such a way that their use no longer requires a philosophical avowal of faith but merely corresponds to findings unemotionally perceived. On the other hand, it is not concerned with those compulsions of our time which would seem dubious, indeed objectionable, particularly—and this brings us back full circle to our introduction—that fatal urge to regard the introducing of the personal element into art, among other things, as superfluous, to transform everything into a completely neutral mathematical operation, and, instead of being touched, stirred, moved, overwhelmed by the beautiful, to cast a cold eye on a chart and determine the degree to which a literary work can be considered beautiful.

This does not mean, however, that we consider the bases for literary evaluation to be totally undiscoverable. We acknowledge the existence of aesthetic pleasure and believe that we can—within certain limits—define its foundations. But we also know that no one can be obliged to concur with the arguments advanced. As Kant has put it, with some complexity, in the *Kritik der Urteilskraft*:

> Here, now, we may perceive that nothing is postulated in the judgement of taste but such a *universal voice* in respect of delight that is not mediated by concepts; consequently, only the *possibility* of an aesthetic judgement capable of being at the same time deemed valid for every one. The judgement of taste itself does not *postulate* the agreement of every one (for it is only competent for a logically universal judgement to do this, in that it is able to bring forward reasons); it only *imputes* this agreement to every one, as an instance of the rule in respect of which it looks for confirmation, not from concepts, but from the concurrence of others.[23]

The decision made here to evaluate a work of art artistically—in the strict sense of the word—rather than politically or morally or religiously—is, of course, in itself contestable and has already been often enough contested, from Xenophanes and Plato down to the leading theoreticians of Marxist literary scholarship. We are not, then, relieved of the responsibility which all who pass judgment must assume. It seems necessary to state this emphatically in an age which tends increasingly to believe that the main object of the sciences is to discharge human beings of their personal burdens.

[*Translated from the German by Leila Vennewitz*]

Notes

1. For the concept of unison and the possibility of demonstrating it in a work of art, cf. E. Staiger, *Die Kunst der Interpretation* (Zürich, 1955), p. 14 ff.
2. Plotinus, Vol. VI, 9, 1, 15.
3. Plotinus, Vol. I, 6, 3, 9.
4. Aquinas, *Summa Theologiae*, Vol. II, p. 145.
5. As quoted by A. Bäumler, *Kants Kritik der Urteilskraft* (Halle, 1922), p. 43.
6. "Dauer im Wechsel," the title of the poem, whose last verse gives us a definition of the beautiful:

> *Lass den Anfang mit dem Ende*
> *Sich in Eins zusammenziehn!*
> *Schneller als die Gegenstände*
> *Selber dich vorüberfliehn.*
> *Danke, dass die Gunst der Musen*
> *Unvergängliches verheisst,*
> *Den Gehalt in deinem Busen*
> *Und die Form in deinem Geist.*

The following is Edwin H. Zeydel's translation, in *Goethe, the Lyrist*, No. 16 of *Studies in Germanic Language* (Chapel Hill, 1955), p. 171:

> Let Beginning now and Ending
> Merge and fuse into a One!
> Swifter than all things attending,
> Let your flight be sooner done!
> Thankful that the Muses' favor
> Brings a boon that ever lives:
> Substance born of heart's endeavor
> And the form your spirit gives.

7. J. W. v. Goethe, Artemis edition, Vol. IX, p. 669.
8. Especially in the letters to Körner, published under the title "Kallias" in the collected edition of Schiller's works, ed. Otto Güntter and Georg Witkowski, Vol. 17 (Leipzig, n.d.), p. 251 ff.
9. Hegel, *Vorlesungen über die Aesthetik*, Vol. 1 (Stuttgart, 1927), p. 160; translation in René Wellek and Austin Warren, *Theory of Literature* (New York, 1956), p. 26.
10. E.g., in the letters to Schiller of June 27, 1797, in which he speaks of the "barbaric composition," and of July 1 of the same year, in which he speaks of the "air phantoms" and the "mushroom family."
11. During his *Italienische Reise*. On March 1, 1788, from Rome, he writes, "I also feel more confident about its [*Faust's*] general tone. I have already completed one new scene, and, if I were to scorch the page, I fancy no one would be able to distinguish it from the rest." Goethe is obviously underestimating the philologist's keen sense of smell here.

12. The break in style is somewhat glossed over by the neutral penultimate verse. The last four verses are:

> O Mädchen, Mädchen,
> wie lieb' ich dich!
> Wie blickt dein Auge!
> Wie liebst du mich!
>
> So liebt die Lerche
> Gesang und Luft,
> Und Morgenblumen
> Den Himmelsduft,
>
> Wie ich dich liebe
> Mit warmem Blut,
> Die du mir Jugend
> Und Freud und Mut
>
> Zu neuen Liedern
> Und Tänzen gibst.
> Sei ewig glücklich,
> Wie du mich liebst!

The following is E. H. Zeydel's translation, in Goethe, the Lyrist, p. 31:

> What love, o maiden,
> I have for you!
> Your eye is beaming
> With love-light too.
>
> So loves the skylark
> Her song on high,
> So morning blossoms
> The balmy sky,
>
> As I love you
> With warmth athrill,
> Who youth and spirit
> And joy instil
>
> For ever new songs
> And dances free,
> Be always happy
> As you love me!

13. As quoted by Bäumler, Kants Kritik, p. 23.
14. Cf. especially the Athenäum fragment: "From the romantic point of view, the aberrations of poetry, even the eccentric and the monstrous, also have their value as materials and preliminary exercises in universality, as long as they contain something, as long as they are original."
15. E. Staiger, Grundbegriffe der Poetik (1st ed.; Zürich, 1946).
16. Cf. "Andeutung einer Musterpoetik," in H. Kunisch's Festschrift, Unterscheidung und Bewahrung (Berlin, 1961).
17. In the Materialien zur Geschichte der Farbelehre, in the section entitled "Julius Cäsar Scaliger," we find: "Greek is unquestionably more classically pure, much better suited to the natural, cheerful, spirited, aesthetic conveying of a happy natural outlook. The practice of speaking in verbs, especially in infinitives and participles, makes every expression admissible; nothing is determined, impaled, fixed, by words, words being merely an indication with which to evoke the object in our imagination."

18. Cf. Hans Peter Jaeger, *Hölderlin-Novalis, Grenzen der Sprache* (Zürich, 1949).
19. In his review of Bürger's poems.
20. Herodotus, Bk. II, ch. 53.
21. Benedetto Croce, *Saggi Filosofici*, Vol. VIII, "La Poesia" (Bari, 1937).
22. In Schlegel's *Georg Forster, Fragment einer Charakteristik der deutschen Klassiker* we find: "In a certain sense . . . no European need fear any classical author. I say: fear, for absolutely supreme prototypal images represent insurmountable boundaries of perfection. In this sense one might say: Heaven preserve us from eternal works!"
23. I. Kant, *Kritik der Urteilskraft*, § 8. English trans. by James Creed Meredith, *Kant's Critique of Aesthetic Judgement* (Oxford, 1911), p. 56.

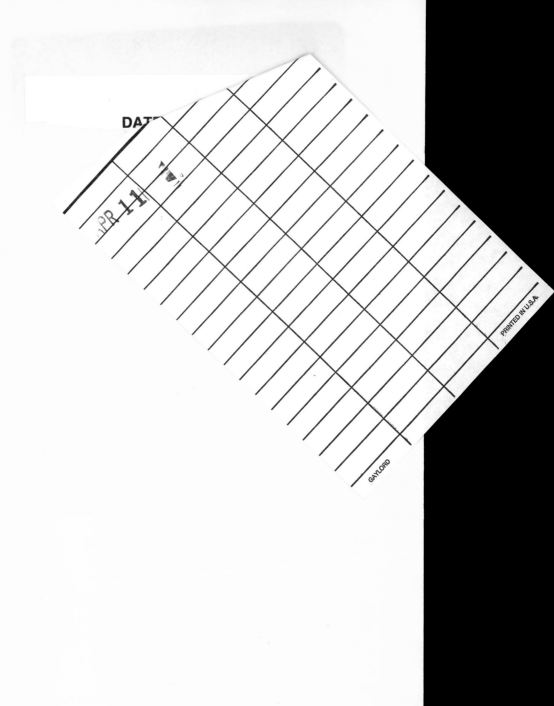